WASHINGTON

Birder's GUIDE TO WASHINGTON

Diann MacRae

Illustrations by Elizabeth A. Mills

Gulf Publishing Company
Houston, Texas

Birder's Guide to Washington

Gulf Publishing Company
Book Division
P.O. Box 2608 ☆ Houston, Texas 77252-2608

10   9   8   7   6   5   4   3   2   1

Library of Congress Cataloging-in-Publication Data

MacRae, Diann.
    Birder's guide to Washington / Diann MacRae ; illustrations by Elizabeth A. Mills.
        p.   cm.
    Includes bibliographical references (p.   ) and index.
    ISBN 0-88415-126-3
    1. Bird watching—Washington (State)—Guidebooks.   2. Washington (State)—Guidebooks.   I. Title.
QL684.W2M33   1995
598′.07234797—dc20   95-1573
                                                                              CIP

To two gentlemen of the old school . . .
Earl R. Gillis, who is my uncle,
and
Frank Richardson, who was mentor and friend.

Where is the man who owes nothing to the
land in which he lives? Whatever that land
may be, he owes it to the most precious thing
possessed by man, the morality of his actions
and the love of virtue.

—Jean Jacques Rousseau

Contents

White-Tailed Deer. Boots Satterlee Black River Preserve. Rainbow Falls State Park.

3. North Puget Trough

Point Roberts. Blaine. Birch Bay State Park. Cherry Point. Lake Terrell HMA. Tennant Lake. Lummi Flats. Bellingham. Chuckanut Drive. Samish Flats. Padilla Bay National Estuarine Research Reserve. Bay View State Park. Skagit Flats. Stillaguamish Delta. Valleys and Foothills East of I-5. Lynden Area. Trumpeter Swan Concentrations. Kayak Point Regional Park. Everett. Wallace Falls State Park. Monroe. Snoqualmie Wildlife Area.

4. Puget Sound and Islands

San Juan Islands. Fidalgo Island. Whidbey Island. Camano Island. Kitsap Peninsula. Hood Canal. Bainbridge Island. Vashon Island.

5. South Puget Trough

Seattle. East of Lake Washington. Tacoma. Fort Lewis. Nisqually NWR. Olympia. Kennedy Creek Estuary. Mima Mounds Natural Area Preserve. Ike Kinswa State Park. Ridgefield NWR. Hulda Klager Lilac Gardens. Columbia River Levee Road.

6. Western Cascades and Crest

Mount Baker-Snoqualmie National Forest. Nooksack River Bald Eagles. Mount Shuksan. Mount Baker. Everett Lake. Howard Miller

Steelhead Park. Skagit River Bald Eagle Natural
Area. North Cascades National Park. Sultan Basin
Recreation Area. Stevens Pass. Snoqualmie Pass.
Mount Rainier National Park. Chinook Pass.
White Pass. Mount St. Helens. Mount Adams.
Steigerwald Lake NWR.

Hart's Pass. Methow River Valley. Nighthawk.
Sinlahekin HMA. Loup Loup. Lake Chelan.
Chelan Butte HMA. Wenatchee National Forest.
Lake Wenatchee. Fish Lake. Wenatchee
Confluence State Park. I-90 Corridor. Lake Easton
State Park. Cle Elum Area. Blewett Pass. Red Top.
Teanaway River Valley. The Colockum HMA. L.T.
Murray and Oak Creek HMAs. Yakima River
Canyon. Vantage.

The High Road: Oroville to Bonaparte Lake.
Curlew Lake State Park. Colville National Forest.
Sherman Pass. Franklin D. Roosevelt Lake. Big
Meadow Lake. Pend Oreille Area. Sullivan Lake.
Salmo-Priest Wilderness Area. Calispell Lake.
McLoughlin Canyon. Crawfish Lake. Tunk and
Aeneas Valleys. Colville Indian Reservation.

Central Ferry Canyon. Bridgeport State Park. U.S.
Highway 2. Grand Coulee. Banks Lake. Wilson
Creek. Creston. Hawk Creek. Channeled

Scablands. Spokane. Mount Spokane. Reardon
Slough. Fishtrap (Miller Ranch). Turnbull NWR.
The Palouse. Walla Walla County. McNary NWR.
Juniper Forest Management Area (Juniper Dunes
Wilderness). Umatilla NWR. Bickleton. Yakama
Indian Nation. Toppenish NWR. Fort Simcoe
State Park. The Hanford Reach of the Columbia
River. Crab Creek HMA. Othello Settlement
Ponds. Columbia NWR. Potholes HMA. Dodson
Road. Quincy HMA. Moses Coulee.

Blue Mountain HMAs. Cloverland Grade. Chief
Timothy State Park. Asotin. Savage Road Ponds.
Anatone Flats. Fields Spring State Park.
Department of Fish and Wildlife Access Areas.
W.T. Wooten HMA.

A Checklist of Washington Birds. Contacts for
Birders. Selected References.

Acknowledgments

Good guidebooks are written with the help of innumerable people. In the often frustrating tangle of facts, directions, and notes, sometimes just a kind comment or two does wonders to help the process along. I want to express my sincere thanks to many special people: to Dorothy Richardson for providing a warm place to visit and access to Frank's library; to Ann van der Geld, who accompanied me for years on birding trips and patiently typed reams of observation notes; to Libby Mills for her wonderful artwork; to Jim Morrison for donating many of his detailed maps to the book; to Todd Thompson, who sent loads of lists, maps, and brochures, gave me a guided tour through the Juniper Dunes Wilderness Area, and invited me to Fishtrap; to Walter Harm for his helpful comments on the San Juan Islands and his yearly leadership of the Orcas Island Christmas Count; to Carole L. Vande Voorde, who sent me wonderful information on the Blue Mountains Region, the part of the state I know the least; to Jean Cross for her excellent help on Spada Lake and Marbled Murrelets; to Maurice Vial's great notes and directions to Spokane birding areas; to Randall W. Hanna and his staff at Fort Lewis for updates and information on what the U.S. Army is doing to help wildlife; and last, but not least, to the ladies of the Mill Creek Writer's Salon, Sharon Sneddon, Helen Smith, and Anila Prineveau, for their unflappable support.

I owe a lot to the Birder's Bag Lunch group at the University of Washington and to Chuck Evans, who keeps the group going properly. My thanks to Chuck, Dale Wesley, Ellen Meyer, Fran Wood, Charles Easterberg, Dick McCabe, Bob Vandenbosch, Gussie Litwer, Eugene Smirnov, Charlotte Albright, and all the others. My knowledge of birding sites and what to find at each was greatly enhanced over the years, thanks to them. Thanks also to Weldon and Virginia

Clark, Fred Sharpe, Gene Hunn, Thais Bock, Steve Williams, Jerry Hickman, Randy Hill, Catherine Secor, James O. Sneddon, Ted Morris, John Scarola, Stephen R. Stout, Helen Grande, John P. Ashley, Michael James, William M. Overby, Eric Watilo, Hawlel Cole, Robin DeMario-Hodges, Brian Carter, Elaine J. Zieroth, J. Quarnstrom, Robert G. Utz, Sharon Riggs, Terry Stevens, Glen Alexander, Kathy Armstrong, Marguerite Hills, John Heublein, David Fouts, Dennis Paulson, Mike Houck, Patty C. Burel, Edward L. Schultz, Bill Gardiner, George T. Lemagie, and Anne Marocchini for their interest, guidance, and expertise.

Responses for information from the Washington State Department of Fish and Wildlife, Washington State Parks Department, Washington State Department of Natural Resources, Bellevue Parks Department, King County Parks, and the Seattle Parks Department were prompt and helpful.

Washington birding references already in print by Howard Ennor, Gene Hunn, Earl Larrison and Klaus Sonnenberg, Mark Lewis and Fred Sharpe, Dennis Paulson and Terry Wahl, and Joe La Tourette were helpful in pointing out several new places and for species verification in some instances.

Very special thanks are due friends and family who made the project workable: to Christopher MacRae who never failed to take care of my geese, dog, and cat when I went wandering; to Colin MacRae for reading and commenting on much of the manuscript and for keeping my dinosaur of a computer running; to Isabel Landsberg and others who helped roam the backroads and provide input, and to my mom, Diann Gillis, in Portland, Oregon, for support and understanding. Last, but far from least, my appreciation to Claire Blondeau, my editor, for her prompt and clear answers to my many questions and for her good humor and understanding as the book progressed.

Foreword

 If you took a Raven's-eye view of Washington and flew across its midsection, from the coastal waters and beaches at Cape Elizabeth to the rolling hill country above Spokane, you would pass over a country as diverse as any place on earth. Threaded by rivers, there are still impressive fragments of ancient forests. Lakes, marshes, meadows, and hardwood stands are abundant. Crossing the Cascades, fir stands give way to alpine forests and glaciers, with pine forests characterizing the eastern slopes, to the edge of grasslands where plateaus of sage are interspersed with desert lakes and ponds. Each distinct habitat is home to a community of specialized life. Birds are the emissaries of these places.

When I come into new country, my first inclination is to watch and listen for the bird life there. By form, behavior, and color, they are typically suited to fit the requirements of surviving in these locations, and what they do provides me with the first glimpses of the ecological dynamics of the setting. Before reaching the edge of a favorite marsh that I regularly visit in early summer, I listen for awhile to be tantalized by the emerging mixture of sound and song-telling of Mallard, Marsh Wren, and Blue Heron. On the water, I've watched Hen Wood Duck lead a string of ducklings into shadows as Barn and Violet-green Swallows whip into clouds of hovering insects. Snipe have burst from underfoot as male Redwings chase females through cattails. If you are patient and watch any one of these species for awhile, their stories begin to unfold. I've learned how this place sustains and nurtures them. Each bird has its own way to introduce me to the intricate linkages they have with other species. Together they form an essential part of the composition of the marsh.

Diann MacRae has compiled a book of places that is as much a tool for discovery as it is a means of seeing different species of birds throughout the year. Timing your visits to correspond with the species' activity and migratory habits, you now have an opportunity to step into the life story of your subject. A bird's survival strategies, feeding habits, social arrangements, and interaction with life around it are but a few of the curious if not dramatic moments that await you. *Birder's Guide to Washington* is your passport.

Tony Angell
Artist/Naturalist/Educator

About the Author

Diann MacRae, an almost-native Washingtonian, has spent much of her adult life wandering the state's backroads seeking birds and other wildlife, and looking for pristine scenery. She is a freelance writer, photographer, and avid birder whose works have appeared in *Birder's World, Bird Watcher's Digest, Beautiful British Columbia, Colorado Outdoor Journal, Northwest Wilderness Journal, Field Guide of the Roger Tory Peterson Institute, Pacific Northwest,* and many other publications.

She presently is education chair and a member of the board of directors of the Hawk Migration Association of North America. Since becoming a member in 1978, she has served as chairman, vice chairman, continental editor, and regional editor in northern New England and the Pacific Northwest. Diann also is a member of the Raptor Research Foundation, the American Ornithologists' Union, the Washington Ornithological Society, and the Seattle Photographic Society. She taught "Birds of Prey in Washington State" for four years at the University of Washington extension, and led and assisted in tours of Washington state and Vancouver Island, British Columbia.

In writing this book, Diann visited almost every site mentioned. She often was accompanied by non-birding friends, who offered insight into other activities and interests for the sites.

Introduction

Diversity is the norm in Washington state. Its birds are varied and can be exotic because of this diversity. Washington's beaches border on the world's largest ocean, the Pacific, which produces a more temperate marine habitat. The only temperate rain forest in the lower 48 states is found on the Olympic peninsula; the channeled scablands of eastern Washington also are unique. Puget Sound, an inland saltwater sea, is connected to the Pacific Ocean by the Strait of Juan de Fuca. Puget Sound extends south nearly 90 miles to Olympia, Washington's capital city. The Cascade Mountains divide the state from north to south and are crowned by Mount Rainier, which, at 14,412 feet, is the second-highest peak in the continental United States. East of the Cascades, the vast inland desert of the Columbia Plateau covers the central and southern part of the state. The Okanogan Highlands stretch across the northeast. Two mountain ranges, the Selkirks to the north and the Blues in the far southeast, extend into these two regions, bringing with them Rock Mountain species that help make Washington's bird life extremely interesting, challenging, and distinct.

The number of bird species in Washington state as of this writing is 430 (accepted records). The species vary from the state's largest, the Trumpeter Swan, to its smallest, the Calliope Hummingbird. Endangered species in Washington state are the American White Pelican, Peregrine Falcon, and Sandhill Crane; threatened are the Bald Eagle and Ferruginous Hawk. Twenty-eight other species are listed as "sensitive"—ten of these are birds of prey.

The primary north-south migration route across western North America is the Pacific Flyway, which passes through Washington state. Huge numbers of migrant waterfowl head south from nesting grounds in the Arctic late each summer. Easily viewed are the thousands of swans, geese, and ducks that stay in the more pleasant wintering areas of western Washington. Raptors, likewise, drift south, usually less communally, except for the Turkey Vulture. Although vultures, Ospreys, and Swainson's Hawks are absent during the winter, Washington is rich in winter raptors.

Songbirds pass through from late August well into fall. When daylight fails, often myriad calls can be heard in the evening hours as migrants pass overhead. Sandhill Cranes are conspicuous travelers along the coast and east of the mountains. Many other species also match their internal rhythms to the seasons and make semi-annual journeys through our state. No matter what your special avian interests, Washington state can provide tempting birding.

Diann MacRae

Chapter 1
The Olympic Peninsula

 The Olympic Peninsula is a land little-changed since Spanish sea captain Juan Perez first recorded the area in 1774. It is a land of superlatives. The world's largest Douglas-fir, western hemlock, subalpine fir, and yellow cedar are all found within Olympic National Park. The largest herd of Roosevelt elk also is found within park boundaries. Northern Goshawks hunt the forests and meadows. Marbled Murrelets and Spotted Owls nest in the ancient trees. Seven Indian nations have left their mark on the river valleys and beaches: the Makah, Hoh, Quileute, S'Klallam, Queets, Quinault, and Skokomish. Wilderness beaches and remote backcountry hiking coupled with the usual amenities of our national parks make this beautiful area unrivaled.

The valleys of the Hoh, Quinault, and Queets rivers on the Olympic Peninsula are temperate rain forests, an entity found only here, in southern Chile, and in New Zealand. These rare forests thrive on moisture: More than 12 feet of rain a year falls in the valleys. "The land where the air turns to water" is a translation of the Indian name for the peninsula. The geographical location—between the Pacific Ocean and the Olympic Mountains—is what makes these lush rain forests thrive.

The range of the Olympic Mountains is a new range with some of the rocks only three million years old. The Olympic range began forming about seven million years ago and now rises from nearly sea level to its highest point at 7,965 feet, the summit of Mount Olympus. It is composed mostly of quartzites and slates; there are no volcanic cones.

The Olympic range is not made up of high mountains, but its north-south orientation is enough to stop the flow eastward of moist Pacific air, which condenses and falls as rain and snow. Mount Olympus has both the highest amount of rainfall in the contiguous United

1

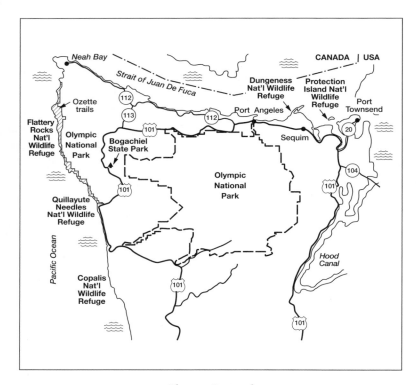

Olympic Peninsula

States, 200 inches a year, and the heaviest snowfalls, 40 feet a year. Harsher eastern weather also is deflected from the peninsula by the Olympics, ensuring a milder climate. Don't be discouraged about the rain, however; the birds don't mind it, and most of it falls between early October and late March. In Sequim (skwim), 40 miles to the west of the Olympic rain forests and nestled in the rain shadow of the mountains, rainfall averages about 17 inches a year.

The Olympic Peninsula is bordered by the Strait of Juan de Fuca on the north, the Pacific Ocean on the west, Hood Canal on the east, and Grays Harbor, US 12, and SH 8 to the south. Access to the peninsula from the east is by ferry from Seattle or Edmonds. Ferries also run to the peninsula from Whidbey Island to the northeast, and Vancouver Island, British Columbia, to the north. To the south, you can leave I-5 for either US 12 or US 101 to reach the peninsula. For Washington ferry schedules and information call (206) 464-6400, statewide 1-800-84-FERRY, or contact the Washington State Ferries, Colman Dock/Pier 52, 801 Alaskan Way, Seattle, WA 98104-1487; for Sidney, BC, ferries, call (604) 381-1551 or (604) 656-1531.

Clallam, Jefferson, Mason, and most of Grays Harbor counties make up the Olympic Peninsula. The peninsula includes about 8% of Washington state with Olympic National Park taking in nearly 60% of the peninsula. Roads—no freeways—encircle the area, and there are several entrances to the park.

NORTHEASTERN OLYMPIC PENINSULA

The Hood Canal Bridge, eastern gateway to the Olympic Peninsula, is the longest saltwater floating bridge in the world. The Olympic Mountains rise in all their glory to the south and, to the north, the low hills of the Kitsap Peninsula with the Cascade Mountains far in the distance greet the eye. SH 104 crosses the bridge, and from it you can see just about anything from a Trident submarine heading for its base at Bangor, to whales and porpoises, to Bald Eagles, Western and Red-necked Grebes, Surf and White-winged Scoters, Greater Scaup, Buf-flehead, mergansers, gulls, and other marine birds. Being stopped for the "Bridge Open" sign is almost a pleasure.

Shine Tidelands State Park

This 124.6-acre primitive state park at the west end of the Hood Canal Bridge just off SH 104 is a good place to picnic or look for what you've seen when the bridge is not open and you can't stop. Bywater Bay extends north from the campground to a sand spit connecting Hood Head with the mainland. A small lagoon is formed here, and at low tides it becomes a tide flat that can abound with Sanderlings, Dunlin, and other shorebirds. Walk up the beach from the park, across the spit, and onto Hood Head for great views across the water. Look for Common Loon, Western, Red-necked, and Horned Grebes, Surf and White-winged Scoters, and Bufflehead in the bay; and for Bald Eagles in the trees to the west.

Twenty basic, rather cramped campsites are found here, and there is a tiny substation visible nearby. The birding, clamming, crabbing, and beachcombing are very good, however, and the view is excellent. To reach Shine Tidelands, take the first right after crossing the bridge (Paradise Bay Road), then an immediate second unmarked right. At the bottom of the short hill is a "Y"—right for the boat ramp, left for the beach and campground. Be sure to check out the tiny marsh just before the small substation for ducks, grebes, and rails. For further information contact Fort Flagler State Park.

Fort Flagler State Park

Fort Flagler, located on the northern tip of Marrowstone Island, faces Admiralty Inlet, the water connection between Puget Sound and the Strait of Juan de Fuca. Port Townsend Bay and Kilisut Harbor border its other sides. Due to its marine prominence, it is both an excellent birding spot and, during two world wars, a strategic defense and training post.

Point Wilson. Located at the very northern tip of the park, this is one of the best spots to see Harlequin Duck; Oldsquaw; scoters, including Black Scoter; Double-crested, Pelagic and Brandt's Cormorants; and other ducks. Tufted Puffin, Rhinoceros Auklet, Ancient and Marbled Murrelets, and numerous other alcids are seen offshore. Black Oystercatcher, Dunlin, plovers, other shorebirds, and gulls also frequent the edges of the shore. Whimbrels and Sanderlings can be seen on the beaches during spring migration. The grassy areas in the park host sparrows, quail, and American Kestrel, and the wooded sections contain Downy and Hairy Woodpeckers and the usual passerine retinue of the western lowland coniferous forest.

Three of the State Environmental Learning Center camps are located here, as is a U.S. Fish and Wildlife marine lab and an underwater park. The abandoned Coast Artillery gun emplacements located in the fort are a point of historical interest. Park facilities include standard, RV, group, and primitive campsites; picnic areas; interpretive displays; boat launches and moorage docks; a fishing pier; hiking and nature trails; a youth hostel; and a grocery/snack concession.

Tufted Puffin

To reach Fort Flagler, turn north off SH 104 to Port Hadlock on Oak Bay Road. Just before Port Hadlock, turn east on Flagler Road and follow the signs 6.6 miles to the park. You will cross a bridge to Indian Island, then another bridge to Marrowstone Island. Check at both bridges for shorebirds, alcids, and waterfowl. For information, contact Fort Flagler State Park, Nordland, WA 98358-9699; (360) 385-1259.

Port Townsend

Victorian architecture is prevalent in Port Townsend, which was the official Port of Entry city for Puget Sound in territorial days. It is now a National Historic District, and many of the old mansions are hotels, restaurants, and bed-and-breakfast establishments. Port Townsend's unique flavor lingers, however, and it is a fine center for birding activities with comfortable lodging, good restaurants, and interesting shops for browsing.

Port Townsend is located on SH 20 at the northeast tip of the Quimper Peninsula. For specific bird information, contact the Admiralty Audubon Society based in Port Townsend. For local information contact the Port Townsend Chamber of Commerce, 2437 Sims Way, Port Townsend, WA 98368; (360) 385-2722.

Old Fort Townsend State Park. This is one of the oldest of the peninsula forts, dating back to the Indian War of 1855–56. An interpretive trail describing the fort, a nature trail, and another 6.5 miles of hiking trails are here. The fort is on a high bluff facing Port Townsend Bay. On its rocky, pebbly beach, Whimbrel, Dunlin, yellowlegs, and other shorebirds can be found. The old fort's wharf is now reduced to pilings that provide perches for cormorants, gulls, and occasional Bald Eagles. Most of the campsites are in a heavily wooded area where numerous forest birds such as Ruby-crowned Kinglet, American Robin, Red-breasted Sapsucker, Steller's Jay, Song Sparrow, plus wrens, nuthatches, and chickadees can be seen.

To reach Old Fort Townsend State Park, go four miles south of Port Townsend on SH 20 and turn east for 0.5 mile on Old Fort Townsend Road. For information, contact Old Fort Townsend State Park, 1370 Old Fort Townsend Road, Port Townsend, WA 98368; (360) 385-3595.

Fort Worden State Park and Conference Center. Located just outside the north city limits of Port Townsend, Ford Worden was one of three fortifications built in the early 1900s to guard the entrance to Puget Sound. It was a large fort with massive gun emplacements. Today, it is a center for the performing arts and many conferences. Its location on a bluff overlooking Admiralty Inlet and the Strait of Juan de Fuca guarantees good looks at marine birds, including Harlequin Ducks, Rhinoceros Auklets, occasional Peregrine Falcons, scoters, grebes, loons, ducks, and geese. Shorebirds are often on the sandy beach during migration.

Fort Worden State Park has its own reservation system and is often quite busy. For information contact Fort Worden State Park, P.O. Box 574, Port Townsend, WA 98638; (360) 385-4730.

PROTECTION ISLAND NWR

In 1792, Captain George Vancouver was quite taken with a small, nearly treeless island just over a mile from the mouth of a large bay. His comments about the island led to its name, Protection Island. His log states that the island was instrumental in guarding the bay "against all attempts of an enemy, when fortified." The bay was subsequently named after his ship *Discovery*. Nearly 200 years later, this island is the nesting site for nearly 72% of all Puget Sound seabirds. Rhinoceros Auklets, nearly 17,000 strong, burrow deep in the island's hillsides, Pigeon Guillemots construct driftwood nests at the high-tide mark, and Glaucous-winged Gulls nest in grassy hollows at the east and west end of the island.

Also burrowing four to six feet into Protection Island's hillsides are Tufted Puffins. They can often be seen flying in and out of the area to feed their young. Rhinoceros Auklets seldom emerge during daylight hours, waiting until the protection of nightfall to feed their young. The island is closed to the public, and boats must stay at least 200 yards offshore. Good views can be had from the mainland shore, especially with a scope.

Diamond Point

Diamond Point sits at the northeastern edge of the Miller Peninsula jutting into the mouth of Discovery Bay. It is one of the closest points to observe Protection Island. Just east of the point is Gardiner Beach and some excellent pelagic birding—from shore. In the bay can be seen Pacific, Red-throated, and Common Loons; grebes; White-winged and Surf Scoters; Oldsquaws; Common and Barrow's Goldeneyes; mergansers; and many others, depending on the season. Shorebirds are often common at low tide during migration. Other habitats are a pond that hosts even more ducks, Red-winged and Brewer's Blackbirds, Song Sparrows, and other passerines, and a timbered area in which there are frequently Bald Eagles and Great Blue Herons.

To reach Diamond Point turn north off US 104 on Diamond Point Road and travel 4.1 miles to the point. It is a developed area of small beach houses, but there is public access.

SEQUIM

The S'Klallam tribe called this lovely valley home long before Europeans arrived. Situated in the Olympic rain shadow, Sequim is a town that gets lots of western Washington sunshine, and half the rain Seattle gets. Dairies and farmlands abound and even need irrigation. Sequim, named after the S'Klallam Indian word meaning "quiet water," is 17 miles east of Port Angeles and has all the amenities of any bustling small town. It is also near many fine Olympic birding areas. The Olympic Peninsula Audubon Chapter is located in Sequim, and birding information can be obtained from the chapter.

The Rainshadow Bookstore at 108 W. Washington, (360) 681-0300, carries field guides, local checklists, information on where to bird locally, and books on the Olympic Peninsula.

Railroad Bridge Park. In 1992, an old railroad trestle that crosses the Dungeness River was refurbished. Located in a wonderful riparian habitat, there is now wheelchair access up onto the bridge and for 0.5 mile across the bridge where it joins a paved pathway. This lovely, wooded habitat is home to Downy and Hairy Woodpeckers, Common Flicker, Red-breasted Nuthatch, Winter Wren, Bushtit, Golden-crowned Kinglet, Rufous-sided Towhee, Varied Thrush, American Dip-

Winter Wren

per, and many warblers, vireos, and flycatchers during summer nesting time. To reach the park, turn north on 5th Avenue off US 101, then left on Henrickson. Follow Henrickson to its end, past a Dead End sign and through some curves to end at a parking area at the trestle.

Non-birding but interesting activities in the Sequim area are: the Manis Mastodon site where archaeologists have uncovered mastodon bones; the Cedarbrook Herb Farm; and the Neuharth and Lost Mountain wineries. All welcome visitors. Sequim is located on US 101.

John Wayne Marina

The boat basin on the western side of Sequim Bay is named, of course, after the actor who often spent time at his property here. It is home to an active Osprey nest (behind the marina); Bald Eagle, Peregrine Falcon, and Great Blue Heron sometimes perch in the tall evergreens along the bay; shorebirds crowd the beaches during migration; and many of the marine waterfowl, alcids, cormorants, and gulls found in the area are here, especially in winter. There are interpretive panels on the marine wildlife of Puget Sound located at the north parking lot. An open, paved shorefront trail from which to view the marine life is wheelchair-accessible. A few blocks south of the marina, there is a large freshwater marsh; be sure to check for marsh birds and waterfowl. The John Wayne Marina is located 0.5 mile north of US 101 approximately four miles east of Sequim city center; it is well-signed.

Dungeness Forks

Dungeness Forks is a small (ten campsites), quiet, inexpensive Forest Service campground at the confluence of the Gray Wolf and Dungeness Rivers. Varied and Hermit Thrushes, Red Crossbill, Red-breasted Nuthatch, Chestnut-backed Chickadee, warblers, woodpeckers, and the usual western forest birds are found here. From US 101 four miles east of Sequim, go south for eight miles on county and then Forest Service roads to reach the campground. For information contact Quilcene Ranger Station, Box 280, Quilcene, WA 98376.

Jamestown Beach

Watch for Bald Eagles and Peregrine Falcons in the trees along the shore. Eelgrass beds make the area attractive to Black Brant and American Wigeon. Glaucous-winged, Thayer's, and Bonaparte's Gulls; Hooded Merganser; Eared and Red-necked Grebes; and Barrow's Goldeneye are some of the special birds here. The shorebirds are impressive during the spring and fall migrations.

To reach Jamestown Beach, follow US 101 to Sequim and turn north at the Sequim Avenue traffic light. Follow Sequim Avenue 3.4 miles to Jamestown Road, then turn east and go about a mile to Jamestown Beach. Be sure to check surrounding fields for raptors and migrants.

Three Crabs area

The Three Crabs is a longtime beachfront restaurant specializing in seafood. It is located in the middle of some interesting birding habitats: freshwater pond, beach grass and field area, sandy beaches, and wide open bay. The area is reached by continuing on Sequim Avenue (do not turn at Jamestown Road) to Dungeness Way. Continue 0.6 mile on Dungeness Way, past the Dungeness Tavern on the left and a "bottle tree" on the right until you reach the parking area.

Dungeness Valley

The valley, including Sequim Prairie, is relatively flat; mostly farmland and spotty developments. Northern Harriers and Short-eared Owls occasionally can be seen quartering across fields and grassy stretches hunting for mice and small birds. Red-tailed Hawks are common on utility poles and the larger trees that still spot the area. Accipiters are seen sporadically and American Kestrels are often on utility wires. Grassland birds such as Lincoln's, Golden-crowned, White-crowned, Fox, and Song Sparrows; American Goldfinch; Western Meadowlark; Mourning Dove; Rufous-sided Towhee; and House Finch can be seen across the valley. Brewer's and Red-winged Blackbirds, Virginia Rail, and Marsh Wren are often by ponds and ditches.

One way to see the valley and some of the prime birding spots is to follow Sequim-Dungeness Way north from the town of Sequim. The road goes for several miles then turns west, eventually running into Cays Road. Follow Cays Road South for about two miles then turn west on the Old Olympic Highway, which in about five miles returns to US 101 just east of Port Angeles.

DUNGENESS NATIONAL WILDLIFE REFUGE

This 756-acre refuge was created in 1915 as a resting and wintering area for Black Brant and other migratory birds. More than 250 species have been recorded here through the years. A variety of habitats are found in the refuge: marine, protected bay, tide flats, salt marsh, sand spit, and grassy meadows predominate with a smaller section of shrub and coniferous forest.

A 0.5-mile hiking trail begins at the entrance gate and meanders through upland forest to a viewpoint on the bluff above Dungeness Spit. It is not paved, but it is an easy walk. Birds to look for along the trail and in the conifers include Bald Eagle, accipiters, Western Screech-Owl, Steller's Jay, Red-breasted Nuthatch, Brown Creeper, Winter Wren, Varied Thrush, Western Tanager, Townsend's Warbler, and Black-headed Grosbeak.

A short, steep, downhill section of the trail brings you to a shrub and grassy meadow habitat where Rufous Hummingbird, Willow Flycatcher, Bushtit, Bewick's Wren, Cedar Waxwing, and Black-throated Gray Warbler often are seen. Another few steps and you are on the spit where some of the finest coastal birding in the state is found.

Dungeness Spit, the longest natural sand spit in the United States, stretches 5.5 miles into the Strait of Juan de Fuca. The spit acts as a barrier between the sometimes wild water of the strait and the bay and estuary on the inner side. More than 15,000 Black Brant winter here, feeding on eelgrass, their staple food. Tens of thousands of waterfowl comprised of Canada Geese, Mallard, Northern Pintail, Green-winged Teal, American Wigeon, Bufflehead, White-winged and Surf Scoters, Greater Scaup, Oldsquaw, Harlequin Duck, and Common and Red-breasted Mergansers also appear during the spring and fall migrations, many staying for the winter. Orca, harbor seals, and porpoises often are seen.

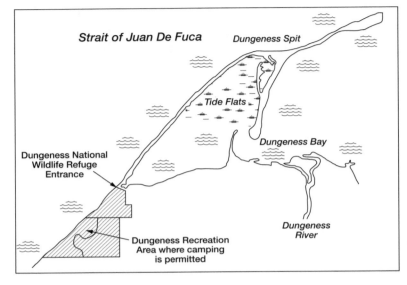

Dungeness NWR

Birds found in open water and on the spit, inner bay, and tide flats in winter include loons; grebes; cormorants; Short-eared Owl; Dunlin; Black-bellied Plover; Surfbird; Sanderling; Pigeon Guillemot; Red-necked Phalarope; Glaucous-winged, Thayer's, Mew, and Bonaparte's Gulls; Caspian Tern; plus herons, corvids, and varied small passerines. Winter rarities are Peregrine Falcon, Yellow-billed Loon, Short-tailed Shearwater, European Wigeon, Glaucous Gull, and Ruddy Turnstone.

Nesting birds at the refuge include Northern Pintail; Green-winged Teal; Common Merganser; Cooper's Hawk; Northern Harrier; Northern Pygmy-Owl; Virginia Rail; Sora; California Quail; Band-tailed Pigeon; Vaux's Swift; Rufous Hummingbird; Pileated Woodpecker; Willow, Hammond's, and Pacific-slope Flycatchers; six species of swallows, and many others—approximately 91 species in all.

Follow US 101 west past Sequim for 4.7 miles to reach the refuge. Turn north on Kitchen-Dick Road and go three miles to the Dungeness Recreation Area. Drive through the recreation area to the refuge parking lot. If you are taking a valley loop drive, there are signs directing to the refuge at several points. There is a $2 charge, and no pets are allowed in the refuge. Because of the wildlife, only low-key activities such as hiking, fishing, boating, and bird-watching are allowed in the refuge. In the adjacent Dungeness Recreation Area, there are 67 campsites and a picnic area—pets allowed. For further information and a Wildlife Check List contact Washington Coastal Refuges, 1638 Barr Road South, Port Angeles, WA 98382; (360) 457-8451.

PORT ANGELES

Abraham Lincoln was signer of the decree establishing a town site and military reservation here in 1862, but Spanish explorer Francisco Eliza discovered and named the harbor area Puerto de Nuestra Señora de Los Angeles (Port of Our Lady of the Angels) in 1791. Its name was later shortened to the present form and given to both harbor and town.

Port Angeles is the largest city on the Olympic Peninsula, headquarters for Olympic National Park and the southern end of the 45-minute ferry ride to Victoria, British Columbia. It is located on US 101, 17 miles west of Sequim. Motels, campgrounds, gas stations, and restaurants are plentiful. For area information contact the North Olympic Peninsula Visitor and Convention Bureau, P.O. Box 670, Port Angeles, WA 98362; (206) 452-8552.

Port Angeles City Pier

There is an observation tower here with an accessible beach running along the harbor edge. Loons, cormorants, gulls, terns, waterfowl, and shorebirds can be seen here in season, and passerines are on the shrubby, but developed, hillsides. There is a nice motel next to the pier with small decks looking out onto the harbor; excellent restaurants are in the adjacent City Pier where you can bird while you eat. The ferry landing, an excellent visitor center, and the Arthur D. Feiro Marine Lab, which is open to the public, also are located at the pier. The City Pier is one block off US 101W at Lincoln Street.

Ediz Hook

The Elwha River spent centuries depositing sand and silt into the Strait of Juan de Fuca at the mouth of Port Angeles Harbor. The resulting sand spit now is called Ediz Hook and is an excellent place for shorebirds and gulls, in season. It is also home for a Coast Guard Air Station and the command center for many Coast Guard installations on the peninsula. To reach Ediz Hook, follow US 101W into town, then continue west on Front Street, which turns into Marine Drive. The public road allows access through the Daishowa America paper pulp mill. (Check the small lagoon just before the mill for birds.) It is two miles from the paper mill to the parking area at the entrance to the Coast Guard Air Station, the end of public access. After passing the mill, there are lots of places to pull off on the right side of the road; a breakwater to the strait is on the left. Further on, there are extensive log rafts on the right and tremendous views of the bay and Port Angeles with the Olympic Mountains in the background. There are rest rooms, picnic tables, boat amenities, and disabled parking at the end of the road.

The waters are calm inside the spit. Along the inner beach and in the log storage areas watch for Black-bellied Plovers, Surfbird, Whimbrel, Dunlin, Sanderlings, and other shorebirds. The log raft areas are favored resting places for gulls, including Heermann's, Thayer's, Bonaparte's, and Herring Gulls; Brandt's Cormorant; Great Blue Heron; Killdeer; Black Turnstone; and Belted Kingfisher. Scan the harbor for Barrow's Goldeneye, Oldsquaw, and possible Yellow-billed Loon. Other loons, grebes, and waterfowl are also present, in season. The ocean side of the hook in winter hosts large flocks of Common Murres, gulls, and other alcids. During fall migration, Parasitic Jaegers, Common Terns, and rare gull species occasionally are seen.

OLYMPIC NATIONAL PARK

Presidential decrees helped create Olympic National Park as we know it today. In 1897, Grover Cleveland set aside much of the Olympic Peninsula as the Olympic Forest Reserve. Twelve years later, Theodore Roosevelt used his presidential authority to bring into being the Mount Olympus National Monument. The 600,000 acres he set aside was created as a refuge for the declining Roosevelt elk, named after him, and became the center of what is now Olympic National Park. Woodrow Wilson, bending to the will of the timber harvesters of that day, chopped many thousands of acres off the park in 1915. Finally, in 1938, Franklin D. Roosevelt signed a bill creating Olympic National Park. And in 1953, Harry Truman added the 57-mile roadless ocean frontage and the Queets Corridor.

Olympic National Park now contains 900,000 acres—95% of it wilderness. It is nearly surrounded by more than 600,000 miles of National Forest. The park contains a trio of native environments together found nowhere else in North America: the temperate rain forests, the last wilderness ocean beaches in the lower 48 states, and a striking alpine backcountry. Found in these varied environs are at least 180 species of birds, 50 species of mammals, and 500 types of plants. Preserved within the park's boundaries are nine wildflower species, five species of mammals, and two species of fish found no other place on earth.

Spectacular scenery, undisturbed natural processes, scientific value, and diversity of plants and animals has earned Olympic National Park status as a Biosphere Preserve and World Heritage Site from the United Nations UNESCO program.

There are no roads through the park or into its heart. US 101 borders the park on three sides, and spur roads give beach and park access. It is approximately a two-hour drive from Seattle to Port Angeles, where access to Hurricane Ridge and the main visitor center is located. The route is by ferry from Seattle or Edmonds, then west to Port Angeles. Two other main routes are via I-5 to Tacoma, then north on US 101; and I-5 to Olympia, then west on US 101 keeping west (to Aberdeen) on SH 8. At Hoquiam turn north on US 101.

Two main visitor centers are open all year: Olympic Park Visitor Center (which includes the Park Headquarters and the Pioneer Memorial Museum) in Port Angeles, and the Hoh Rain Forest Visitor Center at the west-central edge of the park. Ranger stations open all year are located at several other places in the park: Hurricane Ridge, Elwha, Ozette, Mora, Quinault, and Staircase. Ranger stations open in the summer only are found at Storm King, Fairholm, Soleduck, Bogachiel, Kalaloch, Queets, Dosewallips, and Deer Park.

The park has 17 established campgrounds (927 campsites) that have tables and fireplaces, toilet facilities, and piped water. Campsites are available on a first-come, first-served basis. Laundry facilities, showers, and utility connections are *not* available at the park campgrounds.

There are 600 miles of trails in Olympic National Park, and more than 95 backcountry camping locations that have water and are located on the maps. The best way to see variety within the park in the shortest time is by taking day hikes. When writing for information on the park, ask for the two-page flyer "Suggested Day Hikes—Olympic National Park." The flyer also gives wheelchair-access information.

Designated disabled parking with ramps and accessible rest rooms are available at all visitor centers. A guide to Hurricane Ridge is available on cassette tape. Olympic Park Visitor Center has telecommunications devices for the deaf (TDD). The paved, 0.25-mile Hoh Mini-Trail in the Hoh Rain Forest and Madison Falls Trail at Elwha Entrance Station are wheelchair-accessible. Paved paths through Hurricane Ridge's subalpine meadows are accessible with assistance. Seeing-eye dogs are allowed on park trails. The Kalaloch Lodge has a large, wheelchair-accessible log cabin designed for disabled visitors. All campgrounds have rest rooms that are wheelchair-accessible except Deer Park, Erickson's Bay, and July Creek.

The Olympic Park Visitor Center has exhibits on the park wildlife and plants, Native American whaling, and old-growth forests. Rangers are on duty to issue backcountry permits, give information on weather and trail conditions, and conduct walks and evening campfire programs. Maps, books, and other park literature are available. The visitor center is located on a spur, Mount Angeles Road, heading south off US 101 from downtown Port Angeles. The road is well-marked in both directions with brown national park signs. For further information on the park write Olympic National Park, 600 East Park Avenue, Port Angeles, WA 98362; (360) 452-4501.

Nature education courses ranging from photography to archaeology are taught in the park by visiting professionals. For more information contact Olympic Field Seminars, HC 62, Box 9T, Port Angeles, WA 98362; (360) 928-3720.

Hurricane Ridge

Hurricane Ridge offers some of the most spectacular views of alpine scenery in the park. With its sweeping meadows and clusters of mountain hemlock, subalpine fir, and Alaska yellow cedar, the area itself is a fine example of a subalpine environment. Olympic marmots, pika, and black-tailed deer are common. We also have seen black bears, mountain goats, and snowshoe hares from near Hurricane Ridge Lodge Visitor Center (a day-use lodge). Hawk watches have recorded all three accipiters, Golden Eagle, Osprey, Northern Harrier, and Turkey Vulture. Magnificent summer wildflower displays, including glacier lilies, grace the meadows and slopes.

Turkey Vulture

The high elevation and somewhat limited area precludes a large and varied bird population, but what is there is definitely worth looking for. Blue Grouse, Gray and Steller's Jays, Common Raven, Dark-eyed Junco, Horned Lark, Red Crossbill, Black-capped Chickadee, American Kestrel, and Red-tailed Hawk all nest in this area. Other birds to look for are Pine Grosbeak, Northern Pygmy-Owl, Black Swift, and Gray-crowned Rosy Finches.

From the deck of the lodge, the rugged inner ridge of the glaciered Olympic Mountains is spread out 180° before you. Gray Jays, Olympic marmots, deer, and pika are quite trusting here. Displays of alpine plants and wildlife are found inside, and a ranger is usually on duty to give trail and other information. Interpretive programs are held, and snowshoes are available for rent in the winter. A gift shop, small lunch counter, and rest rooms are on the lower level. The trails near the lodge are all asphalt-paved.

Hurricane Ridge is at the end of a picturesque, wide, well-paved 17-mile highway on which one can travel from sea level to 5,229 feet in about 45 minutes. From the Olympic Park Visitor Center, turn right and continue following the signs to Hurricane Ridge. There are many places to turn off the road for viewing. On the way up, watch for Swainson's, Varied, and Hermit Thrushes, Steller's Jay, and migrant passerines in season.

Elwha River

The Elwha River has the longest drainage of any river in the park. The usual forest campground birds are here: Varied and Swainson's Thrushes, Red-breasted Nuthatch, Chestnut-backed Chickadee, Golden-crowned Kinglet, American Robin, and Winter Wren plus the possibility of Spruce Grouse, Spotted Owl, Golden-crowned Sparrow, Pacific-slope Flycatcher, and MacGillivray's Warbler. There are 41 campsites, evening ranger programs, and hiking trails. To reach the Elwha River Campground, continue out of Port Angeles on US 101 for ten miles, then turn west and continue along the river for three miles to the campground.

Olympic Rain Forests

Hoh Rain Forest. Sitka spruce, Douglas-fir, western redcedar, western hemlock, and red alder are the primary rain forest trees. Beneath these moss- and epiphyte-draped giants are vine maple, huckleberry, ferns, bunchberry, oxalis, vanilla leaf, fungi, lichen, and liverworts. A chorus fills the dim, sun-dappled greenness in spring: Douglas squirrels with their piercing "chip" note; the low drumming of the Ruffed Grouse; the high-pitched tinkling notes of kinglets, chickadees, and warblers; and the raucous laughter of the Pileated Woodpecker. For a rain forest ecosystem sampler, walk the 0.75-mile Hall of Mosses trail starting at the Hoh Visitor Center. Watch for a possible Great Horned Owl.

The Hoh is 91 miles south of Port Angeles. Follow US 101 12 miles past Forks, then turn east at the park sign and travel 19 miles on a spur road along the Hoh River to the visitor center.

Queets and Quinault Rain Forests. The Queets River is the one Olympic Park river preserved from the mountains almost to the sea. It is kept in a near-wilderness condition. Solitude and a chance to see more forest birds from your car is probably best acquired on the Queets Valley Road. The entrance to the Queets is about 12 miles south of Kalaloch on US 101. The Quinault Rain Forest road is 15.8 miles south on US 101 from the Queets Corridor. The forest is rainy and dark, but tourist amenities are numerous near Lake Quinault. There is an excellent short loop trail off the South Shore Road, the Quinault Rain Forest Trail (Big Tree Grove Nature Trail), which goes through a grove of 500-year-old Douglas-firs. The trail is 1.3 miles from US 101; there is a picnic area and other hiking trails. A variety of forest birds are in the rain forests with remote possibilities of Spotted Owl, Marbled Murrelet, and Spruce Grouse; more likely are Blue Grouse, Vaux's Swift, American Dipper, Varied Thrush, Rufuous Hummingbird, and the common northwest forest birds.

Olympic Park Beaches

Except for 11 miles along US 101 between Ruby Beach and Kalaloch, the Olympic Park beaches are mostly undisturbed and unpeopled, enough so that cougars, bears, elk, deer, and other wildlife occasionally stroll down the beach. Sea stacks and pristine tide pools are highlights on the 30 miles of beach wilderness trail. Be sure to do your homework and carry a tide table on any of the beach hikes; unprepared beach hiking can be very dangerous. At all beaches watch for Common, Pacific, and Red-throated Loons; grebes; migrating Black Brant; scoters; mergansers; Harlequin Duck; Oldsquaw; Tufted Puffin; Pigeon Guillemot; Common Murre; auklets; shearwaters; Bald Eagle; Osprey; Peregrine Falcon; Merlin; Wandering Tattler; Rock Sandpiper; turnstones; phalaropes; gulls; terns; and shorebirds, in season. In March, April, and May, nearly 20,000 gray whales pass just offshore on their 6,000-mile migration from Baja, California.

Lake Ozette. This is Washington's largest freshwater lake—20 miles long. The area is remote and unsettled with only a ranger station and small campground. Bald Eagles and Osprey cruise over the lake, fishing is good, and trails to Cape Alava and Sand Point start here.

Cape Alava. Cape Alava is the western-most point in the contiguous states. This dramatic and historical beach is reached via a 3.3-mile, flat, boardwalked trail over spongy wetlands. Views of offshore islands are magnificent; Point of Arches is just to the north. An ancient Indian village buried in mud centuries ago was discovered here in 1970. The archaeological dig, now closed, unearthed artifacts from 500 years ago; these items are now on display at the Makah Museum in Neah Bay. A loop can be made by hiking three miles south on the beach to the Sand Point Trail. Fifty-six Indian petroglyphs are found along this stretch of beach.

La Push-Mora-Rialto beaches. An 18.5-mile wilderness trail north to Cape Alava begins here. To reach this area, turn west off US 101 just north of Forks. The road is paved and there are some amenities.

Ruby Beach. Tiny garnet crystals make up the pinkish sand of Ruby Beach and, like most of the north Olympic coast beaches, the view is spectacular. US 101 rejoins the coast at this point, and six different beaches, accessed by short pathways, are found between Ruby Beach and Kalaloch. Information is available at the Mora and Kalaloch Ranger Stations.

Kalaloch. There is a campground with 179 sites, a large, comfortable lodge, and a ranger station at Kalaloch. All are on a bluff overlooking the beach.

NORTH OLYMPIC PENINSULA COAST

Elwha Delta

Another site that is rewarding for gulls and marine birds is where the Elwha River meets the Strait of Juan de Fuca. The dike at the end of the road is a good spot for gulls including Glaucous and Glaucous-winged, Herring, Heermann's, and Thayer's; occasional Black-legged Kittiwakes have been seen. The usual marine ducks, alcids, cormorants, and grebes can also be seen. To reach the Elwha delta, follow US 101 for about six miles west out of Port Angeles then onto SH 112 (signed to Neah Bay). At 2.1 miles turn north onto Place Road for two miles, then east onto Elwha Dike Road. At 0.1 mile, park on the shoulder area on the south side of the road. A short trail leads to the log-strewn beach and the river delta.

Salt Creek Recreation Area

The Salt Creek Recreation Area is on the Strait of Juan de Fuca. It includes Tongue Point, Striped Peak, and the Salt Creek Estuary; Crescent and Freshwater Bays are adjacent. These are interesting and varied areas in which to bird. Turkey Vultures congregate here in large numbers in the fall, most having just made the more than 13-mile overwater journey from Vancouver Island. Alcids and sea ducks are found along the rocky shores of the Strait of Juan de Fuca, and marsh and land birds abound in the estuaries and forested areas.

Tongue Point. Salt Creek County Park and Recreation Area cover much of Tongue Point. The extensive kelp beds make this one of the top skin diving spots in Washington. It is a Marine Life Sanctuary and is maintained by the Clallam County Park System. At low tides, one can walk out on the rocks of Tongue Point, view the tide pools, and see the birds in a better perspective. Black Turnstone, Surfbird, Wandering Tattler, and Rock Sandpiper occasionally can be seen on the rocks; Black Oystercatchers nest on them. Harlequin Duck, Surf Scoter, Double-crested and Brandt's Cormorants, Common Murre, Tufted Puffin, Rhinoceros Auklet, and other alcids are seen regularly in the water offshore.

Harlequin Duck

Salt Creek County Park. There are 90 campsites at Salt Creek Park, some closely spaced in a large, open meadow looking out to the strait; others in a somewhat open, windswept treed area with a fair amount of room and privacy. There are excellent views looking toward Vancouver Island, British Columbia. Sea otters and seals can be seen around the undulating mats of seaweed and driftwood, and a Great Blue Heron usually rides on top. Gray whales, orca, California sea lions, and harbor seals can be seen further offshore. Heermann's Gulls are common in late summer and early fall.

The campground hosts the usual northwest chorus of Golden-crowned Kinglet, Red-breasted Nuthatch, and Chestnut-backed and Black-capped Chickadees, and each campsite is guaranteed to have a resident Winter Wren scolding the transient occupants. Blue Grouse, Band-tailed Pigeon, Belted Kingfisher, Red-breasted Sapsucker, Common Flicker, Swainson's Thrush, Solitary Vireo, and several warblers also have been seen.

Salt Creek Estuary. This is a good spot to see Great Blue Heron, Bald Eagle, and Osprey. Coho Salmon, Cutthroat, and Steelhead all use the creek for spawning. There is a small parking lot belonging to the park just before Crescent Beach. Half of Salt Creek, which empties into Crescent Bay, is park-owned, and half is privately owned and not open to the public except for a fee.

Crescent Bay. The county road parallels the low dunes of Crescent Bay beach, and there are good views from the roadside or from a car. There is a $3 charge to walk the private beach. Many wintering ducks including Oldsquaw, Harlequin Duck, all three scoters, mergansers, plus Common, Red-throated, Pacific, and, occasionally, Yellow-billed Loons can be seen at Crescent and Freshwater bays. Grebes and several species of gulls are also found here. Watch for shorebirds on the beach during migration.

OLYMPIC VULTURE STUDY

Grants from the Hawk Migration Association of North America and advice from birding friends led me to research the overwater Turkey Vulture migration from Canada's Vancouver Island. I chose the Salt Creek Recreation Area as the focal point for the Olympic Vulture Study, finally settling on Salt Creek County Park as the official site. The park is almost directly across from the Rocky Point military base and Sooke Park on Vancouver Island, where most of the 1,000-plus British Columbia-summering vultures are counted by Victoria birders.

During the three years of the study, more than 1,000 vultures have been counted each year coming in off the water. The birds generally fly on pleasant, warmish days with light winds. The last week in September and the first week in October are peak flight times, with several hundred vultures often coming across at once. At times, they continue on over the trees; other times, they delight us by landing in trees all around us and spreading their wings, or by soaring high over our heads on thermals as they reach land.

Other raptors are also on migration during the study, and we have recorded, in order of abundance, Red-tailed Hawk, Sharp-shinned Hawk, Bald Eagle, Cooper's Hawk, Northern Goshawk, Osprey, Peregrine Falcon, and Merlin.

To reach the Salt Creek Recreation Area, follow US 101W from Port Angeles—keeping right at SH 112 (to Joyce)—for 13.7 miles. Turn right at Camp Hayden Road and follow the road 4.2 miles to the campground. To reach Crescent Bay and the Salt Creek estuary, continue on Camp Hayden Road past the campground entrance about 0.3 mile.

SH 112 LOOKOUT SITES

Between the Salt Creek area and Neah Bay are several spots to pull off and scan the beaches and offshore waters for loons, grebes, waterfowl, alcids, cormorants, shorebirds, and raptors. Orca are occasionally seen. These handsome, toothed whales were revered by coastal Indian tribes and regularly appear on their totems and artwork. Good stopping places along SH 112 include Pillar Point, Clallam Bay, and Kydaka Point. Seal and Sail Rocks are offshore sites for nesting colonies of cormorants, puffins, and gulls. The rocks are visible from the shore.

NEAH BAY

Neah Bay and the surrounding area is a center for fishing and is located within the Makah Indian Reservation. *Please respect tribal laws.* Birding is excellent in the area, and be sure not to miss the handsome Makah Research and Cultural Center, one of the northwest's finest museums. The museum is located on the south side of the road at the eastern edge of town. Neah Bay is located 70 miles west of Port Angeles on SH 112.

Cape Flattery. Cape Flattery, the northwestern-most point in the contiguous US, was almost discovered by James Cook in 1778. His journal reads: "There appeared to be a small opening that flattered us with hopes of finding a harbor there," hence Cape Flattery. His discovery proved fruitless, however, and it wasn't until Capt. George Vancouver returned to the area in 1792 that he located Cook's true Cape Flattery. Flattery Rocks, to the south, are charted as Cook's original discovery.

Ancient Sitka spruce and western redcedars throw out their roots seemingly to bar visitors from the impressive views awaiting them at the end of the short trail. Watch your step! While meandering through the trees and shrubbery, watch for Rufous Hummingbird, Rufous-sided Towhee, Chestnut-backed Chickadee, Golden-crowned Kinglet, Varied and Swainson's Thrushes, and many other passerines, in season. At the end of the trail, there are several viewpoints from a high bluff overlooking the merging of the Pacific Ocean and the Strait of Juan de Fuca. Gray whales pass just below these cliffs in the spring. Large flights of Sandhill Cranes often in "V" and line formations high overhead are also observed in the spring heading north to British Columbia and Alaska.

The bluff on the cape allows wonderful views of large caves carved by centuries of pounding waves. Pigeon Guillemot, Tufted Puffin, Black Oystercatcher, Common Murre, and other seabirds can all be seen at close hand, especially with a scope. Many nest on Tatoosh Island. Cape Flattery trail can be reached from the west edge of Neah Bay by a loop road; the left road is paved to the Makah Air Force Station, the right road gravel. The parking lot is 8.5 miles from Neah Bay.

Tatoosh Island. Tatoosh Island was the home and burial ground of the Makah Indians long ago. The island, about a half mile off Cape Flattery at the entrance to the Strait of Juan de Fuca, now is owned by the U.S. Geological Survey and is a base for oceanographic studies. The lighthouse on the island, built in 1847, is one of the oldest in the northwest. Tatoosh Island is also home to many seabird colonies including alcids, Pelagic Cormorants, Black Oystercatchers, and Glaucous-winged Gulls, all of which can be seen on the island and around the waters offshore. Also scan the cliffsides. Nesting on the island but active only at night are Cassin's Auklet, and Leach's and Fork-tailed Storm-petrels.

Mukkaw Bay. By turning south at the Air Force Station and crossing the Waatch River Bridge, many shorebirds and various waterfowl can be seen. Wandering Tattler; Rock Sandpiper; Surfbird; turnstones; Whimbrel; Sanderling; Harlequin Duck; Common Merganser; Common, White-winged, and Black Scoters; eagles; falcons; and many others may be seen.

Hobuck Beach. Continue a few miles further to Hobuck Beach for good views of swans, ducks, shorebirds, marine birds, gulls, and raptors. Marine mammals often are seen here, and the tide pools are excellent. This 2.5 mile stretch of beach often is deserted, but is custom-made for birding.

Bahokus Peak. Bahokus and Archawat Peaks are about 1,400 feet in elevation and located more or less in the center of the Cape Flattery "peninsula." The peaks and their ridgeline are separated by the Waatch Valley from the rest of the Olympic Peninsula. The Falcon Research Group, beginning in 1983, started hawk watch studies here. Now monitored by the Ad Hawk group, these studies have escalated through the years and have established this remote site as a major raptor migration route. The Strait of Juan de Fuca, 13 miles wide, is the first major water crossing north of Mexico. To give an idea of its importance, in 1990, during an approximately four-week period, nearly 9,000 migrating raptors were counted, and this count excludes Bald Eagles. Red-tailed Hawks account for nearly 75% of the total, Sharp-shinned Hawks another 10%. Golden Eagle, Cooper's Hawk, Osprey, and Turkey Vulture also are prominent in their passing but in much smaller numbers. For more information on the Cape Flattery Hawk Watch Project, contact Donna Chapman, Wildlife Biologist, Makah Tribal Center, Neah Bay, WA 98357.

WASHINGTON ISLANDS REFUGES

Copalis NWR, Needles NWR, Quillayute NWR, and Flattery Rocks NWR

This series of national refuges extends for more than 100 miles along Washington's Pacific coast and contains 870 rocks, reefs, and islands. These refuges are in the midst of abundant ocean food sources and are protected from land predators.

Fourteen species of seabirds nest here including Tufted Puffin; Cassin's Auklet; Leach's and Fork-tailed Petrels; Brandt's, Pelagic, and Double-crested Cormorants; Rhinoceros Auklet; and Common Murre. The total count of waterfowl, seabirds, and shorebirds is probably more than a million during migration.

These islands are closed to the public and boaters are asked to *please stay at least 200 yards offshore to avoid disturbing wildlife*. There are interpretive sites telling about the island wildlife at Lake Ozette, Rialto Beach, Second Beach, Ruby Beach, and Kalaloch. The islands can be viewed from a distance, and the birds often fly near the coastline. For more information contact Nisqually NWR Complex, 100 Brown Farm Road, Olympia, WA 98506; (360) 753-9467.

OLYMPIC COAST NATIONAL MARINE SANCTUARY

On July 16, 1994, this newest sanctuary was formally dedicated. Marine sanctuaries are similar to national parks—created to protect resources of special national significance—but are administered by the Commerce Department's National Oceanic and Atmospheric Administration (NOAA).

The intertidal habitat in the Olympic sanctuary is some of the most productive in the country. The seabird colonies, some of the biggest in the lower 48 states, feed on the vast variety of fish that live in the underwater canyons and submarine plateaus of the sanctuary. Whale, dolphin, and porpoise species plus varieties of kelp are more numerous here than anywhere else in the world.

While protecting this vast marine habitat, sanctuary status also means no oil or gas development. A proposal to designate the majority of the sanctuary as an "area to be avoided" by oil and chemical-bearing ships is hoped to be adopted in the near future. The 3,000-acre sanctuary extends from Cape Flattery to Copalis.

BOGACHIEL STATE PARK

Bogachiel is the only developed state park on the northwest Olympic peninsula. It is a rain forest environment, but many deep-forest birds can, with luck, be seen here including Spotted Owl, Spruce Grouse, and Gray Jay. There is excellent steelhead and salmon fishing on the river. Only 20 acres of the park's 119 are developed; the 41 campsites are here. Several hiking trails are available. Bogachiel State Park is located 4.4 miles south of Forks on US 101.

Chapter 2
South Coastal and Willapa Hills

 The South Coastal area extends from Grays Harbor at the southern edge of the Olympic Peninsula to the mouth of the Columbia River, approximately 6% of the state. Three hundred years after Columbus' voyage in 1492, Robert Gray, the Yankee fur trader captain of the *Columbia Rediviva*, crossed the intimidating bar of a new river and changed North American history. Named after Gray's ship, the 1,214-mile-long Columbia, which drains more than 259,000 square miles of the Pacific Northwest, went on to become an avenue of exploration into Oregon, Washington, and British Columbia.

The South Coastal and Willapa Hills region is a focal point for salmon fishing, razor clam digging and, in recent years, whale-watching trips for gray whales. The southern part of Grays Harbor County, at Bowerman Basin, is the staging ground for more than a million shorebirds each April, one of the largest gatherings on the west coast. Black bears and Spotted Owls share the forests of this region. The inland farming valleys of the area are bucolic and offer good fishing on uncrowded rivers and lakes.

This area is bordered by I-5 on the east and the Columbia River, geographical boundary between Washington and Oregon, to the south. Again, there are no freeways once you leave I-5, except for a stretch on US 12 toward Westport. SH 4 and SH 6 cross the area east to west.

These highways are two-lane, but traffic is usually light. Always expect log trucks in western Washington! SH 4 follows the Columbia River for the most part and passes by one of Washington's few surviving covered bridges at Grays River.

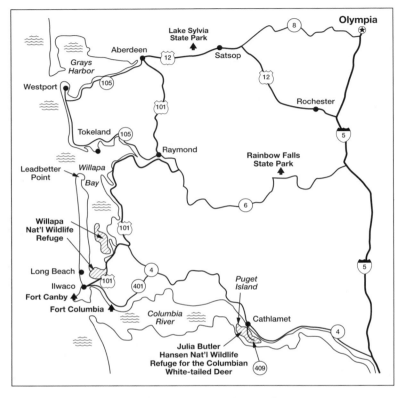

South Coastal and Willapa Hills

The gently rolling Willapa Hills extend west to east between SH 4 and SH 6, a breach in the lengthy coast range. The oldest rocks here are pillow basalt, of a greenish-black or black color; the bedrock is sandstone and shales. This is a humid, ridge-and-ravine countryside, never over 3,000 feet. It is drained by the Willapa and Chehalis rivers, which flow into the Pacific. Western hemlock, Douglas-fir, western redcedar, and Sitka spruce predominate, and there is lush undergrowth everywhere. Pacific and Wahkiakum counties, plus parts of Cowlitz, Lewis, Thurston, and Mason counties are contained in this southwestern section of Washington.

SATSOP RIVER VALLEY

The Satsop River Valley offers a variety of habitats, including old-growth forest, tree farms, open meadows, farmland, and riparian areas. The valley contains areas of near-rain forest habitat due to 80–90 inches of annual rainfall, as well as an oak-grassland habitat common to drier inland areas south of Fort Lewis and Olympia. Look for a variety of marsh birds and freshwater ducks, woodpeckers, swallows, warblers, sparrows, and other passerines.

Schafer State Park. The park takes in about 120 acres along the East Satsop River. Birds common year-round are Red-breasted Merganser, Red-tailed Hawk, Townsend's Warbler, Evening Grosbeak, Varied Thrush, Cassin's Finch, American Dipper, Chestnut-backed and Black-backed Chickadees, Steller's Jay, American Goldfinch, Ruffed Grouse, Green Heron, Long-eared Owl, and many others.

Schafer State Park has campsites, picnic shelters, and hiking trails heading to several types of habitats. The park is reached by heading west from Olympia on US 12. At Brady, turn north on East Satsop Road (or Middle Satsop Road) and proceed ten miles to the park.

LAKE SYLVIA STATE PARK

Lake Sylvia State Park is a small park forested with hemlock, cedar, and alder. Lake Sylvia is a long, narrow lake with Common Merganser, Bufflehead, Northern Shoveler, Wood Duck, Pied-billed Grebe, and Great Blue Heron. At the north end of the lake, there are water channels between several marshy islands. Look for American Bittern, Virginia Rail, blackbirds, and wrens. During spring migration, the woods are full of warblers, flycatchers, and vireos. The park has 37 campsites, hiking trails, and other recreational facilities. It lies one mile north of Montesano off US 12.

GRAYS HARBOR

Grays Harbor was named for Captain Robert Gray, an American fur trader who discovered both the harbor and the Columbia River in

1792. Gray named the harbor "Bullfinch," in honor of the owner of his ship, but Lieutenant Joseph Whidbey, whose charts were published soon after, renamed the area Grays Harbor. The 95-square-mile bay has miles of sandy shore and tide flats, and extremely interesting and challenging birding.

Ocean Shores. This area was a cattle ranch until 1960 when it was purchased and developed. Ocean Shores area offers a variety of interesting pursuits. Located on Point Brown to the north of the entrance to Grays Harbor, it hosts huge numbers of shorebirds. Point Brown's diverse habitats—forest, mudflats, freshwater lake, salt marshes, sand dunes, and open beaches—are the drawing cards for its wildlife. State records abound from here: Ruff; Dotterel; Hudsonian and Bar-tailed Godwits; Buff-breasted and Upland Sandpipers; and many others. The rock jetty at the end of Brown Point is excellent for Wandering Tattlers, Black Turnstones, shearwaters, and gulls. Rock Sandpipers and Surfbirds winter there, and in summer Brown Pelicans are seen. Elegant Terns occasionally appear in great numbers. In July 1992, up to 300 were counted at Ocean Shores; at Tokeland, a bit further south, observers saw nearly a thousand Elegant Terns in mid-August.

Lesser Golden-Plover, Buff-breasted Sandpiper, Whimbrel, Horned Lark, Lapland Longspur, and others often can be found in the grassy dune areas to the east of the jetty. In winter, Bald Eagles, Peregrine Falcons, Merlins, Snowy Owls, and Snow Buntings sometimes are seen.

Ocean Shores is reached by traveling west from Hoquiam on SH 109, then turning south on SH 115. To get to the Point Brown jetty, take Ocean Shores Boulevard south until reaching a parking area at the very southwest tip.

The Oyhut Game Habitat Management Area. The Oyhut Management Area, covering 682 acres, is a prime resting stop for the Dusky Canada Goose on its fall migration. American Wigeon, Mallard, Northern Pintail, and Green-winged Teal also are seen. Large flocks of Marbled Godwits are often on the beach, and the salt marsh area is good for waders and shorebirds. Oyhut is a large saltwater intrusion—a "sink"—with sand dunes on three sides and the North

Brown Pelican

Jetty of Grays Harbor on the north. Watch for migrant sparrows and warblers near and in the dunes. Oyhut is reached by heading west at the junction of SH 115 and Point Brown Avenue. It is signed and next to the sewage treatment plant.

Ocean City State Park. The fall passerine migration is usually quite good here, and it is one of the best spots for Palm Warblers. Between the park and the highway, Virginia Rails, Bitterns, blackbirds, and marsh wrens nest. Great Egrets are sometimes seen. Ocean City State Park, with 181 various types of campsites, is central to all of the Point Brown activities. It is located two miles north of Ocean Shores on SH 115.

Bowerman Basin. One of the most crucial stopovers for hundreds of thousands of migrant shorebirds on the west coast is Bowerman Basin. Located at the northeast edge of the Grays Harbor estuary, it is bordered by SH 109 on the north, Paulson Road on the east, the Bowerman Field Airport on the south, and by a row of trestle pilings on the west. Bowerman Basin is an ideal habitat for the voracious appetites of the shorebirds. The basin lies at a bit higher elevation than the rest of the harbor, making it the last spot to be flooded at high tide and the first spot exposed as the tide recedes, thereby giving the birds extra time to feed. Tiny, shrimplike organisms that are abundant in the mud provide food. The salt marsh areas surrounding the flats offer cover and roost sites.

The birds begin showing up in early April, but the biggest concentrations are in late April, from approximately the 18th to the 26th. The last of the migrants dwindle away in mid-May. Best observation times are the hour before and the hour after high tide. Western Sandpipers account for more than 85% of the total. Dunlin, Short-billed and Long-billed Dowitchers, Semipalmated Plovers, and Red Knots make up most of the rest. Nearly 50,000 Dunlin also winter in the area. Peregrine Falcons, Merlins, Red-tailed Hawks, and Northern Harriers often are seen in the vicinity, as are a variety of waterfowl, gulls, terns, and passerines.

To reach Bowerman Basin, follow SH 109 for 0.5 mile out of Hoquiam, turn left on Paulson Road, then right on Airport Way until you reach signs for Bowerman Basin and parking. The birds can be

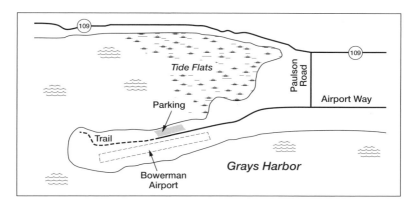

Bowerman Basin

viewed from the paved parking area; views are best with binoculars or scope. There are also openings along a rather muddy trail leading to the point of the peninsula. *Do not go beyond the marked viewing-area boundary.* For further information and tide times, contact: Grays Harbor NWR, c/o Nisqually NWR, 100 Brown Farm Road, Olympia, WA 98506; (360) 753-9467.

Aberdeen Sewage Treatment Ponds. Aberdeen is the largest city on the coast and lies at the eastern end of Grays Harbor. Its sewage treatment ponds, behind dikes on the north side of SH 105, sometimes yield interesting species, including Stilt Sandpiper and Hudsonian Godwit. The ponds are about 0.5 miles west of the entrance to Grays Harbor College.

Bottle Beach. This beach boasts one of the finest mudflat shorebird areas in Grays Harbor. Semipalmated Plover, Black-bellied Plover, American Golden-Plover, Whimbrel, Willet, Greater Yellowlegs, Red Knot, Least Sandpiper, and Long-billed Dowitcher are just a few that might be seen. Scan the bay for mergansers, ducks, geese, loons, and grebes. Bottle Beach is reached by driving 2.5 miles west of the Elk River bridge on SH 105. Take the one-lane (difficult to see) road at the spot where the road curves to the left away from the diked fields. Park where you can, and follow a path to the beach.

Westport. At the south entrance to Grays Harbor is the Westport area. Two state parks, three rock jetties, a fishing pier, and whale-watching boat trips (with sometimes fine views of seabirds, gulls, and kittiwakes) make this another excellent birding spot. Whale-watching is best from March to May. Brown Pelicans, Caspian Terns, and Double-crested Cormorants are common in summer, and Parasitic Jaegers may be seen in migration from the South Jetty. Westport is located south of Aberdeen on SH 105 and is well-signed.

ELIZABETH A. MILLS
1976

Greater Yellowlegs

PELAGIC TRIPS

Pelagic trips to look for seabirds and rare migrants are enthusiastically attended. On all of North America's coastline, ocean-going bird trips fill up quickly, and only the most inclement weather will cause the cancellation of an excursion. Die-hard birders defy seasickness with patches and pills, the elements with Gore-tex and slickers, and the lack of restaurants with eclectic lunches that only the strong-of-stomach can master. Pelagic birding is for the adventurer.

Pelagic bird trips are not just for seabirds and ducks. Encounters with whales and pinnipeds are not unusual, and raptors and off-course songbirds are not infrequent. One of the most interesting migration spectacles—best seen from a boat—is the semi-annual flight of Sooty Shearwaters. By the tens of thousands or more, these transequatorial petrels travel a course along the North American sea-coasts as they move between nesting areas in the southern hemisphere and winter feeding areas in the north Pacific.

Offshore Seabird Trips from Westport

Since 1966, Terry Wahl has led more than 200 trips to Grays Canyon and the ocean off Washington's coast. Species that are regularly seen include Black-footed Albatross, Northern Fulmar, Sooty Shearwater, Fork-tailed Storm-Petrel, Black-legged Kittiwake, Common Murre, Pigeon Guillemot, Marbled Murrelet, Cassin's and Rhinoceros Auklets, and Tufted Puffin.

Flesh-footed and Pink-footed Shearwaters and Xantus' Murrelet are possible from May to October; Laysan Albatross, Short-tailed Shearwater, and Ancient Murrelet are possible both early and late in the season. Buller's Shearwater is likely from mid-August to October; Leach's Storm-Petrel and Long-tailed Jaeger in July and August; Red-necked Phalarope and Arctic Tern in May, and from July to September; Red Phalarope and South Polar Skua from July to October; Pomarine and Parasitic Jaegers and Sabine's Gull in May, and from July to October.

Along with the above birds, about a dozen species of gulls, Caspian and Common Terns, loons, cormorants, sea ducks, shorebirds, migrant land birds, and a variety of sea mammals can be seen in season. Most of the trips from Westport go to Gray's Canyon, about 25–30 miles offshore.

Trips leave from Westport on the Pacific Ocean and are usually full a month or so before the scheduled date. There are often last-minute cancellations, so it can be profitable to check if you are late signing up. Most trips last eight to ten hours. Coffee and hot water are supplied; participants bring their own lunches.

Weather on pelagic trips can be cold, windy, and wet, so dress for the worst—in layers of warm clothing with a water-repellent top layer. Don't forget a cap, gloves, and warm boots. There is a warm cabin on the boat. Photography is possible on trips.

Trips are usually scheduled from July through October, and the cost is $70 per person. The boat leaves about 6 a.m. and returns about 4 p.m. for the Gray's Canyon trips. The occasional longer trips going farther offshore leave during the night. They are more rigorous, take fewer people, and cost $160 per person. For information on Westport Seabird trips, contact Terry Wahl at 3041 Eldridge, Bellingham, WA 98225; (360) 733-8255.

RAYMOND AREA

The Raymond Airport was one of the first spots in Washington where White-tailed Kites were routinely spotted. Occasional sightings have been reported from other spots along the coast, but the airport location was the first verified breeding site in the state. The parking lot at the airfield is the best viewing area if the kites are present. The extensive brushy fields around the airport support flocks of passerines and blackbirds all year, and Northern Harriers and various falcons are also seen in the vicinity during migration and in the winter. To reach the airport, drive west of Raymond on SH 105 for about three miles; the route is well-signed.

In the past three years, the White-tailed Kites most often have been seen between the towns of Lebam and Frances on SH 6, approximately ten miles east of Raymond. By following Elk Prairie Road south of SH 6 for about a mile and scanning the fields, kites are a good possibility.

North River. West of the airport on SH 105, wintering Willets are regularly seen on the mudflats east of the mouth of the North River. Whimbrels, Long-billed Curlew, and Marbled Godwit also can be found on the flats. Be sure to check flocks of godwits for possible Hudsonian and Bar-tailed Godwits.

JOHN'S RIVER HABITAT MANAGEMENT AREA

The John's River Area, which includes Markham Island, has 1,528 acres of tidal mudflats, grass, brush, and spruce bottoms, and hillsides of second-growth alder and fir. The extensive estuary provides resting and feeding habitat for migrating and wintering waterfowl and shore-birds. Peregrine Falcons and other raptors can be seen. Upland game birds are found in the drier habitats. Black-tailed deer, Roosevelt elk, and black bear are in this area; salmon and steelhead fishermen also take advantage of the site. John's River is 12 miles southwest of Aberdeen on SH 105.

TOKELAND

SH 105 passes through the Shoalwater Indian Reservation where the turnoff to Tokeland is located. The town, in an area famous for oysters and crabs, is settled on the south side of a three-mile spit at the northern entrance to inner Willapa Harbor. Toke Point, at the tip of the spit, is named after a local Indian chief whose reputation includes being a glib teller of legends, the area's fastest canoe paddler, and a leader of war parties against the settlers. The Tokeland Hotel, built in 1885, is listed on the National Register of Historic Sites and is open for dining, lodging, and tours.

Birding for waterfowl, shorebirds, raptors, terns, gulls, and migrating passerines is very good here. West of the road approaching the town is a large tidal marsh. Marbled Godwit, Long-billed Curlew, Whimbrel, Greater Yellowlegs, and dowitchers can be seen in winter and during migration.

LONG BEACH PENINSULA

The Long Beach Peninsula is a barrier beach between the Pacific Ocean and Willapa Bay, a comparatively undisturbed estuary. It stretches 28 miles north from the town of Ilwaco. The peninsula is made up of small fishing villages, miles of sandy beaches, estuarine marshes, dunes, and coniferous forests. This is a premier west coast birding spot that hosts hundreds of thousands of waterfowl and shorebirds during spring and fall migration, and also in winter.

Two day-use parks provide beach access from SH 103 north of the town of Long Beach. Loomis Lake State Park, nine miles north, and Pacific Pines State Park Recreational Area, 15 miles north, provide parking, rest rooms, picnic areas with windscreens, and facilities for the disabled.

WILLAPA NATIONAL WILDLIFE REFUGE

The Willapa National Wildlife Refuge, created in 1937 to provide a wintering area for Brant, is a fragmented area on and around the Long Beach Peninsula. Eleven thousand acres of diverse habitat are found in the five main sections of the refuge: Leadbetter Point, Long Island, Willapa Bay, the Riekkola Unit, and the Lewis Unit.

Long Island. Long Island, accessible only by boat, is a birder's paradise for kayakers. It is the largest estuarine island on the Pacific Coast. Its 5,000 acres include 274-acre Cedar Grove, an old-growth remnant forest, salt grass tidal marshes, mudflats, and extensive wet coastal forest. The extensive eelgrass beds found on the west side of the island attract brant from October through May. Nine species of owls are present, and many woodpeckers and songbirds nest here.

Cedar Grove offers an extensive pallet of old-growth forest wildlife from canopy to floor. The 0.75-mile Trail of the Ancient Cedars gives visitors the opportunity to see Blue Grouse, Winter Wren, Northern Saw-whet and Barred Owls, Vaux's Swift, Pileated and Hairy Woodpeckers, Solitary Vireo, Western Tanager, Olive-sided Flycatcher, Golden-crowned Kinglet, Steller's Jay, Common Raven, and Bald Eagle. Black bears are abundant, and several species of squirrels, bats, and salamanders—along with pine marten, raccoon, bobcat, and cougar—are found here.

(text continued on page 43)

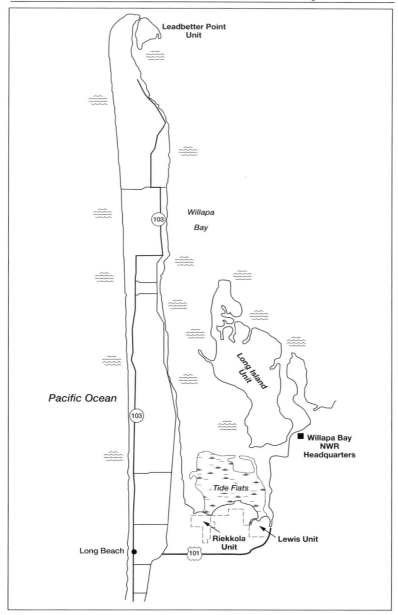

Long Beach Peninsula

Bald Eagle

(text continued from page 40)

There are five primitive campsites on the island. You must have your own boat or secure the services of a competent captain. The trip to and from the island can be difficult and occasionally dangerous due to tidal fluctuations, currents, and extensive mudflats.

Leadbetter Point State Park Natural Area. Leadbetter Point is at the northern tip of the Long Beach Peninsula. Located three miles north of Oysterville on Stackpole Road, it is a day-use park. Shifting sand dunes, freshwater ponds, marshes, grasslands, and forests provide habitats for outstanding birding. Parking areas are found at Stackpole Slough and at the northern end of the park. Easy hiking trails start at both points, and there are trails to the ocean beach off the main road. Peak seasons for viewing migrants are late April and early October.

Shorebird migration is excellent here with Red Knots, Pectoral Sandpipers, golden-plovers, Western Sandpipers, Sharp-tailed Sandpipers (fall), and other common shorebirds. Dunlins, Sanderlings, and gulls are found on the outer beaches, and Snowy Plovers nest there. Some beach segments are closed April–August to protect the plovers, but they can be seen from a distance. Loons, grebes, mergansers, cormorants, Brown Pelicans, gulls, terns, Trumpeter Swans, ducks, and raptors are present in good numbers, except during the summer. Good views of vast flocks of Sooty Shearwaters on their way from summering in Alaska to their nesting islands off the coast of New Zealand can be seen east of the point; lesser numbers are seen in the springtime. White-fronted Geese can be seen in May, and the shrubby grasslands are good spots to search for migrant passerines.

Lewis Unit. At the south end of Willapa Bay near the mouth of the Bear River is the Lewis Unit. American Wigeon, Canvasback, scaups, Green-winged Teal, and Bufflehead use the freshwater marshes for both resting and wintering habitat. Trumpeter Swans often winter here. To reach the Lewis Unit, follow US 101 to just west of Bear River. Turn north on Jeldness Road for about 1.5 miles to parking and trailhead. Both the Lewis and Riekkola units have extensive diked hiking trails.

Riekkola Unit. The Riekkola Unit provides feeding areas for migrant geese, ducks, and shorebirds. The area is especially important for the dusky race of the Canada Goose. Geese are basically grazing animals, and grassland meadows are planted, improved, and maintained for them on an ongoing basis. To reach the parking lot and trailhead, take Yeaton Road out of Long Beach for about four miles.

The refuge headquarters is located 13 miles north of Ilwaco on US 101. Maps, directions, and brochures can be found there. To request information by mail write to: Refuge Manager, Willapa National Wildlife Refuge, HC 01, Box 910, Ilwaco, WA 98624-9707; (360) 484-3482.

FORT CANBY

Fort Canby was established in 1862 to guard the entrance to the Columbia River. The fort became a park in 1957 and encompasses nearly 1,900 acres with 190 campsites and 16 miles of hiking trails. There is an interpretive center featuring the Lewis and Clark Expedition plus local military and maritime history. Fort Canby is 2.5 miles southwest of Ilwaco on US 101. For information or reservations: Fort Canby State Park, P.O. Box 488, Ilwaco, WA 98624-0488; (360) 642-3078.

The North Jetty. The jetty, built between 1914 and 1916 to aid in keeping the shipping channel open, is the prime spot for viewing birds. The jetty provides views of Bald Eagles, Sooty Shearwaters, Black-legged Kittiwakes, Brown Pelicans, Heermann's Gulls, loons, alcids, sea ducks, and cormorants. Shorebirds, including tattlers, turnstones, Surfbirds, and Rock Sandpipers can be seen along with migrant passerines.

FORT COLUMBIA

Fort Columbia is a day-use park featuring a Chinook Indian exhibit and a history of coastal artillery. It is listed as a National Historic Site, and there is a youth hostel in the park. It is located on the Columbia River two miles southeast of Chinook on US 101.

Cathlamet. In 1982, when President Ronald Reagan and Congress selected June 20th as National Bald Eagle Day, Cathlamet chose this theme for its annual summer festival. More than a decade later, it is still possibly the only community in the nation to set aside a day to celebrate the Bald Eagle.

PUGET ISLAND

Puget Island's 8,000 acres are an interesting link via bridge and ferry between Washington and Oregon. It has, through the years, been diked, logged, farmed, and used as pasture for dairy cattle. Less than 300 acres of native woodland are left, but there is varied birding in the area, plus opportunities to view the endangered Columbian white-tailed deer. During migration and the winter months, waterfowl are abundant.

To reach Puget Island, take SH 409 about 1.5 miles south of Cathlamet, then south over the bridge to the island. A short drive across the island brings you to the tiny ferry and the 15-minute ride to Oregon ($2.50). We have seen migrant Sandhill Cranes and swans from the ferry in November.

ROBERT W. LITTLE PRESERVE

The Nature Conservancy's Robert W. Little Preserve also is located on Puget Island. The preserve furnishes native tidal spruce swampland significant in the preservation of the Columbian white-tailed deer. Wetland wildlife—including herons, songbirds, beaver, and raccoon—is also found here.

The preserve is open from February to August and is reached by traveling west on West Birnie Slough Road for 0.75 of a mile to Crossdike Road Junction. Turn onto Crossdike Road and go about 1.5 miles to North Welcome Slough Road. The preserve lies along North Welcome Slough Road at that point for 0.4 mile. Best viewing is from the road.

LEWIS AND CLARK NATIONAL WILDLIFE REFUGE

The Lewis and Clark NWR, accessible by boat only, takes in the expansive estuary of the Columbia River and its islands. It encompasses 35,000 acres of mudflats, islands, sand bars, and tidal marshes of Washington and Oregon. Peak populations of up to 3,000 Tundra Swan, 2,000 Canada Geese, and 50,000 Mallard, American Wigeon, Canvasback, Lesser Scaup, and Northern Pintail have been observed here.

The deeper channels of the estuary provide fish for diving grebes and cormorants. Spruce, cottonwoods, and willows on the islands provide perching and nesting sites for Red-tailed Hawks and Bald Eagles. Passerines nesting in the area include Orange-crowned Warbler, Black-throated Gray Warbler, Common Yellowthroat, Wilson's Warbler, and Savannah, Song, and White-crowned Sparrows, to name just a few. Gulls, shorebirds, and Great Blue Herons can be seen on the sandy beaches and mudflats.

October through April is the best time for observing large numbers of birds. The refuge is open all year. Two boat landings are near Skamokawa in Washington, and at Aldrich Point and John Day in Oregon. Much of the river and islands can be seen from shore. For a map and further information, contact Lewis and Clark NWR, c/o Willapa NWR, Ilwaco, WA 98624; (360) 484-3482.

JULIA BUTLER HANSEN NWR FOR THE COLUMBIAN WHITE-TAILED DEER

The Julia Butler Hansen NWR is located on the Columbia River in Washington and Oregon. The 4,757 acres of diked floodplain is critical habitat for the deer; Roosevelt elk and coyotes are common. It is also prime wintering habitat for more than 100,000 waterfowl. American Wigeons make up more than half this total, and more than 1,000 geese, primarily Dusky and Lesser Canadas, are here. Tundra Swan, Mallard, Northern Pintail, Great Blue Heron, Common Snipe, and loons are also common. In the spring, American Goldfinch, Varied Thrush, Golden-crowned Sparrow, Bewick's Wren, Wilson's Warbler, and many other songbirds are found. Marsh birds and raptors, including possible White-tailed Kite, are common.

The refuge is located two miles west of Cathlamet on SH 4. At Steamboat Slough Road, just west of the Elochoman River bridge, is the refuge entrance. Best viewing is from the road encircling the main refuge. The islands in the refuge are accessible only by boat.

Tenasillahe Island. The island has a nine-mile diked hiking trail and occasionally hosts large numbers of Band-tailed Pigeons in the fall. Mink, river otter, beaver, and nutria can also be seen. The annual precipitation here is about 106 inches. Boots might come in handy.

BOOTS SATTERLEE BLACK RIVER PRESERVE

The Nature Conservancy's Boots Satterlee Black River Preserve covers nearly 22 acres and is one of the largest pristine riparian environments in western Washington. It is accessible only by canoe or kayak. Paddling through the dense stands of Oregon ash and red alder edged with thickets of red osier, you can see Yellow, MacGillivray's, and Yellow-rumped Warblers; Black-headed Grosbeak; American Bittern; Green Heron; Mallard; and Wood Duck. Otter, beaver, and mink also might be spotted.

There are two boat launches to the reserve: To reach the easternmost launching site, go 12 miles south of Olympia on I-5 turning west at the Rochester exit, US 12. Follow US 12 through Rochester and past Albany Street. Proceed about three miles, turning right on Moon Road SW, and again right into the lot. A second launch site is reached by turning right at Albany Street and continuing approximately six miles upriver on SH 121/Littlerock Road SW to the site on the left. These boat launches also give access to the Black River Habitat Management Area on the opposite river bank.

RAINBOW FALLS STATE PARK

Rainbow Falls State Park is a CCC-constructed park that features a swinging bridge over the Chehalis River. An old-growth forest fragment is located in the park, and there are hiking and nature trails. Hermit Warblers have been found here in the trees near the playground. Screech-owls sometimes nest in snags in the same area. There are 47 standard campsites and three primitive sites. Rainbow Falls is located 17 miles west of Chehalis on SH 6.

Chapter 3
North Puget Trough

 The complete length of the Puget Trough extends south through western Washington from the Fraser River lowlands in British Columbia to the Willamette Valley in Oregon. For ease, I have divided this long area into two regions: the North Puget Trough and the South Puget Trough.

The North Puget Trough is bordered on the north by British Columbia, on the east by the foothills of the Cascade Mountains, on the west by the eastern shore of Puget Sound, and on the south by the King County line. This region is the second-most populated in the state and probably the most heavily birded. Rolling hills, often densely forested, some drier prairie-like areas, and many rivers, lakes, and miles of saltwater shoreline make up its habitats.

The region is part of the humid transition zone with extensive forests of Douglas-fir, western redcedar, and western hemlock. Bigleaf maple, black cottonwood, red alder, and Pacific dogwood are found along streams. Some of the more common birds of this zone are the Wood Duck, Bald Eagle, Ruffed Grouse, Band-tailed Pigeon, Downy and Hairy Woodpeckers, Steller's Jay, Vaux's Swift, Rufous-sided Towhee, Black-capped and Chestnut-backed Chickadees, Winter Wren, Black-throated Gray Warbler, American Goldfinch, and Purple Finch.

This region includes the western parts of Whatcom, Skagit, and Snohomish counties. The primary north-south highway is Interstate 5. Main east-west highways are US 2 out of Everett and SH 20 from the Mount Vernon area.

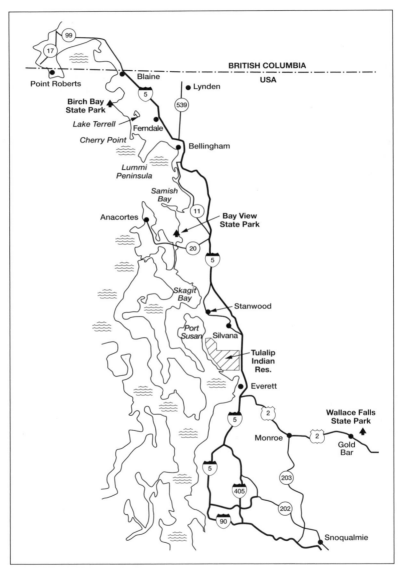

North Puget Trough

POINT ROBERTS

Point Roberts is somewhat of an anomaly: It is U.S. soil, but you must go through a foreign country, hence through two customs stations, or over water, to get there. Birding can be great, especially for water birds. Point Roberts became part of the United States during 1872 arbitrations over the international boundary through the San Juan Islands. Cut off from Canada by the 49th parallel, this well-developed five square miles of northwest Whatcom County is reached by driving about 25 miles through British Columbia. Visit it in the winter to reap the raptorial and other benefits of the wonderful birding on the Fraser River Delta.

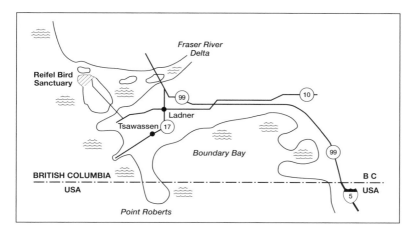

Point Roberts

Strong marine currents push large numbers of birds toward the peninsula shore. Lighthouse Park, which juts into the Strait of Georgia, is one of the best viewing spots. All loon species can be seen here, including Yellow-billed, with luck. Brant, all three scoters, Harlequin Duck, Oldsquaw, an occasional King Eider, scaups, Northern Pintail, Canvasback, and many others make up the thousands of ducks and geese that winter on the strait and Boundary Bay to the east. Alcids are plentiful and include Marbled and Ancient Murrelets, Pigeon Guillemot, Common Murre, and others. Watch for kittiwakes; Parasitic Jaegers; Thayer's, Glaucous-winged, Mew, and Heermann's Gulls; terns; and other migrants during the fall.

Shorebirds, such as Black-bellied Plover, Sanderling, and Black Turnstone, can be seen, especially on the beaches on the Boundary Bay side; Bald Eagles, cormorants, grebes, and a variety of passerine migrants also can be found at the point. The hilly areas offer western lowland forest birds such as Hutton's Vireo, Red Crossbill, Pine Siskin, and many others, especially during migration.

To reach Point Roberts, take I-5 through the border at Blaine and continue on Highway 99 for 21.1 km (13 miles). At the Highway 10 interchange, take the Ladner Trunk Road for 7 km (4.3 miles); scan the bordering fields for large flocks of gulls, and the poles, barns, and air for raptors. Turn south on Highway 17, Tsawwassen-Ferry Road, then in about another 7 km turn south again on the Point Roberts Road. Follow this road through the town of Tsawwassen, U.S. customs, and on to Point Roberts. *Note:* The Reifel Wildfowl Refuge and the Boundary Bay dike area are two outstanding birding areas, both within a few miles of Point Roberts.

BLAINE

Blaine is one of Washington's border cities and home port for many commercial fisherman. Early residents were from Iceland and found

Marbeled Murrelet

a home here where they could continue the work of their ancestors: fishing on the high seas. Because Blaine is located at the boundary line of Washington and British Columbia, there is a customs station. On weekends, the border can be extremely congested; if so, a check of the truck route into Canada, about a mile to the east, is advised.

Peace Arch State Park

This tiny state park is not a destination in itself, but a good spot to stop for a rest or picnic and a look out over Drayton Harbor for waterfowl and a bountiful number of other species. The park is made up of five acres of formal gardens that include heathers, rhododendrons, azaleas, and thousands of annuals. The Peace Arch itself is a six-story, white stone monument straddling the international border. The arch commemorates U.S.-Canadian harmony, its doors stand open always, and sealed inside are parts of the *Mayflower* and the Hudson Bay Company's first west coast steamboat, the *Beaver*. To reach Peace Arch State Park take Exit 276 for Blaine from I-5, then continue north on Second Street for 0.5 mile to the park entrance.

Drayton Harbor

Drayton Harbor is a large, shallow estuary bordering the town of Blaine. In winter and during migration, it is a mecca for many water birds including Brant, cormorants, marine ducks, loons, grebes, gulls, terns, alcids, and shorebirds. Good viewing spots are from the public pier, at the tidal flats, and from the county park at Semiahmoo Spit at the west edge of the harbor.

BIRCH BAY STATE PARK

Birch Bay lies at sea level to the east of the Strait of Georgia. The state park's mile of waterfront, looking out over extensive eelgrass beds, is one of the best spots to view wintering species and migrants. The park spreads across 193 rather heavily wooded acres of Douglas-fir, western redcedar, hemlock, alder, and birch. Wood Duck, Great Blue Heron, Belted Kingfisher, Pileated Woodpecker, robins, Red-winged Blackbird, and many other passerines can be found at the park.

On Birch Bay, look for all of the loon species. Red-necked, Western, and Horned Grebes, with a possibility of Eared Grebe; flocks of Brant, especially in April; Black, Surf, and White-winged Scoters; Oldsquaw; Harlequin Duck; American Wigeon; Northern Pintail; plus gulls, terns, cormorants, murres, and other alcids also can be seen on the bay. Groups of herons from one of the state's largest Great Blue Heron rookeries to the east of the park often feed at the ebbing tide line.

Belted Kingfisher

Terrell Marsh Nature Trail

At the south end of Birch Bay State Park, Terrell Creek flows through a 40-acre freshwater marsh. The Terrell Marsh Nature Trail is a half-mile loop; there is a guide pamphlet at the trailhead. Listen for Virginia Rail and American Bittern, especially in the spring; watch for teal, Mallard, Marsh Wren, American Goldfinch, Red-winged Blackbird, Common Yellowthroat, swallows, and a variety of other passerines as you walk along the trail.

Birch Bay State Park is a popular and well-used park. There are 167 smallish campsites (only a few have partial hookups), rest rooms with showers, fireplaces, a picnic area, and a boat ramp. To reach the park follow I-5 for 11 miles south of Blaine (or three miles north of

Ferndale), then west on Grandview Road for seven miles, following signs to the park entrance. For more information contact the park at 5105 Helwig Road, Blaine, WA 98230; (360) 371-2800.

CHERRY POINT

Cherry Point is a beachfront area facing the Strait of Georgia about halfway between Point Whitehorn, at the southwest tip of Birch Bay, and Sandy Point, at the northwestern edge of Lummi Bay. Large flocks of loons, scoters, gulls, murres, and other species feed during the herring spawning season, which is April to May. To reach Cherry Point follow the directions to Birch Bay State Park, but turn south on Jackson Road from Grandview Road for about two miles.

LAKE TERRELL HABITAT MANAGEMENT AREA

The 1,320-acre Lake Terrell area is one of the first migration stops for southbound Canadian-breeding ducks. All western Washington duck species—including Mallard, Green-winged Teal, Canvasback, Northern Pintail, Gadwall, and Ring-necked Duck—can be found here. The area is officially managed for ducks and Ring-necked pheasants; there is hunting here, in season. There is an interpretive center at the lake, and fishing for catfish and cutthroat trout. To reach the Lake Terrell HMA take Exit 260 west from I-5 on SH 540, which is Slater Road, then north on the Lake Terrell Road for three miles.

TENNANT LAKE

Tennant Lake is part of the Hovander Homestead Park, just south of the town of Ferndale. Waterfowl and raptors are found on the lake and nearby during migration and winter; Canada Goose, Wood Duck, Blue-winged and Cinnamon Teal, Mallard, Great Horned Owl, Western Screech-Owl, Common Barn-Owl, Virginia Rail, Common Yellowthroat, Red-winged Blackbird, and Marsh Wren nest here. Other species—such as American Wigeon, Northern Shoveler, Ring-necked Duck, Lesser Scaup, Bufflehead, Northern Pintail, Barrow's and Common Goldeneyes, and Ruddy Duck—are common in winter. A braille-signed and barrier-free trail is found in the park. A boardwalk is built through the swamp to Tennant Lake, and there is an observation tower at the interpretive center. A leaflet and bird checklist are available from the Tennant Lake Natural History Interpretive Center, 5236 Nielson Road, Ferndale, WA 98248; (360) 384-5545.

LUMMI FLATS

The flats of the Lummi peninsula are much like the Skagit and Samish flats: alive with raptors in the winter! Possibility of Peregrine Falcon and Merlin, Bald Eagle and Northern Harrier, Rough-legged and Red-tailed Hawks, Short-eared Owl, and a sprinkling of accipiters and kestrels makes the area intriguing. Tundra and Trumpeter Swans, Green-winged Teal, Greater Scaup, Greater Yellowlegs, Dunlin, Ring-billed and Glaucous-winged Gulls, Northern Shrike, Lincoln's and Harris' Sparrows, and occasional rarities such as 1993's Snowy Egret and Brambling, and you have a birder's delight of winter wildlife.

Caspian Tern and interesting passerines such as Bewick's Wren, Swainson's Thrush, Cedar Waxwing, Orange-crowned and Yellow Warblers, Black-headed Grosbeak, White-crowned Sparrow, Brewer's Blackbird, and Purple Finch can be seen late spring to early fall. Red River Road often is good. The land area on the peninsula is both private farmland and Lummi Indian Reservation property. In the summer, birds are harder to come by and raptors seen less often, but for something different, come in June for the Stommish Water Festival at Gooseberry Point on the Lummi Reservation; the war canoe races and traditional dancing are fun to see.

Lummi Flats is reached by taking SH 540 west from I-5 for about two miles, then turning south on the Ferndale Road. In another two miles, take Kwina Road west. Kwina crosses both Lummi Shore Drive, which follows the east side of the peninsula, and Haxton Way, which follows the west shore. For best results, cover most of the peninsula by crisscrossing on the farm roads both north and south of SH 540. Red River Road is off SH 540 east of Haxton Way.

Gooseberry Point

This is the landing site for the Lummi Island Ferry. Gooseberry Point is located at the southwest tip of the peninsula and extends into

Hale Passage, the waterway between the Lummi peninsula and Lummi Island. Just west of the ferry landing is a good spot to scan for grebes, waterfowl, alcids, gulls, terns, and other waterbirds. Gooseberry Point is reached by following Haxton Way south from SH 540.

Nooksack River Delta

The Nooksack River flows down from the high Cascades near Mount Baker to empty into Bellingham Bay. Its delta is much like the Skagit and Samish river deltas: rich in raptorial birds. Trumpeter and Tundra Swans, Brant, waterfowl, waders, and shorebirds also may be found here, plus a variety of passerines including Western Meadowlark and Brewer's and Red-winged Blackbirds. The delta area is reached by following Ferndale Road south from SH 540 watching along the way, then west on Kwina and south on Lummi Shore Drive to Fish Point.

BELLINGHAM

In 1904, four small communities were united under a city charter and became the city of Bellingham, county seat of Whatcom County. The name Bellingham unites it with Bellingham Bay, which it borders. Both city and bay were named after Sir William Bellingham, a controller who personally checked Captain Vancouver's supplies before he left England in 1791. Bellingham is now the home of Western Washington State University, a thriving industrial center, and jump-off point to Mount Baker. Bellingham is 18 miles south of the Canadian border and straddles I-5. It is a good base for birding the northwestern Puget Sound area.

Whatcom Falls Park

Once the site of the first local sawmill, this area once again is forested. Both a riparian (along Whatcom Creek) and woodland (from the cemetery down to Lake Whatcom) habitat, this site has a multitude of interesting passerines: Hooded Merganser, American Dipper, Common Yellowthroat, Wilson's Warbler, and many others are common nesting species. Near the lake, the marshy areas host Marsh

Wren, Red-winged Blackbird, Pied-billed Grebe, and others. There are good hiking trails in this 241-acre city park. Whatcom Falls Park, at 1401 Electric Avenue, is reached by turning east from Exit 253 on I-5, then following Lakeway Drive. Bay View Cemetery, in the same area, also is good for passerines.

Sehome Hill Park and Arboretum

Sweeping views of the San Juan Islands, Bellingham Bay, and the city are found from the top of Sehome Hill Park. Three-and-a-half miles of forest hiking and interpretive trails in the park give access from the city, or you can drive to the top. A variety of unusual and interesting plants and trees are found in the 165-acre native plant preserve, plus a variety of birds.

Maritime Heritage Park

This city park is located in the historical Fairhaven district and is at the mouth of Whatcom Creek. There is a salmon hatchery and fish ladder and a variety of walks and spots to picnic. The Chinook salmon return to the area about Labor Day and the spectacular migration of the Chum Salmon occurs between Halloween and Thanksgiving, a fine time to see Bald Eagles and other wintering birds.

CHUCKANUT DRIVE

This dramatic scenic drive winds through tall evergreens and past rocky cliffs from south Bellingham to the Samish Flats along Chuckanut and Samish bays. Bald Eagles often are seen in the trees along the drive; there are pullouts for observing Samish Bay and possible waterbirds. To reach Chuckanut Drive follow SH 11 south out of Bellingham's Fairhaven District.

Larrabee State Park

Hanging above Samish Bay with 3,600 feet of shoreline, Larrabee State Park is basically a Douglas-fir, grand fir, western redcedar, and madrona forested area; it is Washington's first state park. Eight miles

Bald Eagle

of hiking trails to view western woodland bird species such as Black-capped and Chestnut-backed Chickadees, Band-tailed Pigeon, Hutton's Vireo, kinglets, warblers, wrens, and Brown Creeper are found in the park. The park has 87 campsites, 26 with full hookups, running water, and rest rooms with showers. Tide pool exploring, swimming, fishing, and boating are all possible. Larrabee is seven miles south of Bellingham on SH 11 (Chuckanut Drive).

Interurban Trail. The trailhead is across from the south Larrabee park entrance; car parking is inside the park's main gate. The five-mile Interurban Trail follows the old Bellingham to Mount Vernon interurban line, which operated from 1912–1930. It is open to hikers, horseback riders, and mountain bikers, and allows access to Chuckanut Mountain. Birds to be encountered along the trail might include

Ruffed and Blue Grouse; Barred Owl; Band-tailed Pigeon; Downy, Hairy, and Pileated Woodpeckers; Black-capped and Chestnut-backed Chickadees; Brown Creeper; Golden-crowned Kinglet; Red-breasted Nuthatch; Winter Wren; Rufous-sided Towhee; Varied Thrush; and robins. In summer, add Western Tanager, Hutton's Vireo, Pacific-slope Flycatcher, and a variety of finches and warblers. Special luck would produce a Northern Pygmy-Owl or accipiter.

Cleaton Road. At 1.2 miles north of the north Larrabee Park entrance (Milepost 16), turn east on High Line Road, which leads to Cleaton Road. Cleaton Road gives car access to a bit of lower Chuck-anut Mountain. Winding 3.5 miles up the west side, it is a good gravel road bordered by Douglas-fir, maples, alders, and sword and bracken ferns. In summer, ocean spray, foxglove, daisies, and fireweed add color. Varied Thrush, Steller's Jay, Pileated Woodpecker, Ruffed Grouse, and deer often can be seen from the car. At the road's end there is a large parking lot and an extensive view of the islands and Samish Bay.

SAMISH FLATS

As Chuckanut Drive winds down from the coniferous forests above Samish Bay, the landscape turns to low, flat farmlands laced with estuaries and sloughs: the delta of the Samish River. This is the most outstanding spot in western Washington for raptors from fall to spring. All five falcons often are seen here. Bald Eagle, Rough-legged Hawk, Red-tailed Hawk, and Northern Harrier are numerous and easy to observe. Snowy Owls are often present near the shoreline, and Short-eared Owls hunt the fields. Gyrfalcons are annual visitors and in 1994, the Falcon Research Group radio-tagged a second-year gray morph female that they followed for some time.

Mid-winter censuses show that "the big four"—Bald Eagle, Red-tailed and Rough-legged Hawks, and Northern Harrier—make up 90% of the total. The winter density of raptors has stayed remarkably uniform. Based on a study area size of 151 square miles, each square mile has an average of about four birds of prey, a high density for winter. Figures for the 1991 Skagit Flats Winter Raptor Census were

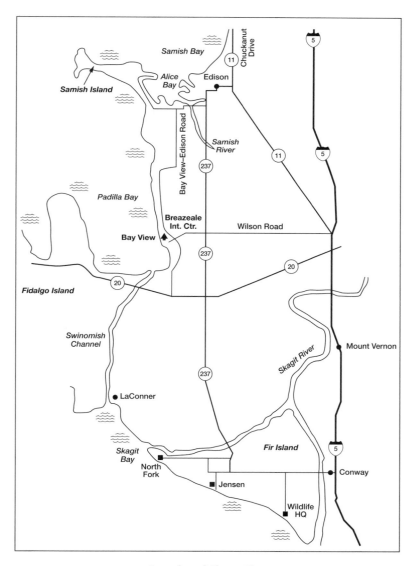

Samish and Skagit Flats

Bald Eagle, 308; Red-tailed Hawk, 181; Northern Harrier, 77; and Rough-legged Hawk, 39—and this was a low count year!

The stubble fields of the many farms abound with Northern Pintail, American Wigeon, and Mallard. A variety of usual and unusual passerines such as Horned Lark, Western Meadowlark, Lapland Longspur, and Harris', American Tree, and Fox Sparrows frequent the brambles and field edges.

The Samish Flats are best viewed from the roadside because most of the land is private. Be sure to pull all the way off the road before looking and, for the most part, use your car as a blind so you won't stress migratory or nesting birds. Mileage-wise, the flats are not extensive, but you can easily spend a day looking over the fields, ponds, and shorelines. The usual route local birders take (coming from the north) is south on Chuckanut Drive (SH 11), west at the intersection of Chuckanut Drive and West Bow Hill Road, SH 237 (Rhododendron Cafe, excellent!). Continue through Edison with its right-angle turns, then at the intersection of SH 237 and Bay View-Edison Road, just past the liquor store, turn west again. Follow Bay View-Edison Road west until it turns south. Go straight on Samish Island Road to Samish Island. Retrace the Samish Island Road route east to the Bay View-Edison Road, then turn south. Side roads such as D'Arcy and Sullivan off Bay View-Edison Road are usually very good, and both connect with SH 237. Descriptions of some special viewing spots on the flats follow.

Smith Road. After entering the eastern limits of Edison, 3.1 miles from where the Chuckanut Drive bridge meets the flats, turn north on Smith Road keeping to the right along the field edges. At 0.3 mile there is a gate at the edge of the Department of Fish and Wildlife area; parking is very limited. The dike can be walked from here, and Snowy Owls, Bald Eagles, Rough-legged Hawks, and Red-tailed Hawks are often on the pilings and beach driftwood; waterfowl are both in the bay and in the fields. Loons, alcids, grebes, and other marine birds frequent the bay, and sparrows and other passerines use the brush and brambles for cover.

West Edison boat basin. A little south of Edison, turn west from SH 237 onto Samish Island Road. At 0.5 mile (Milepost 9) there is a small bridge over the Samish River and a boat basin on the north. There is roadside parking west of the bridge. Gyrfalcons seem to find this area and the Smith Road site to their liking. Northern Harriers, Short-eared Owls, and a variety of waterfowl, raptors, and roadside passerines can be seen.

Western Grebe

Samish Island Road. The fields along this road are some of the very finest in the state for raptors. From late fall through early spring Bald Eagles abound and an occasional Golden Eagle makes an appearance; Northern Harriers quarter the fields; Red-tailed Hawks and Rough-legged Hawks are numerous on fenceposts, utility poles, and barn rooftops; and all five North American falcons can, with good luck, be seen. Short-eared and Common Barn-Owls hunt the fields, and in some years Snowy Owls are plentiful. Great Blue Herons prowl the ditches and sloughs.

The fields and brambles reveal Western Meadowlark, Horned Lark, sparrows, juncos, and occasional warblers, Lapland Longspur, and Snow Bunting. Sandhill Cranes are seen infrequently during spring migration. This under-three-mile section is extremely productive, and the Seattle hot line is up-to-date on anything appearing here and on the Skagit flats. Roadside parking is okay, but there is extra space and good field views at a right-angle turn at the west end of the road near two outbuildings (just before paralleling diked Alice Bay). The buildings are private property, so stay on the roadside parking area.

Alice Bay. Alice Bay is embraced by some small islands to its east, a dike which is partially paralleled by the Samish Island Road, and .5 mile of the road (with houses) on the north edge (actually, part of the island). Towards Scotts Point and at the northeast end of Alice Bay is a large heron rookery. Great Blue Herons can be seen in small numbers on the islands in the bay in winter, but in July after the young herons have fledged, the islands are wall-to-wall with herons. On a recent August trip I counted nearly 200 at one time. This bay also shelters a wealth of shorebird and waterfowl species, with the aforementioned raptors and passerines nearby.

Samish Island. Samish Island is mostly forested and mostly private property. A few pull-off areas on the road edge afford decent viewing of northwest marine birds. There is one spot, a Department of Natural Resources public access, that is accessible and has about 1,500 feet of rocky beach to explore. Harlequin Duck, Oldsquaw, and Black Oystercatcher are here in winter, and various rock sandpipers sometimes are seen. The park is near the end of Samish Point Road and to the north. A recent August warbler invasion included several hundred birds in the space of eight hours. Species included Orange-crowned Warbler (60%), Wilson's Warbler (25%), Townsend's Warbler (10%), Yellow Warbler (3%), MacGillivray's Warbler (2%), and one each of Black-throated Gray and Nashville Warblers. Interspersed with the warblers were Pacific-slope Flycatchers, Northern Orioles, and Western Tanagers. Watch the trees as well as waters!

PADILLA BAY NATIONAL ESTUARINE
RESEARCH RESERVE

The Padilla Bay National Estuarine Research Reserve is one of 22 such reserves in the United States. It is home to more than 237 species of birds, 14 mammals, and 57 species of fish. There are 64 upland acres and 10,700 tideland acres, with more proposed. The 7,500 acres of eelgrass meadows offshore along with Padilla and Fidalgo bays support one of the largest wintering flocks of Brant in the United States.

The reserve was established in 1980, and funding was provided in 1981 with a $2.2 million grant from the U.S. Department of Commerce NOAA to acquire tidelands, develop nature trails, construct an interpretive center, and develop education and research programs. Since 1983, the reserve has been the focus of a number of major studies to learn about the habitat, ecology, and productivity of Padilla Bay, as those topics apply to management concerns of estuaries across the United States.

The Breazeale Interpretive Center is located within the reserve. The center is a fine natural history center offering exhibits of local wildlife, a well-stocked library, classrooms, rest rooms, and maps and brochures of the area. A one-mile upland nature trail provides access to grasslands and woodland habitat. A new observation deck provides beach access below the Interpretive Center, while a 2.25-mile interpretive trail, located one mile south of the center, stretches along the south end of Padilla Bay and Indian Slough.

The center is located directly across the road from the reserve. Thousands of Bufflehead, Surf Scoter, Greater Scaup, Canvasback, Northern Pintail, American Wigeon, Mallard, alcids, grebes, loons, herons, and other water and marsh birds inhabit these waters. Active Bald Eagle nests and Great Blue Heron rookeries are nearby. Peregrine Falcons and Merlins occasionally hunt from bayside perches in winter.

To reach the Padilla Bay Reserve and Breazeale Interpretive Center take the Anacortes exit off I-5, continue for six miles to the Farmhouse Inn intersection (traffic light), then turn north on the Bay View-Edison Road for five miles. Coming from the north, follow directions down the Samish Flats to the Center.

BAY VIEW STATE PARK

Bay View State Park is less than a mile south of the Padilla Bay Reserve. Sixty-eight campsites are on the elevated east side of the road, and 1,300 feet of beach frontage (day-use only) with a great

view is on the west side. All the birds found at the Padilla Bay
Reserve area are here. On the beachfront look for herons, Dunlin,
Black-bellied Plovers, and other shorebirds, plus specialties such as
Canvasback, Eurasian Wigeon, Peregrine Falcon, and Merlin. In the
upland areas of the park check for migrant passerines, and also look
for Ruffed Grouse, Cooper's Hawk, Band-tailed Pigeon, Pileated
Woodpecker, Steller's Jay, kinglets, and Varied Thrush.

Dunlin

Wilson Road

Wilson Road goes directly east out of the tiny town of Bay View,
just south of the state park and north of the Skagit Regional Airport.
During spring through fall (and sometimes in winter), check the
fields to either side for Western Meadowlark, Horned Lark, Red-
winged and Brewer's Blackbirds, Great Blue and Green Herons,
American Goldfinch, and a variety of sparrows. In winter, watch for

waterfowl, including Trumpeter and Tundra Swans, feeding in the open fields.

Padilla Bay Shore Trail. A 2.5-mile interpretive trail along a restored dike separating Padilla Bay Estuary from nearby farmland is quite good for bird viewing. The original dike was built at the turn of the century; it now provides access to the interesting tidal flat and its plants and wildlife. Brant use the extensive sea grass meadows in the bay, but Dungeness crabs, waterfowl, and a variety of invertebrate life also make use of these swaying food stores. Estuaries top the list of the most biologically productive areas on earth; this is a fine chance to see an estuary in action.

The north end of the trail begins just south of Bay View. There is a large, well-signed parking lot on 2nd Street, a short block off the Bay View-Edison Road. At the trail's south end, 2.3 miles further down the road, parking is extremely limited.

SKAGIT FLATS

The Skagit River is the biggest watershed in the Puget Sound basin, second only to the Columbia River in size in the western United States. More than 2,900 streams make up the flow of fresh water into the sound, draining an area more expansive than the state of Delaware.

The Skagit River Delta, or the Skagit "flats" as it is locally called, is rich, alluvial land that supports brilliant fields of red tulips and yellow daffodils in the spring, and endless acres of peas, broccoli, and cabbage throughout the summer and fall. As harvests end and strong northern winds begin to blow, it is time for waterfowl and raptors to be the stars of this seemingly dead landscape.

Flocks of tens of thousands of Snow Geese fill the skies beginning in early November. Tundra and Trumpeter Swans, Brant, Northern Pintail, American Wigeon, and Cinnamon and Blue-winged Teal are only a few of the species gracing ponds, bays, and fields. Black-crowned Night Herons, Western Meadowlarks, and a profusion of passerines can also be found. Raptors are common. It is fall-to-spring birding at its best.

A prime lure of the Skagit is its feeling of isolation—being surrounded by flat expanses of salt marsh and fallow fields—yet being close to all amenities and a short distance from Seattle. As in all of the delta river areas of northwest Washington, it often is best just to wander about crisscrossing the land via farm roads. The following are excellent birding spots on the Skagit flats.

Skagit Habitat Management Area (SHMA)

The Skagit Habitat Management Area's 10,862 acres is the top waterfowl area in western Washington. Twenty-six species either nest or winter here including Trumpeter and Tundra Swans, Canada Goose, White-fronted Goose, Brant, Northern Shoveler, Northern Pintail, Gadwall, American Wigeon, mergansers, and a host of others. More than 200 species of birds have been identified on the Skagit including loons, grebes, grouse, quail, phalaropes, jaegers, gulls, terns, rails, shorebirds, and an extensive variety of songbirds. Some uncommon species include Sandhill Crane, pelicans, American Bittern, Gyrfalcon, Northern Bobwhite, Northern Shrike, Northern Mockingbird, Western Bluebird, and Snow Bunting. River otter, mink, coyote, raccoon, beaver, opossum, blacktail deer, and harbor seal share the area.

Skagit Headquarters. Birding is very good around the spacious parking area. Look for Cooper's Hawk, Yellow Warbler, Black-headed Grosbeak, Swainson's Thrush, and many others, in season. The SHMA as a whole is broken up into two large parcels and several smaller ones, and access to these parcels varies. To make exploring easier, obtain a copy of the *Skagit County Bird Watching Guide* from the Washington Department of Fish and Wildlife, 600 Capitol Way North, Olympia, WA 98501-1091. At the headquarters there are rest rooms, dike trails, and a small interpretive display. Headquarters is reached by taking the Conway exit from I-5 and heading west through Conway on Fir Island Road. Just after crossing the Conway bridge, turn south on Mann Road which follows Wylie Slough; there are directional signs. Watch for possible Bald Eagles and Merlins along the slough, and a variety of species across the farmed areas.

Skagit River Access Areas. There are three access areas—sites with access to dikes that separate sedge-bullrush and cattail salt marsh from the farmlands and that look out to the tide flats and Skagit Bay. These access areas have only parking, and no amenities. A scope is a big help in spotting distant birds. Bald Eagles can be seen perching in tall evergreens, on pilings in the water, and in fields at all accesses from fall to spring.

Big Ditch Access Area. The short road to the Big Ditch parking area goes between two farm fields. Watch the ditches on either side for

ELIZABETH A. MILLS
- 1977 -

Fledgling Hermit Thrush

Great Blue Heron and miscellaneous sparrows and the fields for falcons and Northern Harrier. A dike trail goes both north and south—to the south there are scrubby trees and some shrubbery. Bald Eagles often perch here and Cooper's Hawks have been seen; interesting passerines are often here. The southern trail goes along a small slough and between an extensive cattail marsh and farmland. Huge numbers of Snow Geese, ducks, and swans often raft at the edge of the marsh in Skagit Bay. Raptors are common over the marsh areas. Big Ditch is located on a short spur road that extends west at the junction of SH 530, 102nd Avenue NW, and the railroad tracks, about two miles north of Stanwood.

Jensen's Access. Large concentrations of Dunlin often are seen here, sometimes with a Merlin in hot pursuit. The dike hiking area is very limited. This is the best area to observe the tide flats, and with a scope good views of rafting waterfowl just offshore can be seen. Raptors are abundant here, too. Jensen's Access is on Maupin Road (when Fir Island Road makes a right angle, continue straight); the sign has been down for several years, but it is the last field road going to the south.

North Fork Access. North Fork is especially noted for its Northern Harriers and Short-eared Owls. Often at twilight several individuals of both species will be quartering the cattail marsh area at one time. Waterfowl, other raptors, and a variety of passerines are here. When leaving Jensen's Access, continue west, then north on Maupin Road, then left on Rawlins Road. North Fork is at the west end of Rawlins Road. Scan nearby fields for Snow Buntings and occasional shorebirds during migration.

Fir Island Road

The fields along Fir Island Road are some of the best spots to see huge flocks of Snow Geese and smaller groups of Tundra and Trumpeter Swans. Ducks also are plentiful and falcons occasional. Other raptors frequent the area as they do all of the river deltas in the northwest. A little more than a mile west of the town of Conway and the I-5 exit, there is a pond on the south side of the road that has several deciduous trees on its east side. Scan the trees from November through March to see the small colony of Black-crowned Night Herons that roost there every year. (Park only on the road edge.)

La Conner and Mount Vernon

For amenities while visiting the Skagit flats, two very different possibilities are close at hand. Both allow quick access to the Skagit's birds, tulips, and bicycling.

La Conner. La Conner lies near the mouth of the Skagit River on the Swinomish Channel. It is a tiny town but packed with history, antique shops, and good restaurants—plus an outstanding bakery. Several local inns make this a good base for birding trips. Information: La Conner Chamber of Commerce, P.O. Box 1610, La Conner, WA 98257; (360) 466-4778.

Mount Vernon. Mount Vernon is also historic, the base for the giant Skagit Tulip Festival, but is a bit more mainstream. It straddles I-5, and most of the major motel and restaurant chains are here. Information: Mount Vernon Chamber of Commerce, P.O. Box 1007, Mount Vernon, WA 98273; (360) 336-9555.

STILLAGUAMISH DELTA

Smaller than the Skagit delta area, the Stillaguamish delta offers a variety of habitats and some excellent birding. Raptors and the huge flocks of Snow Geese and swans sometimes are less common here, but waterfowl are plentiful and songbirds abound in the brambles, fields, and coniferous areas. Stillaguamish is a local Indian name meaning "river people." Its delta is reached quickly from Seattle via I-5. Several exits offer interesting drives to the delta area: SH 530 to the south through Silvana, SH 532 directly to Stanwood, and SH 530 to the north at Conway, then south to Stanwood. All lead through interesting birding habitats.

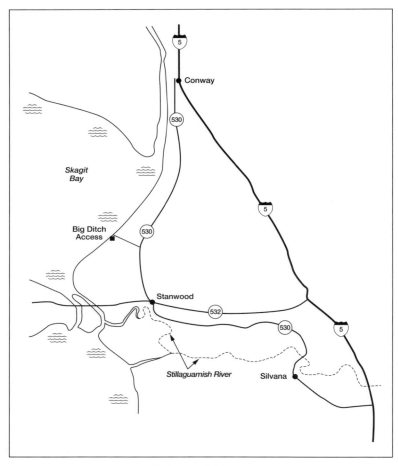

Stillaguamish Delta

Stanwood Sewage Ponds

The ponds are excellent for waterfowl and can be seen south of SH 532 as you approach the town. Both diving and dabbling ducks such as Ruddy Duck, Northern Shoveler, Canvasback, Ring-necked Duck, Lesser Scaup, Mallard, and American Wigeon are a few of the species that can be seen, in season. Flocks of Dunlin and other shorebirds often appear at high tides. Blackberry brambles and fence rows are occasionally a winter home to American Tree, White-crowned, Golden-crowned, Clay-colored and Swamp Sparrows, plus rarities such as Say's Phoebe, Northern Waterthrush, and Mountain Bluebird. The ponds are on Leque Road, and parking is available inside the gate or further along Leque Road near the dike at the large pond.

Douglas Slough. Just west of Stanwood town limits is marsh and wetland area extending to the north and south. You can pull off the road on either side and scan the marsh and waters for waterfowl, herons, and raptors, and the brambly areas for passerines.

VALLEYS AND FOOTHILLS EAST OF I-5

The relatively flat land that extends into low, rolling hills before taking off into the higher Cascade Mountains is a land of dairy and truck farms, lakes, and small cities. It is easily accessed from I-5 which, in turn, means habitats are much more disrupted. Two-lane, SH 9 is an alternative north-south route; it parallels I-5 five to 15 miles to the east. Birding can be interesting along the way. Lakes of various sizes host dabbling ducks, herons, bitterns, and rails, an occasional Osprey or Bald Eagle, and, on their edges, various passerines.

LYNDEN AREA

North and east of Bellingham are miles of flat farmlands that have their own complement of wintering raptors. Occasional Gyrfalcons and Snowy Owls are seen; Peregrine, Merlin, Rough-legged and Red-tailed Hawks, Northern Harrier, and Short-eared Owl also can be seen. Check the brushy roadsides for wintering sparrows, Snow Bunting, Western Meadowlark, and Lapland Longspur.

The area is reached by driving I-5 south a few miles past Blaine, then turning east on the Birch Bay-Lynden Road. Birds are best seen by crisscrossing the many farm roads along the way and north to the border. Lynden, itself, was settled by the Dutch and more than half the population is of Dutch descent, so expect flowers, windmills, and Dutch festivals when here.

TRUMPETER SWAN CONCENTRATIONS

The Skagit and Samish flats host a large number of Trumpeter and Tundra Swans. The Washington State Swan Working Group censuses swans annually each winter. In 1994, official counts were set at approximately 1,100 Trumpeters and 11,000 to 14,000 Tundra Swans. Barley and other grain fields are favored feeding grounds.

Telling Trumpeter and Tundra Swans apart in the field is not always easy, but swans are extremely sensitive to human intrusion, so please stay in your car while observing them. An excellent four-page flyer on swan identification is available from the Trumpeter Swan Society for a long, self-addressed, stamped envelope: 14112 First Avenue West, Everett, WA 98208.

In a small area just north of Mount Vernon, there are excellent prospects of spotting flocks of Trumpeter Swans. Bordered on the west by I-5, on the north by SH 20, on the easy by SH 9, and on the south by SH 538, this farm development area has several lakes that attract swans. When searching for swans, be aware that there are usually interesting waterfowl and raptors in the same habitats. Following are some possibilities.

Barney Lake. Barney Lake shoreline is all private, but views are possible. Take SH 538 east from I-5, go past Skagit Valley College and turn north on Martin Road, then north on Trumpeter Lane (Martin Road curves west). Barney Lakes lies to the east. Fields often are flooded after heavy rains so scan them for waterfowl, and fences and poles for raptors.

Clear Lake. Clear Lake Park, a Skagit County Park, has some possibly good winter waterfowl viewing. Trumpeter Swan, Ring-necked Duck, Redhead, Canvasback, Bufflehead, Lesser Scaup, Mallard, and many others are present on the lake in winter. Bald Eagles may be in the surrounding trees. The town of Clear Lake abuts SH 9, and the park is at the southern end off Beaver Lake Road.

Beaver Lake hosts similar birds as Clear Lake. Also check for sparrows in the grasses and brambles. There is a Department of Wildlife

Trumpeter Swans and Snow Geese

access road at Beaver Lake. Beaver Lake is on Beaver Lake Road, just southeast of Clear Lake.

Francis Road. Francis Road and its bordering fields is another area excellent for waterfowl, including swans, and raptors. Also check for shorebirds such as Common Snipe, Pectoral Sandpiper, Greater Yellowlegs, and Long-billed Dowitcher during migration. DeBay Slough goes alongside the meandering road and is also a good spot; try DeBay's Isle Road. Francis Road goes west from SH 9 at the north end of the town of Clear Lake.

Other sites. Several other sites in western Washington also host wintering Trumpeter Swans, usually in small flocks of 50 birds or less. The following are places you might also look: San Juan and Orcas islands, the Ferndale area, Lake Quinault on the Olympic Peninsula, the Long Beach Peninsula, the Chehalis River drainage near Elma, and the Ridgefield NWR, just off I-5.

KAYAK POINT REGIONAL PARK

This 670-acre, wooded saltwater park is located just north of the Tulalip Indian Reservation on the east side of Port Susan. It sits directly across from Camano Island. The 300-foot-long fishing pier jutting into the bay is a good spot from which to observe birds and marine mammals and to fish and crab. Look for Pacific Loon, Brant, cormorants, scaup, mergansers, scoters, Canada Geese, American Wigeon, Great Blue Heron, Bald Eagle, occasional falcons in winter, gulls, and a large variety of other water birds. California sea lions, which follow the hake and steelhead runs, usually can be seen from December to May. An occasional gray whale may visit. The 3,300 feet of shoreline includes both sandy and cobble beaches and, during migration, shorebirds often are seen.

There are 34 rather private campsites with hookups on the high bluff above the beach; two barrier-free sites are available for the disabled. The upper part of the park is quite wooded with several trails and possibilities of seeing most of the western lowland species. There is a boat launch facility, and the beach area has many picnic shelters and fire pits. An outstanding 18-hole golf course is located across from the park for non-birding companions. The park is reached from I-5 by taking Exit 199 at Marysville. Head west on Marine View Drive through the Tulalip Indian Reservation; the park is about 13 miles on the left. Information: Kayak Point Regional Park, 15610 Marine View Drive, Stanwood, WA 98292; (360) 652-7992.

EVERETT

Everett is the largest city in Snohomish County, the county seat, home of the world's largest building—the Boeing Company's aircraft assembly plant, and site of a great minor league baseball team, the Everett Giants. It also has wonderful sewage treatment lagoons with specialties such as American Black Duck, Black Tern and, recently, a rare Common Black-headed Gull. Everett sits near the delta of the

Snohomish River facing Port Gardner Bay, part of Possession Sound. It has an extensive shoreline, islands with nesting Ospreys, and a variety of birding habitats. The city is bisected by I-5 and is just less than 30 miles north of Seattle.

Jetty Island

Jetty Island is a rich environmental oasis two miles long and a half mile wide. It is a man-made island that sits a quarter mile off the industrial waterfront of the city. It is reached only by boat, but from early July to early September the city sponsors free ferry trips back and forth to the island along with interpretive rangers who conduct classes and activities. The addition of a protective berm to the western side of the island created a new salt marsh complete with newly transplanted native plant species. The sandy beach is two miles long, and the shallow tide flats make the water comfortably warm. Sand dunes have been planted with rye grass and wildflowers that help to make the habitat more welcoming for the many species of birds and mammals that live here.

American Legion Memorial Park

This Everett City Park, dedicated in 1937 by a member of the Tulalip tribe, gives a sweeping view of the Snohomish River delta, from industrial eyesores to the wonderful mudflats, wetlands, pilings with Osprey nests, Jetty Island, Port Gardner Bay with the craggy range of the Olympic Mountains as a backdrop, and Mount Baker to the north. A scope gives the best views, but binoculars are fine. An active Osprey nest is just below the park, Red-tailed Hawks catch lift from the park's bluff, and Bald Eagles perch along the bluff's edge. The huge, isolated trees on the bluff section plus the brush and brambles below the edge are sometimes alive with sparrows, warblers, and other small birds.

To reach American Legion Memorial Park when going north on I-5, take Exit 193, Marine View Drive. Go left onto East Marine View Drive and follow it around and under SH 529. After passing the golf course entrance turn left onto Alverson Boulevard, then pull into a parking area on the right for the bluff section.

Everett City Sewage Lagoons

This is a premier birding site in the urban Puget Sound area. When talking with the person on duty I was told the plant has had bird-watching visitors from all over the world; its entrance hall even has popular bird magazines for reading material. This water pollution control facility, managed by the Everett public works department, sits just east of the Snohomish River and I-5. It is a great half-day trip for visitors.

From late fall until early spring, the ponds and lagoons are full of waterfowl. Northern Pintail, Gadwall, Mallard, American and Eurasian Wigeon, Northern Shoveler, Ruddy Duck, Ring-necked Duck, Canvasback, Lesser Scaup, and many others frequent the northern ponds. Uncommon species to look for among the waterbirds are Tufted Duck, Redhead, Eared Grebe, and phalaropes. A small colony of American Black Ducks also resides here. At the south pond, an aerated lagoon, gulls and terns are special. Black Tern and Franklin's, Mew, Bonaparte's, and Little Gulls have been seen.

In the open area surrounding the sewage ponds, there are often Red-tailed Hawks and Northern Harriers. Great Blue Heron, American Bittern, Sora, and Virginia Rail can be seen, too. The brushy and treed areas to the east are excellent for passerines and sparrows; nesting Great Horned Owls also live here. There is a four-mile trail completely encircling the lagoons that allows visitors to investigate a variety of habitats.

To reach the sewage treatment lagoons when heading north on I-5, take Exit 195 (Marine View Drive) to SH 529 North (Pacific Highway), then take the first exit after crossing the Snohomish River and follow signs to Langus Riverfront Park, where there is parking. When coming from the north, take Exit 198 (North Broadway in Marysville) onto SH 529 South and follow the signs to the park. Park either at the south end of the park or go under I-5 and park and lock vehicles on the side of 4th Street near the plant. Go to the treatment facility office to pick up a permission slip for entry. Permits are free, *but the plant operator should be notified 24 hours prior to arrival by phoning (206) 259-8819 or 259-8821; plant hours are 0730 to 1600 hours.*

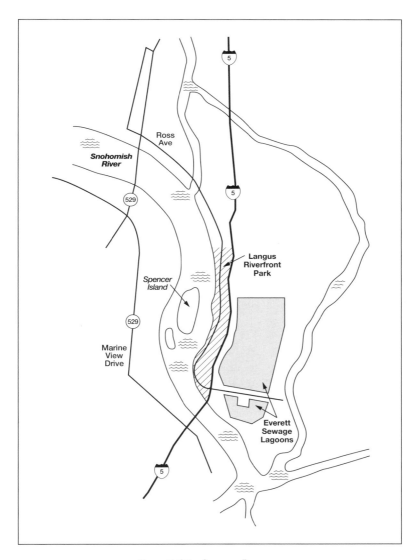

Everett City Sewage Lagoons

Spencer Island. Spencer Island is the very newest of Snohomish County's fine birding areas. Located across from Langus Park at the point where Port Gardner Bay meets the Snohomish River, it well may be one of the largest wetland restoration projects on the west coast. The island's 412 acres were purchased in 1989 by the county and the State Department of Wildlife. Open for three weekends in 1994, it will open full time in 1995 and promises to be a birder's paradise.

When the island opens it will feature two main trails: one atop a 3.5-mile dike that encircles the island and the other a 0.5-mile levee crossing the island. Visitors will be able to encircle the outer edge of the island and look down on its birds, plants, and other possible wildlife in the marshy center. Interpretive signs eventually will appear. No horses, bikes, or motorized vehicles will be allowed. The entrance to the park will be at Fourth Street SE, near the sewer lagoons; parking will be at Langus Riverfront Park, a short hike away. Spencer Island is just west of I-5 and slightly north of Everett.

WALLACE FALLS STATE PARK

In 1977, the Wallace Falls area, named for Sarah Wallace, a woman of the Skykomish Indian Tribe who homesteaded nearby, became a state park. Its 678 acres boast a roaring 265-foot falls on the Wallace River and some great hiking trails. Watch for Varied Thrush, kinglets, chickadees, Brown Creeper, Western Tanager, and Pileated Woodpecker along the trail.

Wallace Falls State Park has six tent campsites, but no RV sites. It is located 30 miles east of Everett and two miles northeast of the town of Gold Bar on US 2 (the Stevens Pass Highway); the route is well-signed. Information: Wallace Falls State Park, P.O. Box 106, Gold Bar, WA 98251.

MONROE

Monroe sits just northeast of the confluence of the Skykomish and Snoqualmie Rivers. The surrounding area is primarily low farmland. Low, rolling, forested hills rise to the east and west of the valley. The Monroe-Duvall Road, SH 203, winds along the eastern edge and gives access to many good birding spots.

Tualco Loop Road

A bit south of Monroe, south of Ben Howard Road, turn west on the Tualco Loop Road keeping straight at the right-angle turn (watch signs). This is another meandering road through farmlands and to the Snoqualmie River. When the Loop Road turns south, there is a parking area and access to the river where you can search for ducks, mergansers, eagles, gulls, and herons, plus warblers, in season (hunting season here is October through January). We have seen Merlin, American Kestrel, Peregrine Falcon, Red-tailed and Rough-legged Hawks, Bald Eagle, and Northern Harrier in the trees and on fence posts in the winter. Scan the fields for possible Snow Buntings and unusual gulls.

Two Rivers Wildlife Management Area. This area features land around and within an old oxbow of the Snoqualmie River. It is recognized as one of the best examples of undisturbed floodplain forest in the region. There are trails and roads, sometimes questionably passable at certain times, that allow access to a variety of habitats. Green and Great Blue Herons, American Bittern, Red-winged and Brewer's Blackbirds, and Marsh Wren frequent the marshy areas.

Wintering sparrows such as American Tree, Swamp, Harris', and White-throated sometimes are present in the deciduous groves of willows and alders. In spring and summer, watch for Willow and Pacific-slope Flycatchers, Warbling and Red-eyed Vireos, Yellow-rumped and Townsend's Warblers, and a mix of other passerines. Specialties in the past have been Rusty Blackbird and Least Flycatcher. There are two parking lots for the Two Rivers WMA, one at the north end on the Loop Road and one almost a mile further, past the prison farm.

SNOQUALMIE WILDLIFE AREA

At about seven miles south of Monroe on the east side of SH 203 lies the Snoqualmie Wildlife Area, a wildlife habitat improvement area administered by the Washington Department of Fish and Wildlife. There are ten acres of ponds, sloughs, fields, and shrubby areas. In late spring, we have seen nesting Canada Geese, Tree and

Violet-green Swallows, American Robin, Red-tailed Hawk, Ring-necked Pheasant, Red-winged Blackbird, American Coot, Common Snipe, and Savannah Sparrow. Birdhouses for swallows and kestrels and dead snags have been erected to enhance the habitat. There is a sturdy, open observation tower that commands a view of most of the area. These wildlife improvements were made possible from the sale of personalized license plates in Washington state.

Snoqualmie Wildlife Recreation Area, Cherry Valley Unit. This land is adjacent to the above unit and offers much of the same type of habitat: ponds, ditches, wetlands, and fields. Fields are mowed with strips of vegetation crossing the areas to act as cover. The area is open to hunting so is best avoided October to January. There is a large parking area just off SH 203.

Chapter 4
Puget Sound and Islands

 Puget Sound, a deep inland sea the result of glacial activity about 15,000 years ago, has more than a thousand miles of shoreline. Islands abound in this watery haven. Vashon, Bainbridge, and Whidbey islands stretch up the middle of the sound between Seattle and the Olympic Peninsula. The Kitsap Peninsula thrusts itself north between Puget Sound; to the north, the San Juan archipelago, lying at the meeting of Georgia, Haro, and Juan de Fuca straits, boasts no fewer than 172 islands.

Captain George Vancouver's expedition in 1792, the first into Puget Sound, marked the beginning of steamroller progress. From fur trading and fishing to Boeing 777s and Starbuck lattés, the Puget Sound area has grown and contributed mightily to Washington's second place in state population of the 13 western states. Luckily, parks, recreational areas, and unsettled lands abound, and birds generally flourish, oil spills and forest cutting notwithstanding.

Puget Sound waters and its environs are home to 57 species of birds, 31 species of which are waterfowl, nearly 70 terrestrial wildlife species, 14 species of marine mammals, and more than 200 kinds of fish, not to mention hundreds of sea stars, shellfish, anemones, and other invertebrates. Diverse water plant ecosystems abound also.

Orca and Dall's porpoises, five species of Pacific salmon, Trumpeter Swan, and Peregrine Falcon all are part of the diverse ecosystem of this region. The innumerable marshes, bays, and estuaries provide comfortable resting spots for migrating waterfowl and shorebirds. Thick stands of Douglas-fir, western hemlock, and western redcedar make up the humid coniferous forests of the region. Salal and Oregon grape, huckleberry, and devil's club help make up the dense underbrush.

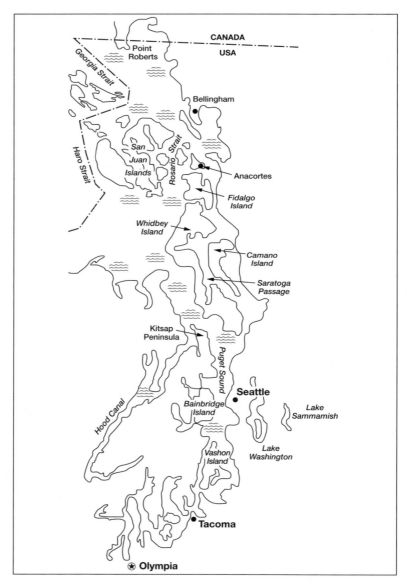

Puget Sound Region

SAN JUAN ISLANDS

The San Juan archipelago covers nearly 900 square miles of dense forest, barren hills reminiscent of the Scottish highlands, farmland, sandy bays, and rocky shoreline. Its diverse ecological resources attract a vast assortment of species. The San Juan environment consists of much hard rock, some of the oldest in Puget Sound environs at 360 million years. Weather is different here, also: Resting in the rain shadow of the Olympic Mountains, climate is generally milder and far less wet.

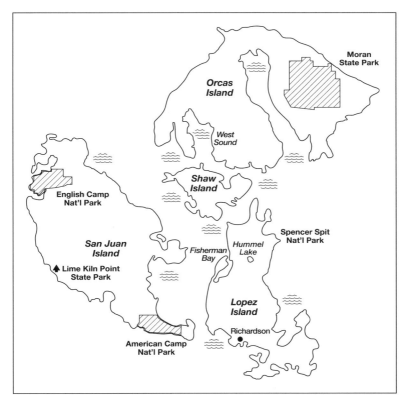

San Juan Islands

The San Juan Islands border on Canada's Georgia Strait and Vancouver Island on the north and west, and the U.S. mainland to the east. The ambience of the islands is rural and laid back—no McDonald's here. From about mid-May until September, three pods of Orca cruise the waters around the islands. Eagles and Ospreys nest on the islands; in fact, the Washington Department of Wildlife has established that the San Juans comprise one of the densest and most successfully reproducing populations of Bald Eagles in the country. In winter, waterfowl, gulls, and seabirds gather by the thousands to rest and feed. Excellent restaurants, shops, small inns, and B & Bs are found on the two largest islands, Orcas and San Juan. There are 17 marine state parks in the islands; most have moorage buoys and campsites.

Anacortes-Friday Harbor Ferry

The ferry terminal lies three miles from the center of Anacortes on Shannon Point. Guemes Island lies due east and Cypress Island is to the north. While waiting for the ferry, spend some time at the Ship Harbor Salt Marsh and brushy area just east of the waiting lanes. Double-crested Cormorants and Bald Eagles occasionally are perched on the old pilings. Peregrine Falcon, Great Blue Heron, American Bittern, Belted Kingfisher, American Crow, blackbirds, waterfowl, and a variety of passerines have been seen here. To the west of the parking lot is a small freshwater lake with riparian habitat that can be investigated for Hooded Merganser, Wood Duck, Downy Woodpecker, Tree Swallow, Cedar Waxwing, Yellow-rumped Warbler, and others. Nearby dirt banks reveal the nesting holes of Belted Kingfisher and Northern Rough-winged Swallow, while both Cliff and Barn Swallows nest on the ferry dock structures.

Leaving Anacortes, the ferry crosses Rosario Strait. Strong convergence areas about halfway across the four-mile strait are important feeding areas for a variety of birds and marine mammals. In winter, Common Murres by the thousands feed here along with Pigeon Guillemots; Marbled Murrelets; auklets; White-winged, Surf, and sometimes Black Scoters; Heermann's and Bonaparte's Gulls; and others. Earlier in the season, Rhinocerous Auklets are seen. Harbor seals, Orca, Minke whales, Dall's and harbor porpoises, and California sea lions all have been spotted in Rosario Strait.

All along the route scan the tall evergreens for Bald Eagles, which nest on most of the islands. Osprey, Turkey Vulture and, very occasionally, a Golden Eagle can be seen from spring to early fall soaring above the islands. Glaucous-winged Gulls nest on several of the smaller rocky islands, and harbor seals often haul out there.

Thatcher Pass, the first narrow channel, runs between Decatur and Blakely islands. Pigeon Guillemots nest on Willow Island at the north end of the pass. Lopez Island is the first ferry stop; it then crosses Upright Channel to Shaw Island, its next stop. After Shaw, the ferry crosses Harney Channel to Orcas Island, the largest of the San Juans. Be on the lookout for Mew, Thayer's, and Bonaparte's Gulls; Common Tern; Brandt's and Pelagic Cormorants; and a variety of alcids and other seabirds. The route from Orcas can go through Wasp Passage, directly to the west between Crane and Shaw Island, or back through Harney and Upright channels to San Juan Channel and Friday Harbor. Friday Harbor has an outstanding variety of marine birds and often hosts rarities. Many boat docks are accessible to the public for good views. Loons, grebes, Greater Scaup, Common Goldeneye, Surf Scoter, Bufflehead, Red-breasted Merganser, an occasional Oldsquaw, Rhinocerous Auklet, Bonaparte's and Mew Gulls, Double-crested Cormorant, and a variety of others can be seen in season. The trip from Anacortes to Friday Harbor takes an average of two hours.

The Anacortes terminal for the ferry through the San Juans is about 80 miles north of Seattle via I-5. At Exit 230, turn west on SH 20 for 16 miles to Anacortes, then follow ferry route signs to the terminal. Some of the ferries also go on to Vancouver Island in Canada. In summer and on weekends it is advisable to arrive *at least* an hour ahead of time. Reservations are not taken for island travel, and time schedules change several times a year.

San Juan Island National Wildlife Refuge

The San Juan Island NWR includes 84 islands set aside as a wilderness refuge for eagles, seabirds, and marine mammals. The islands separate into four habitat types: reefs, rocks, grassy islands, and forested islands. The islands with high cliffs and grassy slopes provide nesting sites for Pigeon Guillemot, Tufted Puffin, Rhinocerous Auklet, Black Oystercatcher, cormorants, Glaucous-winged Gull, and a variety of other birds. Bald Eagles nest in the tall evergreens on forested islands.

Some of the islands, such as Willow, Flower, Turn, Low, and several unnamed rocks, can be observed from the ferry traveling through the San Juans. Detailed maps of the San Juan Islands are posted on all ferries. There are Marine State Parks at Matia and Turn islands with boat mooring, camping, and toilets, but no water. Wildlife observation and photography are allowed on these two islands. Matia has a one-mile wilderness trail. The rest of the islands are closed to the public, and boats should stay at least 200 yards offshore to avoid disturbing nesting birds. Information: San Juan Islands NWR, c/o Nisqually NWR Complex, 100 Brown Farm Road, Olympia, WA 98506; (360) 753-9467.

Guemes Island

Guemes Island is reached by a small ferry that passes through Guemes Channel from downtown Anacortes. Winter is the best time to observe large concentrations of seabirds. Western, Horned, and Red-necked Grebes; loons; Pigeon Guillemots; Marbled Murrelets; Oldsquaw; Pelagic and Brandt's Cormorants; scoters; eiders; and Brant can be seen, in season. Turkey Vultures have been seen in small numbers during late September resting on the beach at Clark Point on the northeast side of Guemes. The island is mostly forested, and there is scattered pastureland.

Sinclair Island Wildlife Area

The 35-acre wildlife area sits on the eastern edge of Sinclair Island, which is about eight miles northwest of Anacortes. It is located on a small bay and is accessible by boat. Its attraction is its uniqueness as a diverse island habitat: 1,000 feet of pebble beach and bay, productive apple orchard and berry fields, 1.6-acre pond and marsh, extensive woodland, distinct vegetation communities, and historical buildings in the form of a homestead and post office. The trip to the island in most seasons will give views of alcids, other seabirds, and possibly marine mammals. Waterfowl and raptors are numerous during fall and winter, and a variety of songbirds nest here in summer. For further information contact the Department of Fish and Wildlife's Region 4 office at 16018 Mill Creek Blvd., Mill Creek, WA 98012; (206) 775-1311.

Lopez Island

The least populated and third largest of the San Juans, Lopez is a cyclist's paradise of gentle, rolling terrain (except for the first hill!). Lopez has more farmland and more public access to beach and shoreline than the other islands. At 12 miles long and five miles wide, there are many spots to get great views of marine birds. Bald Eagles nest at Humphrey Head, a tiny northeastern peninsula of the island. Lopez was named for Gonzalo Lopez de Haro who discovered the island in 1841; the Lummi Indian name for the island was Swa-la-tch.

Spencer Spit State Park. This 130-acre park at the northeast side of the island includes a sand spit that extends into Lopez Sound and almost reaches Frost Island. The park is on a low, wooded bluff above the beach south of Swifts Bay. A mile of beach edges a sizable salt marsh lagoon where Great Blue Heron, Belted Kingfisher, ducks, Canada Geese and, occasionally, loons and grebes can be found. The sandy spit is good for shorebirds such as Killdeer, yellowlegs, dowitchers, plovers, and peeps, especially from July to early September. Shorebirds occasionally attract Peregrine Falcon and Merlin. Lapland Longspur and Snow Bunting also have been seen. In the wooded part of the park look for Pileated Woodpecker, Varied Thrush, wrens, kinglets, chickadees, creepers, nuthatches, and warblers during migration.

The park has 25 campsites (no hookups) and is reached by going south on Port Stanley Road for three miles from the ferry dock. Information: Spencer Spit State Park, Route 2, Box 3600, Lopez, WA 98261; (360) 468-2251.

Hummel Lake. Hummel Lake is a small lake with brambles edging it and a cattail marsh. Look here for Pied-billed Grebe, Bufflehead, scaup, teal, Northern Pintail, American Wigeon, Northern Shoveler,

Marsh Wren, Virginia Rail, Sora, Common Yellowthroat, American Coot, Red-winged Blackbird, swallows, Willow Flycatcher, and Yellow Warbler. Hummel Lake is mid-island where Center Road crosses Hummel Lake Road. The lake is on the east side of the road, and there is a parking lot and boat launch.

Fisherman Bay. To reach Fisherman Bay, go west on Hummel Lake Road, then follow the signs to Lopez Village, which is at the north end of Fisherman Bay. Brambles can be searched for American Goldfinch, Bewick's Wren, Rufous-sided Towhee, California Quail, and Savannah, Chipping, and Vesper Sparrows. The quieter waters of the bay, protected by a long sand spit on the west, are a resting area for Horned Grebe, Great Blue Heron, occasional loons, Double-crested Cormorant, a variety of waterfowl and shorebirds, falcons, gulls, and terns. Fisherman Bay Road follows the edge of the bay south and affords good views.

At the south end of the bay turn west onto Bayshore Drive, which goes north onto Fisherman Spit. To the left of the spit is San Juan Channel, with birds more suited to open saltwater habitat. Lapland Longspur, Snow Bunting, and a variety of sparrows and migrant warblers sometimes can be seen here.

Richardson. Richardson is reached by continuing south on Fisherman Bay Road; it is well-signed. Open farmland areas are especially good spots, in season, to watch for Common Barn-Owl, Short-eared and Snowy Owls, Northern Harrier (which has nested on the island), Red-tailed Hawk, Rough-legged Hawk, Turkey Vulture, Northern Shrike, American Pipit, Brewer's and Red-winged Blackbirds, and a variety of sparrows. North of Richardson, farm ponds have yielded such specialties such as Trumpeter Swan, Ruddy Duck, American Avocet, and Wilson's Phalarope. Marine birds—plus Bald Eagle, Osprey, and occasional falcons—can be seen from the pier in Richardson.

Shaw Island

Shaw Island covers about 5,000 acres, eight square miles, and is the fourth largest of the San Juans. It is an island of evergreen forests and rugged, rocky coastline with little public access to beaches. Two orders of nuns live on Shaw: the Franciscan Sisters of the Eucharist, who run the ferry landing, the fuel station, and the store near the dock; along with the order of Our Lady of the Rock monastery, which operates a dairy and cheese-processing plant and markets herbs and herb products. Birding is as good as on the other islands, amenities aren't.

Blind Bay. Wintering marine birds—such as all the loons and grebes, Marbled Murrelet, Pigeon Guillemot, Red-breasted Merganser, Harlequin Duck, scoters, Bufflehead, Greater Scaup, Common and Barrow's Goldeneyes, Oldsquaw, cormorants, and rock shorebirds—can be seen. In the forested area watch for Great Horned Owl, Pileated and Hairy Woodpecker, Golden-crowned Kinglet, Red-breasted Nuthatch, Brown Creeper, Winter Wren, Dark-eyed Junco, and warblers in migration. Blind Bay is on Blind Bay Road just west of the ferry dock.

A tiny state park on Blind Island at the entrance to Blind Bay is accessible by boat only. It has four primitive campsites (no water, pit toilets). There are few trees, but the rocky shoreline is great for kayaking or boating bird-watchers.

Indian Cove. Indian Cove is at the southeast edge of the island. Shaw Island County Park is here and has a boat launch and access to the sandy beach. Osprey, a variety of shorebirds, and marine waterfowl are here, plus a variety of forest birds.

Squaw Bay. Squaw Bay is excellent for shorebirds including Pectoral Sandpipers, Greater Yellowlegs, Killdeer, and others. The forested area of the park is good for the usual western coniferous species plus a variety of unusual migrants.

Orcas Island

Orcas is the largest, hilliest, and most sprawling of the San Juans. At 56 square miles and with 125 miles of coastline, it is my favorite, but only because I know it so well. All of the islands have their special appeal. Orcas Island has been likened to a saddlebag: two sections divided by East Sound, an eight mile bay about a mile wide that divides the island nearly in half. The eastern half of the island is more hilly with Mount Constitution, the highest point in the San Juans, rising 2,454 feet within the boundaries of Mount Moran State Park. The western half of the island is divided a second time by West Sound, a bay about four miles long. Turtleback is its high point at 1,028 feet. The population and cultural center—the Philadelphia String Quartet and others perform here—is at the town of Eastsound at the narrow northern center of the island.

Birding on Orcas is varied. Mountain species, all of the marine seabirds and waterfowl, lowland forest birds, raptors, and a host of others are here. Christmas count averages have ranged from 103–118 species; species high counts have included Western Grebe, Ring-necked Duck, Glaucous-winged Gull, Marbled Murrelet, American Crow, Chestnut-backed Chickadee, and Winter Wren.

Moran State Park. Five lakes, four campgrounds, and 26 miles of hiking trails are in this beautiful 4,604-acre park. The campgrounds, trails, log shelters, ranger residences, and the stone tower atop Mount Constitution, modeled after 12th-century European watchtowers, were all built by the 4,768th Company of the Civilian Conservation Corps (CCC) from Fort Snelling, Minnesota. Moran State Park is a mix of dense forest, open fields, and lakes. Douglas-fir, western hemlock, grand fir, Sitka spruce, and western redcedar predominate at the lower elevations, while at the top of Mount Constitution lodgepole and western white pine thrive in the rocky soil. Columbia blacktail deer, river otter, muskrat, raccoon, Douglas squirrel and a variety of bats are some of the resident mammals.

Osprey have nested near the west entrance to the park for several years. Cascade Lake, with good fishing for brook trout, cutthroat trout, and Kokanee, a landlocked type of sockeye salmon, is on the right shortly after the entrance. A flock of 11–16 Trumpeter Swans in winter plus Hooded and Common Mergansers, Common Loon, Wood Duck, Mallard, and Pied-billed Grebe all have been seen on the lake. Bald Eagle, Great Blue Heron, Belted Kingfisher, Vaux's Swift, Evening Grosbeak, Pileated Woodpecker, Tree and Violet-green Swallows, Steller's Jay, and Winter and Bewick's Wrens are also in the area. Cascade and Cold creeks, nearby, have nesting American Dippers.

From the wetter lowlands into the more open forests as one starts up the Mount Constitution Road, look for Sharp-shinned or Cooper's Hawks, Northern Flicker, Band-tailed Pigeon, Hairy Woodpecker,

Horned Puffin

Varied, Hermit, and Swainson's Thrush, Brown Creeper, Townsend's and Yellow-rumped Warblers, Purple Finch, Pine Siskin, Red Crossbill, Western Tanager, Chestnut-backed Chickadee, and Red-breasted Nuthatch. Around the forested edges of higher meadows watch for American Kestrel, Blue Grouse, American Goldfinch, Chipping Sparrow, and Rufous Hummingbird. Mountain Lake, part way up, has similar species as Cascade Lake.

The more open, drier woods at the summit host Townsend's and Yellow-rumped Warblers, Varied Thrush, Gray Jay, Clark's Nutcracker, Pine Grosbeak, Gray-Crowned Rosy Finch, Hammond's Flycatcher, White-winged Crossbill, Horned Lark, Black Swift, Common Nighthawk, and Common Raven. Birds far less common in the park are Golden Eagle, Peregrine Falcon, Northern Goshawk, and Wild Turkey.

There are 136 campsites (no hookups) within Mount Moran Park. The park is reached by following Orcas Road to Olga Road east out of

Eastsound; it is well-signed. Information: Moran State Park, Star Route Box 22, Eastsound, WA 98245; (360) 376-2326.

West Sound

The winding, very scenic road around West Sound affords good views of the wide bay. Common, Red-throated, and Pacific Loons; Western, Red-necked, Horned, and Eared Grebes; Double-crested, Pelagic, and Brandt's Cormorants; Bufflehead; Common and Barrow's Goldeneyes; Common and Red-breasted Mergansers; Harlequin Duck; Oldsquaw; White-winged and Surf Scoters; scaup; and alcids are seen regularly in the sound. Bald Eagles are resident, and Peregrine Falcons and Merlins are seen occasionally. On Christmas counts, we have seen huge rafts of various seabirds: Pacific Loon, Western Grebe, Marbled Murrelets, and Bonaparte's Gulls are present in the hundreds some years.

The open woodlands of madrona, Rocky Mountain juniper, and Garry oak along the edge of West Sound often are host to rarities or uncommon passerines. Say's Phoebe, Bohemian Waxwing, Townsend's Solitaire, and Northern Pygmy-Owl have been reported; Dark-eyed Junco, Common Nighthawk, Common Flicker, Chestnut-backed Chickadee, and American Kestrel are more common. West Sound is reached from the Orcas ferry landing by following the Horseshoe Highway north and turning west at the first intersection toward West Sound.

Frank Richardson Wildfowl Preserve. In 1990, the Department of Natural Resources selected this marsh as one of top priority in the state for preservation. The San Juan Preservation Trust is still working for full protection of this wonderfully productive freshwater habitat. Nesting species at the marsh include Pied-billed Grebe, Mallard, Cinnamon Teal, Blue-winged Teal, Wood Duck, Hooded Merganser, Ring-necked Duck, American Coot, Sora, Virginia Rail, Common Snipe, Marsh Wren, Common Yellowthroat, and Red-winged Blackbird.

Wintering species or those seen during migration include Trumpeter Swan (although they are rare in this spot), Northern Pintail, Northern Shoveler, American Wigeon, Gadwall, Green-winged Teal, Blue-winged Teal (may nest), Bufflehead, Ring-necked Duck (may

Common Ravens

nest), and dowitcher. Turkey Vulture, Bald Eagle, Red-tailed Hawk, Peregrine Falcon, Merlin, accipiters, Common Raven, and Great Blue Heron have been seen in trees around the marsh or soaring above. Birds of the brambles and brushy areas are Song Sparrow, Golden-crowned and Ruby-crowned Kinglets, Cedar Waxwing, Chestnut-backed Chickadee, Brown Creeper, Orange-crowned Warbler, and other passerines. Five species of swallows—Tree, Violet-green, Barn, Cliff, and Rough-winged—are observable in spring, and some probably nest.

Best seasons for observation at the marsh are March to June and September to November; however, having spent many Christmas counts in the area, it is productive even in mid-winter. More than once we have aroused Virginia Rails in mid-December. The marsh is reached by following the Deer Harbor Road west. Just before the settlement of Deer Harbor, turn right on Sunset Beach Road, and cross the bridge between Deer Harbor and the adjacent lagoon (excellent birding here, too). Continue for less than a mile and the marsh will be on your right.

Yellow Island

Seen from the ferry, Yellow Island glows with color in the spring. This ten-acre preserve is covered with 150 species of native wildflowers, dense in their profusion partly due to the lack of grazing animals on the island. Yellow Island is part of the Nature Conservancy's San Juan Preserve. With a sandy spit at either end for harbor seals to haul out on and trees for perching falcons or eagles, this tiny island represents nearly all of the important classes of flora and fauna in the San Juans. Migrants often stop here for rest and the western reef off the island occasionally has rock sandpipers including Black Oystercatchers, Surfbirds, and Black Turnstones. A variety of seabirds, such as Harlequin Duck and Oldsquaw, are present.

Reached only by boat, Yellow Island is a preserve for scientific study, education, and the enjoyment of nature, and it is requested that visitors stay on marked trails. It is open during daylight hours only; no overnight camping or moorage. Yellow Island lies in San Juan Channel about 20 minutes by boat from San Juan Island.

San Juan Island

The infamous Pig War of 1859 over ownership of San Juan Island finally came to a conclusion when Kaiser Wilhelm I, arbitrating the decision, ruled in favor of the United States in late 1872. During the 13 years before arbitration, both an American Camp and a British Camp were established (because Yankee Mr. Cutlar shot a British pig!) and thrived; their historical remains now are premier birding sites on the island. English Camp and American Camp are well-preserved, and both are part of the San Juan Island National Historic Park. Information: Superintendent, National Park Service, P.O. Box 429, Friday Harbor, WA 98250; (360) 378-2240.

Birding is excellent on San Juan Island with probably the most varieties of habitats of any of the islands. And the island is the only spot in the United States where you can see Eurasian Skylarks. In the settled area of Friday Harbor, look for House Finch; Dark-eyed Junco; White-crowned, Golden-crowned, and Song Sparrows; Rufous-sided Towhee; Black-throated Gray Warbler; Cedar Waxwing; American Robin; House Wren; Violet-green Swallow; woodpeckers; and even

Common Barn-Owl. At freshwater ponds along Roche Harbor Road, watch for Common Snipe and a variety of dabbling ducks, Canada Geese, Killdeer, blackbirds, Common Yellowthroat, Northern Harrier, plovers, and sandpipers.

White-crowned Sparrow

San Juan Island's Friday Harbor is its only incorporated town, the county seat, home of the Whale Museum, a fine exhibit on northwest cetaceans, and site of the University of Washington Friday Harbor Marine Laboratory. The town offers inns, stores, galleries, bike rentals, marine trips to see whales, and fine restaurants. It is the last stop before the international ferry reaches Sydney, British Columbia. Maps are available free at several places in town, and an excellent "Bird and Wildlife Checklist of the San Juan Islands" is available from the San Juan Audubon Society.

Three Meadows. This is probably the best freshwater marsh on the island for birds. The area is a favorite for the Trumpeter Swan population on the island. Great Blue Heron, a possible American Bittern, Pied-billed Grebe, Wood Duck, Blue-winged Teal, Ring-necked Duck, Hooded Merganser, Virginia Rail, Marsh Wren, and Common Snipe are just a few that nest here. Owls, hawks, Band-tailed Pigeon, Bushtit, Rufous Hummingbird, and Western Tanager can be found in the wooded areas. Three Meadows is a privately owned wetland open to birders, preferably with permission from the Three Meadows Association, P.O. Box 1091, Friday Harbor, WA 98250. To reach Three Meadows, follow Roche Harbor Road out of Friday Harbor to Halvorsen Road. Go just past Halvorsen and turn south on the next gravel lane, then in a very short distance, turn right to the marsh.

English Camp National Park. Wild Turkeys frequent the roads near English Camp, sometimes just wandering along like tame chickens. English Camp is situated on Westcott and Garrison bays at the northwest tip of the island. The English Royal Marines left this beautiful spot in November 1872, but much of the history lives on. Madronas, mixed conifers and hardwoods, thickets of salal and brambles, gardens, lawns, and buildings all make up this shoreline habitat. A splendid maple grove is nearby with one tree more than 300 years old. Flycatchers; swallows; Western Tanager; Red-breasted Sapsucker; Downy, Hairy, and Pileated Woodpeckers; Belted Kingfisher; Olive-sided Flycatcher; Solitary and Warbling Vireos; and many others nest here. Passerines on migration are extremely interesting, also. Look for possible American Pipit, Lincoln Sparrow, Ruby-crowned Kinglet, Hermit Thrush, Golden-crowned Sparrow, and Lapland Longspur. To reach English Camp, follow the Roche Harbor Road and signs. The park can be reached by several other routes, too.

Lime Kiln Point State Park. This is the "whale-watching" park; the only park of its kind in the country. Visitors often can get very close views of Orca, gray and Minke whales, both baleen whales, Dall's porpoises (which look something like pint-sized Orca due to their black-and-white color pattern), and Pacific white-sided dolphin. Interpretive signs illustrate what kinds of whales use the area; May to September are the best months to spot marine mammals.

Deadman Bay, where the park is situated, is host to many of the Pacific marine birds of the area: loons, grebes, cormorants, gulls, terns, alcids, waterfowl, and falcons. Bald Eagles, and occasionally Golden Eagles over Mount Dallas to the east, Turkey Vultures, Red-tailed Hawks, and Purple Martins often are seen soaring on the updrafts and thermals from the rocky mountainside. Madrona berries on the trees extending from the park to the bay attract wintering American Robin, and Hermit and Varied Thrushes. Lime Kiln State Park is several miles south of English Camp. When leaving English Camp, go south on West Valley Road, then west on Mitchell Bay Road, and south on West Side Road. San Juan County Park, which has a campground, is about halfway between English Camp and Lime Kiln State Park.

American Camp National Park. American Camp is at the southeast end of the island, about as far away as they could get from the British. It is an open, grassy, windswept area that extends almost to Cattle Point and a state picnic area, the very tip of the island. Sitting on the high hill near the redoubt and facing the Olympics, watch—and listen!—for Eurasian Skylarks. Their courtship flights complete with beautiful song can be seen from March to July. Their presence here was not introduced by man. They *were*, however, introduced to Vancouver Island, just across Haro Strait, in the early 1800s, but it wasn't until 1960 that the first skylark was recorded on San Juan Island, and not until May of 1970 that nesting birds were found.

Pickett's Lane, which heads due south from the American Camp Road and goes to South Beach, is especially good birding. Huge flocks of foraging marine birds are seen here; almost every species seen in Puget Sound. Along with the regulars watch for Black-legged Kittiwake, Northern Fulmar, Arctic Loon, Brown Pelican, storm-petrels, Sabine's Gull, Arctic Tern, shearwaters, jaegers, puffins, and auklets. Such rarities as King Eider and Smew should not be dismissed; both have been recorded in the San Juans.

Dense woods near Cattle Point have nesting accipiters and Great Horned Owl. The regular forest birds—such as Pileated Woodpecker, Winter Wren, nuthatches, chickadees, and creepers—are also here. Along the higher ridge watch for House Wren, a variety of raptors, Common Raven, Common Nighthawk, and Northern Saw-whet Owl. Shorebirds on the beach areas are Sanderling, Whimbrel, Western and Least Sandpipers, dowitchers, Dunlin, and others. Rocky beach areas sometimes have Rock Sandpiper, Black-bellied Plover, Black Oystercatcher, Wandering Tattler, and Surfbird.

One could write forever about birding opportunities in the San Juans. The point is to keep a *very* open mind and be prepared for anything from bluebirds to albatrosses.

FIDALGO ISLAND

Fidalgo Island is named for Spanish explorer Salvador Fidalgo and was settled in the early 1850s like much of the Northwest. Land on the island consists of thick forests, lakes, some prairie land on March Point, and a rugged, rocky coastline. It is marine-influenced on all sides, bordered by Rosario Strait; Deception Pass; Similk, Padilla, and Fidalgo bays; and Swinomish and Guemes channels. There is an interesting variety of birds with abundant sites in a compact area. The Duane Berentson Bridge connects Fidalgo Island via SH 20 to the mainland.

March Point

March Point is a northward-facing peninsula that lies between Padilla and Fidalgo bays just off SH 20. Although partially covered with oil wells, March Point offers excellent birding. Follow SH 20 west from the Bay View-Edison Road (across from the Farmhouse Inn with its delicious pies). After crossing the high bridge over Swinomish Channel, turn right on March's Point Road and follow it through a stand of trees. Turn right across the railroad tracks. Pull off the road and scan for Bald Eagles and Red-tailed Hawks, which nest in the area; Peregrine Falcons in fall through spring; and Great Blue Herons from a nearby coniferous rookery. Cormorants and eagles often sit atop pilings in the bay. A small marsh across the road may yield Virginia Rail and Sora, Marsh Wren, Violet-green and Tree Swallows; look for Western Bluebird during spring migration, and various sparrows in the dry grassy area above the marsh. Low tides and extensive mudflats, especially on the west side of the peninsula, provide good viewing of shorebirds; even in mid-July small flocks often are present.

At the tip of the point and to the east, large numbers of Brant can usually be seen. Redhead, Canvasback, both scaup, Ruddy Duck, wigeons, and Oldsquaw often are seen along with various loons, grebes, cormorants, alcids, gulls, and terns.

Anacortes

Anacortes is located at the northwest end of the SH 20 spur on the Island, 16 miles west of the junction with I-5. It is Skagit County's second-largest city and is the gateway to the San Juan Islands. The economy of Anacortes is based on the port facilities, fishing fleet, shipyards, seafood processing, oil refineries, and tourism. It is an interesting and historic town with a narrow-gauge steam train, lots of B & Bs, an energetic mural project on buildings, and a variety of parks. Birding spots are many and excellent. For more information on Anacortes, contact the Visitor Information Center at (360) 293-3832. *The MacGregor's Visitors' and Newcomers' Guide to Skagit County* is quite informative and has many maps. It is available from the Anacortes Chamber of Commerce, 819 Commercial Avenue, Anacortes, WA 98221.

Cap Sante Park. Cap Sante is a rocky promontory with views across to Guemes Island and back to the city of Anacortes, plus the distant Cascade Mountains and the Skagit Valley. Bald Eagles often are seen here, sometimes scooping up fish from the bay. Waterfowl, alcids, loons, and grebes also can be seen from the viewpoint. In the wooded areas of the park look for chickadees, kinglets, Pileated Woodpecker, Rufous-sided Towhee, Varied Thrush, and many other passerines during breeding season and in migration. To reach Cap Sante Park, go east on Fourth Street to "Y" Avenue, then turn right to the park.

Washington Park. This coastal Skagit County park is excellent for Harlequin Duck, Oldsquaw, Black Oystercatcher, Bald Eagle, Pigeon

Guillemot, Marbled Murrelet, all three cormorants, and a variety of loons, grebes, and marine waterfowl. It is an extremely scenic park with a perimeter road and pull-offs overlooking Rosario Strait. The park has open areas of Douglas-fir, madrona, and Rocky Mountain juniper, and a variety of unusual birds have been seen here, including House Wren, Townsend's Solitaire, Bushtit, and migrant warblers. A boat launch, hiking, camping, and day-use facilities are available.

Pigeon Guillemot

Mount Erie. "Mountain Guardian," a four-foot bronze eagle sculpture perched stoicly on an eight-foot stone column, stands at the top of Mount Erie, a city park about three miles south of Anacortes. Gus Hensler gave 120 acres of Mount Erie to Anacortes and the public as a wildlife sanctuary, and the sculpture is a memorial to him. At an elevation of 1,270 feet, the mountain is a favorite spot for hang gliders, rock climbers, and hikers. It is also an established hawk watch site commanding a tremendous view in all directions. Turkey Vulture, Bald and Golden Eagles, Northern Harrier, all three North American accipiters, Red-tailed Hawk, American Kestrel, and occasional Peregrine Falcon and Merlin all pass by its summit; many species of migrant passerines and waterfowl also can be seen.

Osprey, Bald Eagle, and Common Raven nest nearby, and all can be seen doing their courtship rituals in early spring. Along the upland wooded hiking trails, a variety of passerines can be seen. To reach Mount Erie from Campbell Lake, follow the Campbell Lake road around the mountain keeping right until the sign to the Mount Erie road; from Anacortes, take the Heart Lake Road south and follow signs to Mount Erie.

Campbell Lake

Campbell Lake is 410 acres of excellent fishing for catfish, perch, bass, rainbow trout, and spiny ray. It is nestled at the base of Mount Erie's south side. Hooded Merganser, Lesser Scaup, Bufflehead, Great Blue Heron, Marsh Wren, Common Yellowthroat, and a wide variety of other birds are near and on the lake. Bald Eagles nest here and often perch on the tiny island in the center of the lake. A family of river otters also call the lake home. The north side of the lake has a public access with a boat launch and rest room facilities. To reach Campbell Lake, turn south where SH 20 divides (towards Whidbey Island, not Anacortes); at about two miles turn west on Campbell Lake Road. The lake will be on your left, Mount Erie to the right.

WHIDBEY ISLAND

Whidbey is one of eight islands that make up Island County. In 1985 Whidbey Island, 45 miles in length and with an area of 212 square miles, was officially designated the longest island in the lower 48 states. By a majority vote of the U.S. Supreme Court, it was decided that New York's Long Island was really a peninsula! Early in the 1830s the Hudson's Bay Company planned on Whidbey Island for one of its fur posts, then changed its mind and chose Fort Nisqually, near Tacoma. Logging began, however, and most of Whidbey's old-growth forests were depleted by 1900. Second- and third-growth western redcedar, Douglas-fir, and red alder are the most prevalent trees now with native rhododendrons and madronas interspersed. At least 247 bird species have been recorded for Whidbey Island.

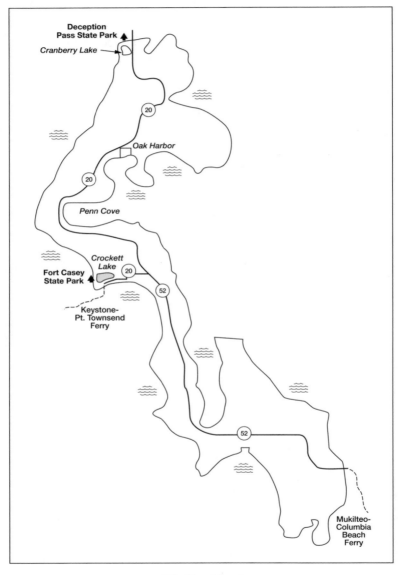

Deception
Pass State Park

Cranberry Lake

20

Oak Harbor

20

Penn Cove

Crockett
Lake

Fort Casey
State Park

20

52

Keystone-
Pt. Townsend
Ferry

52

Mukilteo-
Columbia
Beach
Ferry

Whidbey Island

Whidbey Island is made up of farms, freshwater lakes and ponds, marshes, bays and inlets, and rocky promontories: habitats that support an extremely varied and thriving bird population. Bald Eagles are a prominent nesting species on the island, preferring the upper reaches of Douglas-fir and western redcedars. Eaglets generally hatch in March and April and fledge in July; therefore, parent birds are quite visible coming and going after food for their nestlings. In early August, the fledglings are working on their flight training. By the end of August, Bald Eagles are almost absent from all of the area, only to return in a few short months for the winter's salmon runs.

Whidbey Island is accessed from Fidalgo Island via SH 20 and over the Deception Pass Bridge to the north, by the Mukilteo-Clinton Ferry to the east, and by the Port Townsend-Keystone Ferry, which lands at the west central side of the island. For the very helpful *Visitors' and Newcomers' Guide to Whidbey Island*, contact the Central Whidbey Chamber of Commerce, P.O. Box 152, Coupeville, WA 98239; (360) 678-5434.

Deception Pass

Deception Pass separates Fidalgo and Whidbey islands. The Deception Pass Bridge, a National Historic Monument, is actually two bridges that pass over both Canoe Pass and Deception Pass. The swift and sometimes treacherous waterway beneath the bridge narrows to 200 yards at Canoe Island. On the rocky headlands and heavily forested hillsides of the pass, Bald Eagle, Osprey, and falcons often are seen, Turkey Vultures soar overhead, and a variety of marine ducks and alcids can be seen in the water. The view from the bridge is excellent and a favorite of photographers.

Deception Pass State Park

Deception Pass State Park is one of the most popular parks in Washington. It has 3,000 acres of varied and scenic habitat including 17 miles of salt water shoreline, tide pools, three freshwater lakes with adjacent marsh habitat, much old-growth Douglas-fir, and 20 miles of hiking trails. Some nature trails are specifically designed to accommodate the disabled. A great variety of birds can be seen, from alcids to songbirds. Mammals occasionally spotted in the park include black-tailed deer, raccoons, chipmunks, beavers, muskrats, and several species of bats.

Bowman Bay. This part of the park is just north of the Deception Pass Bridge. There is a small, 16-site camping area that surrounds Bowman Bay; this section of the park is also home to a scientific research facility. Bowman Bay itself is an underwater state park. Various seabirds can be seen on the rocks offshore, including Tufted Puffins, Rhinocerous Auklets, and Pigeon Guillemots. Rosario Head lies to the north and a bit further on is Rosario Bay, where there are tide pools and a variety of marine life. Harlequin Duck and occasional Black Oystercatcher and Rock Sandpiper can be seen here. Reservation Head, on the south side of the bay, is nearly an island. Bald Eagles occasionally rest in the tall firs, and passerines—including Olive-sided Flycatcher, Steller's Jay, Common Raven, Black-capped and Chestnut-backed Chickadees, Bewick's and Winter Wrens, and Varied Thrush—are prevalent in the forested areas.

West Beach. Both stony and sandy beaches are found here, plus sand dunes separating the beach from Cranberry Lake. Shorebirds—such as Black Turnstone; Western, Least, and Pectoral Sandpipers; Short- and Long-billed Dowitchers; and Sanderlings—can be seen on the beach during migration and in winter. Terns, Glaucous-winged and Western Gulls, Marbled Murrelet, all three cormorants, and sea ducks can be spotted offshore. Marine mammals often are present, including Orca and other whales, sea lions, and seals.

Cranberry Lake. The largest of the park's freshwater lakes, Cranberry Lake often has Wood Duck, Mallard, Hooded Merganser, and other dabbling ducks. The marsh-wetland areas on the southwest side are especially good spots to observe Great Blue Heron, Red-winged Blackbird, Marsh Wren, and Virginia Rail; overhead watch for Common Nighthawk and Tree, Violet-green, Cliff, Barn, and Northern Rough-winged Swallows.

Cornet Bay. Cornet Bay is on the more sheltered east side of the park. There is an Osprey nest in this area, and Bald Eagles often are seen fishing nearby. Great Horned Owl, Pileated Woodpecker, Winter Wren, Dark-eyed Junco, Rufous-sided Towhee, and Song Sparrow are all permanent residents. Watch for Black-throated Gray, Townsend's, Wilson's, and Orange-crowned Warblers; Savannah and Lincoln's Sparrows; and Purple and Cassin's Finches in summer.

Deception Pass State Park has 246 standard campsites, five primitive sites, an underwater marine park for divers, a swimming beach, kitchen and picnic shelters, hot showers, boat rental, and an environmental learning center. The main park is located on SH 20 a half mile south of the Deception Pass Bridge or nine miles north of the town of Oak Harbor. For further information, contact Deception Pass State Park, 5175 North State Highway 20, Oak Harbor, WA 98277; (360) 675-2417.

Northeast Whidbey Coast

This section of Whidbey Island faces the Strait of Juan de Fuca and is rich in marine and land birds. There is some beautiful, rich prairie-like farmland on Ebey Road, now part of Ebey's Landing National Historical Reserve. The reserve is committed to protecting farmlands, coastline, glacial geology, Indian prehistory, an 1850s seaport town, and military forts. Marshes and a wealth of coniferous forests complete this special area.

Joseph Whidbey State Park. Joseph Whidbey SP is a day-use park once known as the Civil Service Beach, but it is one of the best on the island for birding. A sandy beach is good for picnics and for viewing the best of Pacific Northwest marine and water birds. Smith Island, which lies about six miles off the shore, is home to nesting Tufted Puffins, Pelagic Cormorants, Pigeon Guillemots, and a few Black Oystercatchers. From SH 20 in Oak Harbor, go west on Swantown Road about three miles. The park entrance is directly ahead of where Swantown Road meets Crosby Road (right turn) and West Beach Road (left turn).

Swantown Marsh. Instead of heading into the state park, turn west on West Beach Road, which soon turns south to go between a line of beach houses on the Strait of Juan de Fuca and the large marsh and

lake on the east. Northern Harriers and Red-tailed Hawks frequent
this very productive marsh most of the year. There is plenty of room
to pull off on the marsh side of the road, and there is beach parking
along the west side. Watch for Caspian Terns, the largest North
American tern, plunging into the surf just off shore during summer.
Loons, alcids including Rhinocerous Auklet, grebes, scoters, cormorants, and Sanderlings also are seen on the beach side. Heermann's, Glaucous-winged, Bonaparte's, and California Gulls; Semipalmated and Black-bellied Plovers; Semipalmated, Pectoral, Least,
Western, and Baird's Sandpipers; Killdeer; yellowlegs; and dowitchers
use the marsh and lake.

Bonaparte's Gull

Libbey Beach County Park. This lovely and bird-productive Island
County park can be reached by continuing south from Swantown
Marsh on the West Beach Road for about seven miles. At Libbey
Road, turn west and continue 0.6 mile to the park (also from SH 20
near Penn Cove by going west on Libbey Road). Libbey Beach is a
small park right on the beach at Partridge Point. Extensive kelp beds
host an exciting assortment of marine life. Bald Eagles perch in trees
along the shore, and the usual plethora of marine birds and shorebirds can be seen. There is a covered, log picnic building, plus rest
rooms and ample parking.

Fort Ebey State Park. Fort Ebey State Park is my favorite on the island. Ring-necked Pheasant, Bald Eagle, an occasional falcon, and a variety of forest passerines are present. The 228-acre park is an outstanding example of glacial "kettle topography." Large chunks of ice were buried 10,000 years ago under soils and gravels. The melting ice caused the rocky debris to collapse, and steep-sided depressions, called "kettles," were formed. Lake Pondilla within the park is, basically, a kettle filled with water. Freshwater dabbling ducks can be found here.

The hilly terrain is what makes this park interesting. There are terrific views of the meeting of the Strait of Juan de Fuca and Admiralty Inlet from high points on Partridge Point. Three miles of hiking trails through old-growth Douglas-fir giants and second-growth mixed conifers allow access to forest birds, and three miles of open, sandy beach offer good views of shore and marine birds.

This park is one of several that originally was part of the World War II defense plan for Puget Sound. Fort Ebey SP has 50 fairly private campsites. It is located south of Oak Harbor on SH 20, the Libbey Road exit. Information: Fort Ebey State Park, 395 North Fort Ebey Road, Coupeville, WA 98239; (360) 678-4636.

Penn Cove

Penn Cove, Coupeville's waterfront, may be named for the grandson of William Penn, but it's best known for its delicious mussels; don't pass up a chance to try this wonderful shellfish. Penn Cove pokes in and almost through Whidbey Island from the east and about a third of the way down. It is a superb spot to see large numbers of scoters in the winter. Five grebe species can be found here, including a local population of Eared Grebes. Waterfowl, loons, and alcids also can be seen in the open water.

Shorebirds—including Surfbird, Black Turnstone, plovers, yellowlegs, Whimbrel, and Spotted Sandpiper—are fairly common; Rock Sandpiper, Ruddy Turnstone, Willet, Wandering Tattler, Solitary Sandpiper, and Black Oystercatcher are much rarer. Oak and Crescent harbors, which continue from the northeast of Penn Cove, have similar species.

Admiralty Inlet

Admiralty Inlet is the waterway between the Strait of Juan de Fuca and Puget Sound. It was named by Captain Vancouver in honor of his supreme commanders, the Board of Admiralty, who managed Great Britain's royal navy.

Fort Casey State Park. This state park, a U.S. Army post in the early 1900s, covers 137 acres looking out to Admiralty Inlet. Migrant warblers are common in the park, and most of the western lowland forest birds nest here. Guillemots, auklets, and murrelets are seen in the open water, along with large rafts of gulls in summer and fall. Fort Casey has an underwater marine reserve, the mile-long Keystone Spit, hiking trails, and 35 campsites. It is located on SH 20 three miles south of Coupeville; it abuts the Keystone Ferry landing area. Information: 1280 Fort Casey, Coupeville, WA 98239; (360) 678-4519.

Crockett Lake. Crockett Lake is northeast of the Keystone Ferry Dock, just inland from a sandy barrier beach. Peregrines and Merlins occasionally are seen. Shorebirds, waders, waterfowl, and raptors frequent the lake and marsh area. Warblers occasionally are seen during migration in the low dune area. There is plenty of parking along the access road.

Keystone-Port Townsend Ferry. This 35-minute crossing of Admiralty Inlet is one of the livelier ferry rides. Alcids, loons, grebes, gulls, and waterfowl may be seen on the crossing. Black-and-white marked Dall's porpoises and their larger Orca cousins follow the large returning salmon runs and frequently are seen in this passage. At the Mid-channel Bank, the area between Marrowstone Island and the entrance to Port Townsend Bay, watch for Pigeon Guillemots, Rhinocerous Auklets, and Tufted Puffins, which come to forage in this rich area from their nesting sites on Protection Island. Glaucous-winged Gulls also feed here in large numbers.

South Whidbey State Park. South Whidbey is an 85-acre Douglas-fir- and Sitka spruce-wooded state park with outstanding views of Puget Sound and the Olympic Mountains. Pileated Woodpecker,

Red-breasted Nuthatch, Brown Creeper, Winter Wren, and Chestnut-backed Chickadee can be seen all year. The Wilbert Trail goes through an interesting section of old-growth forest on the east side of the park. Watch for Varied Thrush, kinglets, and Great Horned Owl. South Whidbey SP has 54 campsites. It is approximately 18 miles south of Crockett Lake via SH 525, then south on Smugglers Cove Road. Information: South Whidbey State Park, 4128 Smugglers Cove Road, Freeland, WA 98429; (360) 321-4559.

CAMANO ISLAND

Camano Island is a heavily forested island nestled close to the mainland west of Stanwood and just east of Whidbey Island. The Saratoga Passage divides the two islands. The Snohomish and Kikialos Indians, early gatherers of game, fish, clams, and berries, named the island Kallutchin, meaning "land jutting into a bay." It was later renamed for Spanish explorer Jacinto Caamano. Pacific lowland forest birds predominate on the land: Pileated Woodpecker, Varied Thrush, Rufous-sided Towhee, Black-capped and Chestnut-backed Chickadees, Brown Creeper, and Red-breasted Nuthatch are among the usuals. The island is reached via Exit 212 off I-5, through the town of Stanwood on SH 532, and over the bridge crossing West Pass.

Davis Slough

Davis Slough is located just over the South Pass Bridge on the eastern edge of the island. A dike provides good views of the marshlands and the upper part of Port Susan Bay. Watch for shorebirds during migration, waterfowl, and occasional raptors. The dike is reached by turning left onto Eide Road. There is also a Department of Wildlife access area 0.25 mile west of the bridge on SH 532.

Camano Island State Park

Camano Island State Park is a quiet, off-the-beaten-path park with good salmon, bottom fishing, and clamming. Bald Eagles often are seen in the trees facing Saratoga Passage, in season, and various alcids and marine waterfowl, including Harlequin Ducks, can be seen in the offshore waters. Bigleaf maple, red alder, stinging nettle, and sword fern form a habitat for the forest birds found here. Mammals—such as deer mice, rabbits, squirrels, raccoons, skunks, opossums, and deer—also are present. There is an excellent trail brochure explaining the half-mile of Northwest specialties found on the Al Emerson Nature Trail in the park. A few 600-year-old Douglas-firs are along the trail, and a large Pacific yew, a wood used for bows, arrows, and fish spears by the Indians, is also here. The park has 87 quiet, wooded, fairly private campsites. Camano Island State Park is reached by following either West or East Camano Road and the signs to the campground. Information: Camano Island State Park, 2269 South Park Road, Stanwood, WA 98292; (360) 387-3031.

KITSAP PENINSULA

The Kitsap Peninsula thrusts itself northward abutting Admiralty Inlet to the north and is bordered by Hood Canal to the west and Puget Sound to the east. The Edmonds-Kingston Ferry and the Hood Canal Floating Bridge give a northern access from the Seattle area to the Olympic Peninsula. Many large bays jut into this contorted land mass and provide shelter for wintering waterfowl and seabirds. The quieter waters of Hood Canal provide habitats for many oyster farms and land birds; waders and raptors often are abundant. Kitsap, meaning "brave," was named after a local Indian medicine man and war chief who fought against the settlers in the Indian Wars of 1855–56.

Edmonds-Kingston Ferry Route

A 25-minute crossing takes the ferry just north of the deepest part of Puget Sound at 900 feet. This is the main basin of the sound and one of the narrowest spots, just under four miles. At the Edmonds terminal, there is an underwater park for divers to the north; marine birds also take advantage of these waters. The new fishing pier, south of the terminal, is an excellent spot to observe Western Grebes, which gather by the hundreds in the winter. Bald Eagles, occasional falcons, scoters, mergansers, goldeneyes, alcids, gulls, terns, and cormorants also can be seen, in season.

At about midchannel, Mount Rainier is visible behind Seattle to the south and the Olympics rise to the west. Swirling eddies, a convergence of ebb and flood tides, attract masses of herring and other small fish that, in turn, attract a variety of alcids, gulls, and waterfowl. Many marine mammals also feed at these spots, including Minke whales and Orca, harbor and Dall's porpoises, and sea lions. At the Kingston terminal, Appletree Cove, scan for eagles, loons, grebes, and a variety of dabbling ducks. Edmonds is about 15 miles north of Seattle via I-5; the ferry route is well-signed.

Foulweather Bluff

Foulweather Bluff is a 93-acre Nature Conservancy Preserve composed of brackish marsh, beach, forest, and saltwater habitats; it is the most northerly point on the peninsula. Red alders, Douglas-fir, and western redcedar form the main part of the 50-year-old, second-growth forest. The preserve is located near the northern tip of the Kitsap Peninsula and borders Hood Canal; it is separated from the cold waters of the canal by a natural, raised barrier of sand. Three important bird species found here are characteristic of a healthy lowland forest: the Winter Wren, which gleans from the forest floor; the Red-breasted Nuthatch, which works down, up, and around tree trunks; and the Chestnut-backed Chickadee, which forages for insects among the branches.

Great Blue Heron, Bald Eagle, Osprey, flocks of Lesser Scaup that stop during migration, Pileated Woodpecker, and a variety of mammals are also here. Loons, grebes, and alcids are found offshore. Foulweather Bluff can be reached via the Edmonds-Kingston Ferry from the mainland. Follow SH 104 for about two miles, then turn north on Hansville Road NE and go to Hansville. The preserve is 2.8 miles further on Twin Spits Road.

Port Gamble

Port Gamble is the oldest operating lumber community in the United States, and is run by Pope and Talbot. It is a historical town, boasting clapboard-style Victorian houses and elm trees brought here around Cape Horn from Maine, Mr. Talbot's birthplace. Port Gamble sits at a point jutting between Hood Canal and Port Gamble Bay. All of the loon and grebe species have been seen from the point, along with

Common and Barrow's Goldeneyes, Oldsquaw, Harlequin Duck, Hooded Merganser, and all three scoters. Jaegers occasionally are seen, and Bald Eagles are often in large evergreens near the harbor. Port Gamble is located on SH 104 about eight miles northwest of Kingston.

Hood Canal Floating Bridge

The three longest pontoon, or floating, bridges in the world are located in Washington state: two across Lake Washington near Seattle, and the Hood Canal Bridge. Birding can be quite good from the bridge. Occasionally, Trident submarines from their base at Bangor pass through, allowing good views plus a long wait on the bridge, which means good birding. The Hood Canal Bridge crosses Hood Canal from Salsbury Point a few miles west of Port Gamble to Termination Point in the west.

Kitsap Memorial State Park

Kitsap Memorial State Park is quite accessible—just four miles from the Hood Canal Bridge—and has many campsites facing Hood Canal with sweeping views of the Olympics to the west. The beach is good for collecting oysters, in season, and clams the year-round. Waterfowl and a variety of seabirds—including loons, grebes, alcids, and gulls—are common. The forested areas are good for passerines in migration.

Fifty-one campsites (no electrical hookups) and a variety of amenities are found here, plus an 18-hole golf course nearby. The park is four miles south of the Hood Canal Bridge on SH 3. Information: Kitsap Memorial State Park, 202 NE Park Street, Poulsbo, WA 98370; (360) 779-3205.

HOOD CANAL

Hood Canal is a 65-mile-long saltwater channel that snakes off Admiralty Inlet at Foulweather Bluff and heads south. This waterway averages about 1.5 miles in width and provides a multitude of bays and inlets for a great variety of water-oriented birds. Fifty miles south, the channel turns northeast for another 15 miles, The Great Bend, finally ending up in an extensive mudflat area. The main road giving access to the canal is US 101 down the west side, approximately between Potlatch in the south to Quilcene in the north. Hood Canal also can be approached from the Hood Canal Floating Bridge, SH 104, then following signs to Hood Canal.

River Estuaries

There are four main rivers originating from the glaciers of the Olympic Mountains and emptying into Hood Canal from the western shore: the Quilcene, Dosewallips, Duckabush, and Hamma Hamma. All have interesting estuaries that support a wide variety of birds. Turkey Vultures and Bald Eagles sometimes feed on the flats, shorebirds can be numerous during migration, and herons are common. Waterfowl, while less numerous than in the more open areas of the sound, are common. Canada Goose, scaup, Bufflehead, Mallard, American Wigeon, Gadwall, mergansers, goldeneyes, Ruddy Duck, and teal are found here in season. The deeper, open waters host loons, Common Murre, and Western Grebe.

Along the wooded shores, there is always the possibility of good migrant passerines and many of the marshy areas provide homes for American Bittern, Virginia Rail, Sora, Marsh Wren, and blackbirds. Spur roads to the west off US 101 lead very quickly into mountain habitats and the possibilities of Northern Goshawk; Blue Grouse; Common Ravens; Gray and Steller's Jays; Horned Larks; Northern Pygmy-Owl; Red-breasted Sapsucker; Hermit, Varied, and Swainson's Thrushes; and many others.

Quilcene Estuary. The northernmost estuary is near the town of Quilcene, about six miles south of the intersection of SH 104 and US 101. Falls View Park, Olympic National Forest, is four miles south of Quilcene and has 38 campsites; it is inland from Hood Canal. This park is set in a heavily forested area, and there is a hiking trail to a waterfall on the Big Quilcene River. A trail leads up 2,800-foot Mount Walker, where raptors including large flocks of Turkey Vultures in the fall often can be seen. Hiking trails lead west into the Buckhorn Wilderness.

Dosewallips Estuary. The Dosewallips Estuary is about 12 miles south of Quilcene on US 101 near the town of Brinnon. Dosewallips State Park is nearby on the canal and has 127 campsites with full amenities.

Duckabush Estuary. The Duckabush Estuary is about two miles south of the Dosewallips on US 101. There are also state recreational areas along the way that have camping.

Hamma Hamma Estuary. The Hamma Hamma Estuary is south on US 101 about two miles from Duckabush. Potlatch State Park is about ten miles south on Annas Bay. There are 35 campsites in a hardwood-conifer forested area. Look for a variety of warblers during migration, including Townsend's Yellow-rumped, Black-throated Gray, Wilson's, and Orange-crowned.

The Great Bend

The area of the The Great Bend stretches from Potlatch State Park past the Skokomish River estuary and on to the mudflats at Lynch Cove. Marbled Murrelets; Western, Horned, and Red-necked Grebes; scaup; Common, Red-breasted, and Hooded Mergansers; dabbling ducks; a variety of gulls; and many others are found here. Just past Potlatch, turn east on SH 106 toward Union and Belfair.

Mary E. Theler Wetland

This 73-acre estuary boasts three types of wetlands and is surrounded by private and Department of Wildlife lands. The total secured area is 135 acres. There are five major wetland types; the three found here are riverine, freshwater swamp, and estuary-salt marsh. More than 150 species of birds, 100 species of insects, and almost 150 species of plants are found here.

A dike trail passing through crabapples and brambles and past salt marsh and freshwater ponds has produced both American and Eurasian Wigeon; Green-winged Teal; Northern Pintail; Northern Shoveler; Cooper's Hawk; Osprey; Merlin; Great Blue Heron; Ring-necked Pheasant; Common Yellowthroat; Willow Flycatcher; Northern Shrike; Harris', Lincoln, and Swamp Sparrows; Western and Least Sandpipers; yellowlegs; Dunlin; and many more. The boardwalk trail also goes through a cedar and alder swamp. Look there for possible Northern Pygmy-Owl; Downy, Hairy, and Pileated Woodpeckers;

Red-breasted Sapsucker; Western Tanager; Hutton's Vireo; and Wilson's and Black-throated Gray Warbler, to name a few!

BAINBRIDGE ISLAND

Bainbridge Island sits directly across from Seattle; a 30-minute ferry ride across Elliott Bay and the central basin of Puget Sound. Even at this busy seaport, birds flourish and can be seen from the ferry. The wharves and various seawalls along Seattle's waterfront are host to a variety of gulls and waterfowl.

Seattle-Winslow Ferry

The Seattle-Winslow ferry route is urban scenic: spectacular views of the Seattle skyline, the tall bluffs of Magnolia to the north, and the prominences of Alki and West points. During the nesting season, watch for Pigeon Guillemots near the Magnolia bluffs. Alcids, mergansers, and other seabirds along with a variety of marine mammals also can be seen along the route. At about 20 minutes along the route, the ferry turns to approach Eagle Harbor where the town of Winslow sits. Belted Kingfisher, Great Blue Heron, Bald Eagle, Rock Dove, gulls, grebes, loons, and waterfowl can be seen in the harbor.

From the ferry, Blakely Rock, part of a raised marine terrace found at points throughout the sound, can be seen against the background of Bainbridge Island. Kayakers and skin divers frequent the area, and it is a roost site for Surfbirds, Black Turnstones, and other rock shorebirds at high tide. Harlequin Ducks also can be seen.

Fay-Bainbridge State Park

Fay-Bainbridge State Park sits on Monroe Point where three branches of Puget Sound come together: Rich Passage, Sinclair Inlet, and Port Orchard Bay. The park, situated on the open beach and a sloping hillside, provides great views of the Seattle night skyline. Vegetation is primarily conifers with a few hardwoods interspersed. The usual campground birds of chickadees, nuthatches, creepers, kinglets, American Robin, and Winter Wren are here, plus a variety of others such as Steller's Jay, Bewick's Wren, Hermit Thrush, Cedar Waxwing, Pacific-slope Flycatcher, Solitary Vireo, and Evening Grosbeak.

There are 36 campsites (26 with water hookups, no electrical). Fay-Bainbridge State Park is located via SH 305. Four miles north of Winslow (eight miles south of Poulsbo), go three miles east on NE East Day Road, north on Sunrise Drive NE, and then into the park. Information: Fay-Bainbridge State Park, 15546 Sunrise, Bainbridge Island, WA 98110; (360) 842-3931.

Fort Ward State Park

Fort Ward State Park is on Beans Point at the southern end of the island where Rich Passage empties into Puget Sound. It is a day-use park with about a mile of beach to explore. A wooded trail goes to the beach, and Steller's Jays, Varied Thrush, and Winter Wren can be seen along the way; black-tailed deer are occasionally here, too. Scan the conifers edging the beach for Bald Eagles and a possible falcon. Shorebirds in migration include Black-bellied Plover, Dunlin, dowitchers, and Western Sandpiper; other peeps can be seen on the beach in small numbers. Waterfowl—such as both goldeneyes, mergansers, loons, grebes, cormorants, and gulls—are in offshore waters. Also watch for marine mammals. Fort Ward is six miles southwest of the Winslow Ferry terminal.

VASHON ISLAND

Vashon Island, 12 miles long, sits between two main channels of Puget Sound: the East Passage and Colvos Passage. George Vancouver bestowed the name Vashon in honor of Capt. James Vashon, a British Royal Navy captain who was honored for his heroism against rebel ships during the American Revolutionary War. Habitat on Vashon is rolling, rural countryside with fragmented coniferous forests.

Fauntleroy-Vashon-Southworth Ferry

The 15-minute ride from Fauntleroy Cove to Point Vashon crosses East Passage. After docking at Vashon, one can continue for another eight minutes across the Colvos Passage and land at Point Southworth on the lower Kitsap Peninsula. In Fauntleroy Cove watch for possible Black Scoter, Harlequin Duck, Red-necked Grebe, Barrow's Goldeneye, Common Merganser, and the usual seabirds of the area. Great

Blue Heron, Red-tailed Hawk, and Bald Eagle may be seen. To the north of Point Vashon lies Allen Bank, a shelf extending for about a mile and up to 70 feet deep. Look especially for alcids and other seabirds, plus gulls.

Crossing Colvos Passage, look to the north to 475-acre Blake Island, a state park accessible only by boat. Nearing Point Southworth, watch for Pigeon Guillemots nesting in the bluff areas. Scoters, loons, and grebes are common, and the eelgrass beds off the point often host Brant, in season.

Banks Road Pond and Mukai Lake

These two small bodies of water are the extent of freshwater habitat on the island. Northern Pintail, Bufflehead, Mallard, Hooded Merganser, Green-winged Teal, Virginia Rail, Common Yellowthroat, yellowlegs, and Solitary Sandpiper have all been seen here. Both lakes are off SW 176th Street; drive to the town of Vashon and turn west on SW 176th at its intersection with 99th Avenue SW. For Mukai Lake, at one-half mile turn south at the "Zippo" sign and park at the end of the street, then follow a trail southwest across a field to the lake. For Banks Road Pond, continue another mile on 176th; the pond is north of the road.

Maury Island

Maury Island is really a peninsula connected to Bainbridge Island by a long stretch of sand between Quartermaster Harbor, known for its Barrow's Goldeneyes, and East Passage. It was wrongly charted as an island and named by Commander Wilkes for the expedition's astronomer and hydrographer, Lt. William L. Maury.

Robinson Point. At the northeastern edge of the "island" is a site noted for Parasitic Jaeger in the fall; Common, Red-throated, and Pacific Loons; Western, Red-necked, and Horned Grebes; Surf and White-winged Scoters; alcids; cormorants; and a variety of waterfowl most of the year. Some specialties recorded here are Short-tailed Shearwater, Merlin, Eurasian Wigeon, and Oldsquaw. To reach the point go east from Portage, where Vashon and Maury join.

Chapter 5
South Puget Trough

 The metropolitan areas of Seattle, Tacoma, and Olympia, plus the eastern communities of Bellevue and the farmlands and subdivisions extending to the Cascade foothills, are cradled in the central portion of the extensive Puget Trough. Puget Sound invades everywhere to make this a truly water-oriented area. Between Seattle and Bellevue is 18-mile-long Lake Washington, which is connected, through Seattle and to Puget Sound, by a system of locks and canals. Forested hills meet the water in many areas, subdivisions are everywhere, and well-developed park systems exist throughout the region.

Tacoma is sandwiched between Seattle and Olympia on Commencement Bay. Olympia, Washington's state capital, sits at the southern end of Puget Sound on Budd Inlet. The extensive Nisqually National Wildlife Refuge lies between Tacoma and Seattle. These three cities, supporting the majority of Washington's population, are within one to two hours of the high Cascade peaks and on the edge of a variety of water environments. Birding is excellent.

South of Olympia and on to the Oregon border is a land of rolling hills interspersed with evergreens. Farming, forest products, light industry, and recreation are prominent in supporting the economy. This is also the I-5 corridor, the main artery north and south for transporting goods.

Climate is a bit milder than the northern section of the Puget Trough, but still basically mild, wet winters and coolish summers. The Southern Puget Trough is made up of western King and Pierce counties, most of Thurston County, parts of Lewis, Cowlitz, and Skamania counties, and all of Clark County.

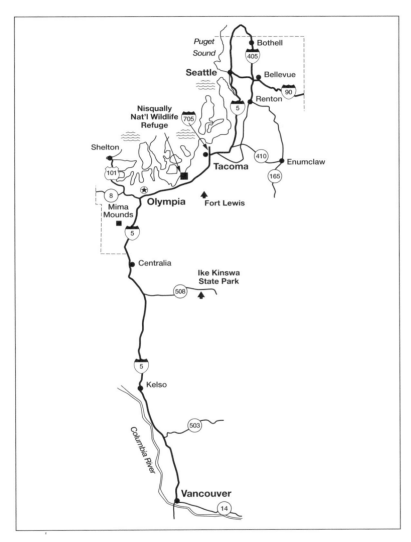

South Puget Trough

SEATTLE

Seattle has come a long way since the Denny party came ashore from the schooner *Exact* to settle on Alki Point in 1851. With no safe boat landing there, the party moved a few months later northeast, to where the city now lies. Seattle's first industry, Henry Yesler's sawmill on Elliott Bay, made good use of the abundant timber and the deep, natural harbor. Now, Seattle is a city of nearly half a million people with skyscrapers rising from the central area, and Elliott Bay is a busy international trade and export center. Its bird life is probably much more varied now than in earlier times. This is a city where Peregrine Falcons maintain an aerie on a downtown skyscraper; Purple Martins, a state candidate species, nest on city buildings; a Burrowing Owl was found wandering in an alley; Bald Eagles successfully nest within the city limits; and a nesting colony of 100 pairs of Glaucous-winged Gulls claim residence on the waterfront.

Seattle was named after a friendly chief of the Suquamps and allied tribes, Noah Sealth. The Indian name for the city was Tzee-tzee-lal-itc which meant "little place where one crosses over." (Phonetically, it sounds like a warbler rendition). There are more than 300 parks covering 5,000 acres of land in Seattle: tiny urban settings with Western Tanagers and Orange-crowned Warblers in the trees, densely forested woodlands with most of the lowland coniferous forest birds, and huge parklands stretching along Puget Sound which host a vast variety of marine birds of all kinds. Small and large lakes abound in the greater Seattle area, and most have a variety of waterfowl, marsh birds, gulls, and passerines.

Woodland Park Zoo and the Seattle Aquarium, both rated world-class, also are administered by the Seattle Park Department and are spots to consider for birding trips. At the aquarium, a variety of marine birds and mammals are on exhibit; close-up views of how alcids swim under water, just what a Tufted Puffin or an otter family looks like face-to-face, and the mechanics of a fish ladder are just a few of the interesting sights. The zoo has an interesting raptor exhibit and special interpretive talks with birds in flight. Woodland Park is a very modern zoo with most of the wildlife shown in as close approximation of their natural environment as possible. There are three free-flight avian environments that visitors can walk through: swamp and marsh habitat, tropical rain forest, and a smaller exhibit of savanna birds.

Parks too numerous to mention offer good birding. A few that you might want to look into that I haven't covered in detail are Seward Park, a peninsula on Lake Washington's west shore that has had nesting Bald Eagle and Osprey; Carkeek Park, a north end Puget Sound-facing, heavily forested ravine park with owls, coyotes, and forest passerines; Lincoln Park, a huge, long, wooded park extending along the edge of Puget Sound to the south of the city—it holds "first" titles to a state record of King Eider and county record of Yellow-billed Loon; and Volunteer Park on Capitol Hill, which has a wonderful conservatory; five linked greenhouses, each with a different collection; plus habitats of mixed forest/parkland that attract a variety of interesting passerines, especially during migration.

The Seattle Parks Department publishes a flyer of all city parks. Information: Seattle Department of Parks and Recreation, 100 Dexter Avenue N, Seattle, WA 98109; (206) 684-4075. The Specialized Programs Office has a full range of activities and field trips for disabled adults and children. Trained staff members will answer questions regarding the accessibility of a park or facility and programs offered; (206) 684-4950.

As any good birder knows, with diligence and patience, interesting and provocative birds can be found almost anywhere. Our own backyards are often special places, so I will start with my own as an example of what can be found by going nowhere. I have no idea if mine is typical or not. I live in suburban Bothell, about 15 miles from downtown Seattle, on two acres of mixed forest habitat—definitely not immaculately manicured by any means—and at a bit higher elevation than most, about 750 feet. A deep ravine lies behind the backyard where my two pet geese hold court. Geese are good in the absence of spotting scopes, and mine have so far observed Bald Eagle, Osprey, Red-tailed Hawk, all three accipiters, Great Blue Heron, miscellaneous gulls, Canada Geese, and a variety of ducks soaring or flying overhead. Their water and grain tempts Mallards, and in midwinter there are nearly 45 present.

Because this is a heavily wooded area, we have a wonderful variety of tree-inclined species such as Western Screech-Owl and Great Horned Owl; Pileated, Downy, and Hairy Woodpeckers; Bushtits;

Brown Creeper; kinglets; Red-breasted Nuthatch; Chestnut-backed and Black-capped Chickadees; Steller's Jay; American Crow; Song Sparrow; Anna's and Rufous Hummingbirds; Vaux's Swift; Tree, Violet-green, and Barn Swallows; Black-headed and Evening Grosbeaks; Winter and Bewick's Wrens; Olive-sided and Pacific-slope Flycatchers; House Finch; Rufous-sided Towhee; Cedar Waxwing; and Black-throated Gray, Yellow-rumped, and Townsend's Warblers. These are, with the exception of a Northern Goshawk, the more common species. Someone else's yard in more urban Seattle would have a different makeup, but still interesting birds.

Magnuson Park

Magnuson Park is a part of the Sand Point Naval Air Station that was deeded to the city. It has extensive frontage on the western shore of Lake Washington and much grassy, brushy, lawn-type habitats. Northern Harrier and Short-eared Owls often quarter the fields in search of prey. Canada Geese, Mallard, and Gadwall nest here every year, and a variety of waterfowl are seen from fall through spring. Barrow's Goldeneye, Merlin, Cooper's Hawk, Common Snipe, Killdeer, Yellow-rumped Warbler, Lapland Longspur, and Snow Bunting also have been seen during winter. Magnuson Park is reached by following Sand Point Way northeast of the university and turning east into the park at NE 65th Street.

Green Lake

The 2.8-mile pathway around very urban Green Lake in Seattle is crowded with joggers, walkers, skaters, and dogs, but it doesn't seem to bother the influx of waterfowl and gulls and a few exotic species that gather here from fall through spring. The park and lake cover 342 acres; lawns slope to the water's edge; huge, old Sequoias and cottonwoods dot the park; and a variety of cattails and brush surround the lake. Domestic ducks and geese—and Mallards of questionable heritage—lure an exciting mix of waterfowl to join them, much to the pleasure of birders. Canada, Greater White-fronted, and Snow Geese; Wood Duck; Green-winged, Blue-winged, and Cinnamon Teal; Northern Shoveler; Gadwall; Canvasback; Redhead; goldeneyes;

mergansers; Ruddy Duck; and American and Eurasian Wigeons are just a few that have been seen. Peregrine Falcon, Green and Great Blue Herons, American Bittern, grebes, Common Loon, and cormorants also have been found here.

A few shorebirds are seen, including Killdeer, Spotted Sandpiper, and Common Snipe. There is outstanding gull-watching at the lake: Bonaparte's, Mew, Ring-billed, California, Herring, Thayer's, Western

Snow Geese

Glaucous-winged, Glaucous, plus hybrids and limited sightings of Franklin's, Little, Common Black-headed, and Heermann's Gulls, plus Black-legged Kittiwake. Soaring overhead, in the proper season, look for Turkey Vulture; Bald Eagle; accipiters; Red-tailed Hawk; Vaux's Swift; and Violet-green, Northern Rough-winged, Cliff, Barn, and Tree Swallows. A variety of passerines—thrushes, wrens, vireos, warblers, sparrows, and finches—also frequent the park. In winter it's not quite as crowded, but recently when the lake was nearly frozen over a Great Blue Heron and a Peregrine Falcon had a tug-of-war over the peregrine's recent kill of an American Coot. The heron was a bit aggressive and advanced toward the peregrine repeatedly; it then stalked haughtily away, leaving the peregrine to dine alone.

Trout fishing is quite good at Green Lake, which is stocked with 15,000–20,000 legal-size trout a year. Power boats are not allowed, but canoes, small sailboats, and paddleboats are. Amenities abound at Green Lake, and some of Seattle's excellent restaurants are nearby. Green Lake is located at Latona Northeast and East Green Lake Drive North, north of the city center and a few blocks west of I-5.

University of Washington

The campus of the University of Washington, founded in 1861, has several outstanding birding areas. The large main campus accommodates 35,000+ students, and has well-landscaped grounds and a variety of plant species. Years ago one winter, more than seven Snowy Owls were perched in the tall conifers overlooking campus lawns. Passerines decorate the mixed forest on campus during migration, Evening Grosbeaks appearing in large numbers in May. Band-tailed Pigeons are present all year. The UW Arboretum, Montlake Fill, and the ship canal with adjacent Foster Island are all special birding habitats.

Montlake Fill. The Montlake Fill is a recuperated garbage dump. Long covered with gravel and grown into habitats of grassland, small ponds, brambles, and freshwater ponds, it is a special urban place for birds and people alike. The fill has a good diversity of ducks, migrants, and residents. Excellent passerines with more than the expected number of vagrants plus a modest number of shorebirds make this site outstanding. Very common, and generally nesting here,

Snowy Owl

are Canada Goose, Mallard, Gadwall, American Coot, Pied-billed Grebe, very few pairs of Ruddy Duck and Hooded Merganser, Spotted Sandpiper, Killdeer, Virginia Rail, Sora, American Bittern, Green Heron, Common Yellowthroat, Savannah and Song Sparrows, and Marsh Wren—plus others including a Common Goldeneye with chicks in 1992. During migration and through the winter, birds invade this area and you might see rarities such as Prairie Falcon, Say's Phoebe, American Avocet, Wilson's Phalarope, Solitary Sandpiper, Yellow-headed Blackbird, Townsend's Solitaire, and Egyptian Goose. Raptors are not uncommon. Accipiters, Red-tailed Hawks, and Bald Eagle are regularly seen, and Northern Harrier, Snowy Owl, and Short-eared Owl visit occasionally.

The actual walking trail around Montlake Fill measures about a mile. Union Bay edges the fill on two sides and is excellent for waterfowl. There are trails through the brambles to the cattail marsh on the east side where Sora and Virginia Rail are most likely; also watch for Marsh Wren, Red-winged Blackbird, and an occasional Yellow-headed Blackbird. Following the brambles paralleling the shore and past cottonwoods, birch, and alders, there are spur paths out to the bay-side where gulls, ducks, geese, and America Coots can be seen. Muskrat, raccoon, and beaver also are found in the area. Main Pond is the best for shorebirds and waterfowl. East Point Pond usually has ducks and a variety of passerines around it. Dime Lot Pond (named for the parking lot that now costs a quarter) with Scotch broom, shrubs, and small trees also attracts miscellaneous land birds. Ring-necked Pheasant can be seen in the grassy areas. The five ponds located on the fill become gradually larger and larger as the rains become more prevalent in the fall, making fall through spring the best time for waterfowl.

Montlake Fill is reached from downtown Seattle by driving north on I-5, turning east at Exit 169, 45th Street, and following 45th Street past the University of Washington campus. Go down the hill, past the shopping center on the north, and turn into Clark Road for one block, then go left on Douglas Road to Parking Lot E5. You also can park on Union Bay Place.

University of Washington Arboretum

The vast, well-manicured lawns and gardens of the University of Washington Arboretum invite walks, picnics, and a chance to see a variety of forest birds, plus migrant passerines. The present arbore-tum was established in 1935. It contains at least 105 genera of trees with about 500 species or varieties, and about 160 shrubby genera with 1,700 species or varieties—something to suit every passing passerine. There are several specialty gardens, such as the Rhododen-dron Glen, the Japanese Garden, and the Winter Garden. The Winter Garden has a 0.5-mile semi-loop trail and is planted with mostly native trees and shrubs—labeled for identification. Watch for Band-tailed Pigeon, Steller's Jay, woodpeckers, and the usual chickadees, nuthatches, kinglets, and Bushtits.

The arboretum is reached via Lake Washington Boulevard from either north or south. The visitor center, near the North Broadmoor entrance, has rest rooms and maps, and the Winter Garden trail begins across the street from the center.

Waterfront or Marsh Trail. Woodland, marsh, and open water make up the habitats over which the mostly elevated marsh trail travels. Beginning at the Museum of History and Industry parking lot and continuing over Marsh Island for half a mile to Foster Island, this scenic and wildlife-filled trail winds through the largest wetland remaining in Seattle (or you can begin at the eastern trail end from the Arboretum Visitor Center, which has maps). Waterfowl predominate; expect to see Canada Goose, Gadwall, Mallard, American and Eurasian Wigeon, Northern Shoveler, teal, goldeneyes, scaup, mergansers, grebes, and occasional Common Loons. The sweeping view looking toward the campus across Union Bay includes a log boom; look here for various cormorants and an occasional Bald Eagle. Osprey sometimes perch on light standards or snags nearby, and local peregrines sometimes hunt the area.

Rare passerines such as Gray-crowned Rosy Finch; Lapland Longspur; American Pipit; Harris', Sage, American Tree, White-throated, and Vesper Sparrows all have been seen. In recent years, three species of owls have been reported: Great Horned Owl, Western Screech-Owl, and Common Barn-Owl. Marsh birds, flycatchers, woodpeckers, swifts, and several species of swallows are possible.

From downtown Seattle, take I-5 north, then SH 520 east to the Montlake Boulevard Exit. At the light, go straight onto East Lake Washington Drive. In one block turn left on Park Drive and cross over the freeway, then continue to the museum parking lot.

Lake Washington Ship Canal and Fish Ladder (Ballard Locks)

The eight-mile-long Lake Washington Ship Canal connects Puget Sound at Shilshole Bay with the fresh waters of Salmon Bay, Lake Union, and Lake Washington. A canal was suggested as long ago as 1853, but it wasn't until 1916 that the small lock was opened to traffic, and 1917 when the channel between Lake Union and Lake Washington was finished. The locks are named for the man who made the waterway a reality, Hiram M. Chittenden. Both commercial and pleasure vessels by the thousands make the more-or-less 40-minute trip through the locks every year.

There is a visitor's center with interpretive displays located in the former carpenter and blacksmith shop. The Carl S. English, Jr. Gardens cover seven acres on the north side of the locks. The gardens attract woodpeckers, kinglets, Brown Creeper, chickadees, Red-breasted Nuthatch, thrushes, and a variety of migrants.

The rebuilt fish ladder is the newest part of the complex. Dedicated in 1976, the structure includes a below-water viewing room where visitors can watch salmon swim up the ladder. The five major species of fish that use the ladders are Chinook (king) salmon, Coho (silver) salmon, sockeye (red) salmon, steelhead trout, and sea-run cutthroat trout. Visitors in winter also can watch sea lions on their annual quest for steelhead at the locks. Everything imaginable has been done to discourage them short of death, so far; steelhead runs in 1994 were the lowest ever. All of the sea lions are named "Herschel."

Various water birds are seen at the locks. Watch for Mallard, Common Goldeneye, grebes, and mergansers, plus gulls and terns. Commodore Park adjoins the grounds of the fish ladder on the south side of the locks. It is nicely landscaped with native trees and shrubs, and a variety of land birds often can be seen including Cedar Waxwing, Rufous Hummingbird, swallows, swifts, Belted Kingfisher, Common Flicker, and migrant warblers.

Discovery Park

Named after Captain George Vancouver's ship, H.M.S. *Discovery*, the park is Seattle's largest at 535 acres. Beaches, cliffs, forests, meadows, and ponds make this a true urban wilderness; more than 50 species of birds nest here, and half of the species recorded in the state have been seen at least once in the park. Discovery Park is a reclaimed historic army base, Fort Lawton. The vintage colonial wooden buildings were built by the Army between 1898 and 1908. The land and buildings were deeded to the city in 1972 to create this wonderful haven.

Discovery Park is a natural area—no food or amenities in the park save rest rooms and parking lots. It is a far cry from the heavily wooded bluff area and the beaches where the Shilsholes made use of the plentiful salmon and shellfish. Eight miles of foot trails wander through the park's modern natural wonders: a 2.8-mile loop trail gives an overview of the park, a self-guided nature trail is located near the

Daybreak Star Indian Cultural Center, and a half-mile fitness path with 15 exercise stations is near the south gate. Four miles of road and hard path also welcome cyclists (bikes are *not* allowed on the natural dirt trails). Driftwood-strewn beaches extend for two miles around the tip of West Point, perfect for picnics and bird- and whale-watching. On the north side of the park is the Indian Cultural Center, sponsored by the United Indians of All Tribes Foundation, which has a gallery of North American Indian art and a variety of educational activities.

Discovery Park is only six miles from Seattle's downtown. There are parking areas at the east, north, and south gates. The visitor center, open 8:30–5:00, is at the east gate located at West Government Way and 36th Avenue West. The north entrance is off 40th Avenue West near Commodore Way, and the south entry is off West Emerson Street and Magnolia Boulevard. There are interpretive walks every weekend led by park naturalists. A bird list is available from the park for 25¢ and a SASE: Discovery Park, 3801 West Government Way, Seattle, WA 98199; (206) 386-4236.

West Point. West Point's historic, still operating, 1881 Coast Guard Lighthouse extends into Puget Sound between Shilshole Bay to the north and Elliott Bay to the south. It is a gathering point for many provocative and elusive birds. Fall to spring are best viewing months, even though birds can be interesting all year. As early as July, the fall migration begins and small groups of shorebirds might be seen, plus a Parasitic Jaeger offshore. All the loons, grebes, and scoters are possible, and Marbled Murrelet and Ancient Murrelet (November), Pigeon Guillemot, Common Murre, and Rhinocerous Auklet have been seen.

Eighteen species of gulls and terns have been recorded at West Point including Sabine's, Little, Thayer's, Heermann's, Franklin's, Glaucous, Western, and Bonaparte's Gulls, and Common Tern. Whimbrel, Wandering Tattler, Black Turnstone, Sanderling, and other shorebirds can be seen on the beach and rocky areas, in season. Rarities, especially after heavy storms, have included Short-tailed and Sooty Shearwaters; Oldsquaw; Caspian, Black, Arctic, and Forster's Tern; and Trumpeter Swan. Waterfowl are not as numerous, but Canada Geese, mergansers, Mallard, Bufflehead, scaup, and an occasional Harlequin Duck are seen. A few passerines and sparrows can be found in the brushy areas near the beach.

Wolf Tree Nature Trail. This 0.5-mile self-guided interpretive trail is located near the Daybreak Star Center. Twenty-two stations explain the intricacies of the forest. Look for Western Tanager, Swainson's Thrush, Bewick's and Winter Wrens, Rufous-sided Towhee, chickadees, Red-breasted Nuthatch, Solitary and Warbling Vireos, Pacific-slope Flycatcher, Black-throated Gray and Yellow-rumped Warblers, and a variety of others. The ponds off the side trails host Great Blue Heron, American Bittern, Mallard, Gadwall, Cedar Waxwing, Anna's Hummingbird, and a variety of swallows.

South Meadow and Bluffs. The large meadows stretching to the southwest from the historic district were once a recreational area for soldiers living at Fort Lawton. Now the meadow hosts a nesting group of Savannah Sparrows, plus Northern Harrier; American Kestrel; Short-eared Owl; Northern Shrike; Ring-necked Pheasant; Killdeer; and Lincoln's, White-crowned, and Golden-crowned Sparrows, in season. Rarities have included Gray-crowned Rosy Finch, Western Kingbird, and Lazuli Bunting. A dense copse of Scotch broom, fireweed, and berries is home to an upland nesting population of Red-winged Blackbirds, plus Willow Flycatcher, Black-headed Grosbeak, Orange-crowned Warbler, and Rufous-sided Towhee. Rufous Hummingbirds mix with Anna's during migration. The view from the south bluff, where Red-tailed Hawks and Bald Eagles often soar, sweeps from Mount Rainier over Puget Sound to the Olympic Range.

North Bluff and Forest. The Cascade Range, Mount Baker, northern Puget Sound, and the Olympics make up the view from the north bluff. Forest trails meander through native alders, maples, and conifers, now home to nesting Barred Owls and a variety of woodland species, including accipiters. Western Screech-Owl, Northern Sawwhet, Great Horned, and Long-Eared Owls also have been noted here, along with migrant flocks of warblers, vireos, and flycatchers.

Schmitz Park

Schmitz Park is a tiny ravine of old growth Douglas-fir and western redcedar nestled in a West Seattle neighborhood. A half-mile loop trail goes up one side of a tiny creek and down the other. Hazelnut, salal, red alder, deer fern, and English holly, a garden escapee, help make up the understory. Forest birds such as Brown Creeper, American Robin, chickadees, nuthatches, and Western Screech-Owl are resident, and Swainson's Thrush, Western Tanager, Black-throated Gray Warbler, and others arrive in summer.

EAST OF LAKE WASHINGTON

A commuter's nightmare awaits any birder trying to cross the floating bridges to the eastern side of Lake Washington during rush hour. Bellevue, now Washington's fourth-largest city, started as a bedroom community for Seattle workers to the west and Boeing employees to the south. It is now a modern, high-tech city. Lake Washington stretches from Kenmore in the north to Renton in the south. Class "A" hydroplane races are held here each August. Lake Sammamish is also a sizeable lake a few miles east of Lake Washington. A little further to the east, you are in the foothills of the Cascades.

Log Boom Park

This small park sits at the very northern tip of Lake Washington on the Burke Gilman Bike Trail. It is reached by following Lake City Way north from Seattle until you reach the town of Kenmore; turn south for one block at the first light, then right into the park. Bald Eagles are quite common here because they nest only a few miles away. Waterfowl such as Canada Geese, Common Merganser, American and Eurasian Wigeon, Mallard, Northern Shoveler, Ruddy Duck, and others gather in large numbers in winter. Double-crested Cormorants often are seen and roost in snags a mile or two around the lake at the Juanita Drive boat launch area. In the fall, watch for Bonaparte's and Franklin's Gulls and Common Tern. Green and Great Blue Herons nest in the area. A nearby Great Blue Heron Rookery has 20 or so nests and is well-situated and well-guarded at a tiny lake just behind the Kenmore Police Station (north of the Park-and-Ride on Bothell Way).

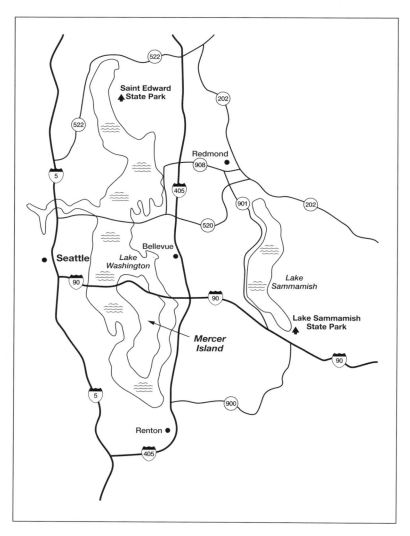

East of Lake Washington

Saint Edwards State Park

The park was once the home of the Supplican Order of Catholic Priests; it was named for Edward the Confessor, founder of Westminster Abbey and King of the West Saxons of England in the 11th century. The largest building on the central grounds is the former Seminary, the steeple of which is home to occasionally nesting Common Barn-Owls. There are manicured lawns and recreational facilities near the buildings—look for American Robin and Killdeer—but the biggest portion of the park's 316 acres is rather wild, undeveloped forest land that edges Lake Washington for almost three-quarters of a mile. The five miles of trails within the park are for foot traffic only, a definite boon to birders.

Great Horned Owl and Western Screech-Owl nest here and, in 1994, were joined by a family of Barred Owls. Accipiters, Winter Wren, Bushtit, Ruffed Grouse, Ring-necked Pheasant, and most of the western Washington forest birds also nest here. Pileated, Downy, and Hairy Woodpeckers; Rufous and Anna's Hummingbirds; Warbling, Solitary, and Hutton's Vireos; Olive-sided and Pacific-slope Flycatchers; and a variety of warblers can be found. To reach Saint Edwards from I-405, take Exit 20A (NE 116th Street) and turn west under the freeway. The street becomes Juanita Drive NE. In about three miles, look for the St. Thomas/St. Edward signs on the right. From the north, take Juanita Drive out of Kenmore and follow it to the signs. Information: Saint Edward State Park, P.O. Box 602, Kenmore, WA 98028; (206) 823-2992.

Carnation Farms

Possum Sweetheart's statue stands at the entrance to Carnation Farms, home of contented cows. In her "hay-day" she broke world records for milk production: 37,381 pounds of milk when she was six years old. Carnation Farms is still a top dairy and now has dog kennels and a cattery on its extensive grounds to test the many varieties of Friskies' foods. Extensive fields, Sikes Lake, native forest, and meandering landscaped gardens are all within the complex and beckon to a rich variety of birds.

Around the main complex of barns and kennels, look for Rock Dove, Brown-headed Cowbird, House Sparrow, and European Starling. When these local standbys of farm locales have been properly observed, go to the west toward the E.A. Stuart Gardens. American Robin, Cedar Waxwing, Black-headed Grosbeak, Northern Oriole, Western Tanager, Dark-eyed Junco, Bewick's and House Wrens, and a variety of other species have been seen here. The hedges backing the gardens are of native hemlocks and cedars; watch for chickadees, kinglets, and Red-breasted Nuthatch.

There is a viewpoint just east of the gardens (in front of the Hippodrome). From this point, the Snoqualmie Valley stretches out with the Snoqualmie River winding through it. In 1974, the farm's 1,200 acres became a state game reserve. Thousands of waterfowl are found here from fall through spring. Canada Geese, American and Eurasian Wigeon, Northern Pintail, teal, Ruddy Duck, Hooded Merganser, and Wood Duck are some that have been recorded. Great Blue and Green Herons, Red-winged and Brewer's Blackbirds, American Bittern, Virginia Rail, Killdeer, and occasional shorebirds also are seen. Turkey Vulture, Bald Eagle, Red-tailed and Rough-legged Hawks, Merlin, Peregrine Falcon, American Kestrel, and occasional accipiters are present, in season.

Marymoor Park

Marymoor Park is 520 acres located along the Sammamish River, ending at the northern end of Lake Sammamish. It started out as a bird-hunting compound for a Seattle banker. His hunting lodge, which evolved into his home, is now the site of the Marymoor Museum. The hunting preserve eventually became a Morgan horse farm, then a dairy farm, and, finally, in 1963 the second-largest King County Park. Marymoor is on the east side bike trail and home to a velodrome, the only one in Washington, where many cycling activities are held. It is a park of large trees and sweeping lawns and several arts fairs throughout the summer. But it does have nesting Common Barn-Owls and Red-tailed Hawks and the two-mile Marymoor Interpretive Nature Trail that leads to the edge of Lake Sammamish.

The first interpretive sign is just past a large open field teeming with voles and mice and other small rodents. Watch for American Kestrel hovering overhead, plus Northern Harrier and Red-tailed Hawks and, occasionally, a Short-eared Owl or Northern Shrike. Savannah Sparrow, Killdeer, American Goldfinch, Ring-necked Pheasant, and Common Yellowthroat also are seen here. Go through the willow thicket and then into a woodland with black cottonwood, alder, and Oregon ash, and finally to a freshwater marsh. Along the way watch and listen for Red-winged Blackbird; American Bittern; Great Blue Heron; Marsh and Bewick's Wrens; Tree, Violet-green, and Barn Swallows; Cedar Waxwing; and Mallard. A variety of warblers, sparrows, vireos, and flycatchers also can be seen along the way.

To reach Marymoor Park from Seattle, take SH 520 over the floating bridge and on to West Lake Sammamish Parkway just before Redmond. Turn south onto the parkway, then east into the main park entrance. Go past the main buildings, and in 0.6 miles turn south on an unpaved road leading to a natural parking lot and the beginning of the trail.

Lake Sammamish State Park

"Sammamish" comes from the Indian word "Samena," meaning hunter. Historically, tribes once gathered at the southern end of Lake Sammamish for their winter festival, or potlatch. At these times they began preparations for winter by hunting game and gathering other provisions.

This 431-acre state park can be filled with people picnicking, swimming, and water skiing, but there are 300 of these acres that are undeveloped and are excellent for nature walks. More than 125 species of birds have been identified in the park. The natural areas of the park are the woods and open fields of an old dairy farm; this acreage is divided by Issaquah Creek. There are dirt trails and a footbridge that spans the creek. Fox, raccoon, coyote, muskrat, opossum, deer, porcupine, and weasel are mammals that might be seen.

The more open areas and forest edges have Ring-necked Pheasant, occasional California Quail, Savannah and Song Sparrows, Bewick's Wren, Rufous Hummingbird, American Goldfinch, and many others. On the forest trails, look for Steller's Jay, American Crow, woodpeckers, Varied Thrush, Pacific-slope Flycatcher, Band-tailed Pigeon, Bushtit, Brown Creeper, and a variety of other species. To reach Lake Sammamish State Park, take I-90 to Exit 15, then turn north. Turn left on SE 56th Street. The park entrance is ahead on the right.

Kelsey Creek Park

Kelsey Creek Park is an 80-acre marvel sandwiched in the very suburban east Bellevue area not far from the high-tech bustle. A family farm with domestic animals and pasturelands is to the southwest, and a thickly forested area lies to the east. Kelsey Creek runs through the park; the creek and its branches drain about 16 square miles of Bellevue and Kirkland. Pacific salmon travel up the creek to spawn, usually in late October. The forest is mixed hardwoods such as bigleaf maple and red alder, with a few evergreens such as western redcedar and Douglas-fir. Raccoons and Great Horned Owls live in large holes in old trees and snags, and a fox occasionally is seen. Red-tailed Hawk nest in this forest, as do Winter Wren, Rufous-sided Towhee, woodpeckers, vireos, warblers, chickadees, nuthatches, Brown Creeper, and many other species. A 0.9-mile gravel trail open to walkers, joggers, and cyclists encircles the pastures, farm, and open spaces.

The Bellevue Parks and Recreation Office is located at this park and has information on Kelsey Creek and other city parks. Facilities are handicapped-accessible. Kelsey Creek Park is located at 13204 SE 8th Place, Bellevue; (206) 455-7688.

Mercer Slough Nature Park

This is a very special park almost in the center of Bellevue; not only are there more than five miles of hiking and interpretive trails, there are developed canoe trails and a special brochure detailing them. Mercer Slough Nature Park covers 320 acres of land around the Mercer Slough channel; the slough connects Kelsey Creek to Lake Washington. There are 170 species of wildlife recorded here, including birds, mammals, and amphibians, and hundreds of species of plants.

Edge of the Marsh Nature Trail. This is a self-guided nature trail with interpretive stations. Most of the trail is over historic bog land which extends nearly 40 feet deep beneath the pathway. In 1916, when the Ballard (Chittenden) Locks were built, Lake Washington was drained about nine feet. The bog-building process ended, but at the top level a wetland took its place. Alders, cottonwoods, and a variety of woody plants took over, and within their branches Yellow-rumped Warbler, Wilson's Warbler, Common Yellowthroat, Marsh Wren, Willow Flycatcher, and Rufous-sided Towhee now flit. Common Flicker and Hairy and Pileated Woodpeckers also live here, along with many other species. To reach the trailhead, park in the small gravel parking lot on 118th near the sign for Bellefields Park. Follow the split-rail fence to the south and look for the trailhead designation posts. For more information, contact the Ranger Station at 15416 SE 16th Street.

Mercer Slough Canoe Trail. Canoes can be put into the water at Enatai Beach Park just south of the I-90 interchange, or at Sweyolocken Park Canoe/Boat Launch just off Bellevue Way SE and north of the I-90 interchange. It is about a four-mile round-trip from Enatai Park. The canoe waterway is outstanding for viewing the hordes of waterfowl that arrive from the north each fall. Canada Goose, Mallard, Gadwall, Northern Shoveler, Green-winged Teal, American Coot, and Pied-billed Grebe are resident; Wood Duck, Northern Pintail, Blue-winged Teal, American and Eurasian Wigeon, Canvasback, Ring-necked Duck, goldeneyes, mergansers, and Ruddy Ducks are part of the many species that visit or winter in the area.

The cattail marsh areas are alive with chickadees and bushtits foraging on the seeds of the cattail. Great Blue Heron, Green Heron, Marsh Wren, Red-winged Blackbirds, and others also live here. Overhead, Tree, Barn, Violet-green, Cliff, and Northern Rough-winged Swallows soar. During migration, they are joined by Vaux's Swifts. From under the I-90 bridge, the gourd-shaped mud nests of Cliff Swallows can be seen on the pillars. May and June are best to watch them in action.

The canoe path leads past bramble and brushy areas where Cedar Waxwing, Willow Flycatcher, Bewick's Wren, kinglets, Veery, Swainson's Thrush, Yellow Warbler, Northern Oriole, Pine Siskin, and Black-headed Grosbeak might be seen or heard. Raptors possible in the park include Red-tailed Hawk, Cooper's and Sharp-shinned Hawk, Bald Eagle, Western Screech-Owl, and Great Horned Owl.

Many of the birds seen from the canoe trail can, of course, be seen from the regular Mercer Slough trail, which parallels some of the waterway. An excellent brochure with bird list is called "Canoeing Mercer Slough" and is available from the City of Bellevue Parks and Recreation Department, P.O. Box 90012, Bellevue, WA 98009-9012; (206) 455-6881, 455-6855. A "Nature Trail Guide to the Quiet Trails of the City of Bellevue" is also available.

Cougar Mountain Regional Wildland Park

Twenty-five miles of trails wind through this magnificent wilderness area located 20 minutes from Seattle. It is the largest of the King County parks covering nearly four square miles of ravines, ridges, forests, ponds, streams, waterfalls, swamps, and meadows. The area is a good example of a healthy lowland Washington ecology. Cougar Mountain has been a site for military installations, it has been mined and logged, and roads and developments have tried hard to inch their way to its 1,595-foot top. Thanks to the Issaquah Alps Trails Club, which formulated a plan for the park and spent years pleading, haranguing, and prevailing upon the local officials to enact the park, the park became a reality in 1984.

Bears and bobcats prowl the backwoods, and porcupines, raccoons, coyotes, flying squirrel, mountain beaver, weasels, rabbits, and a variety of small mammals also make their homes here. Forest birds reign: Pileated Woodpecker; Band-tailed Pigeon; Sharp-shinned Hawk; Hermit, Swainson's, and Varied Thrushes; Brown Creeper; Great Horned Owl; Western Screech-Owl; Ruffed Grouse; and, recently, Common Raven. Along with Cedar Waxwings and Yellow, Wilson's, and MacGillivray's Warblers, the usual bands of chickadees, nuthatches, and kinglets roam the trees.

Radar Park. Radar Park is the only place nearby with rest rooms and a picnic area. An interpretive sign with a map of the park's trails and a history of coal mining on Cougar Mountain is near the rest rooms. This park is basically a large meadow with trees on most sides but with a spectacular view of the Cascade Mountains and the Sammamish Valley to the north. Watch here for Red-tailed Hawks soaring overhead and American Kestrels hunting over the meadow. Bald

Eagles are not known to nest in the area but are occasionally seen passing. Sparrows, Rufous-sided Towhee, and California Quail are on the grassy, woody edges.

Cougar Mountain is the headwaters for Coal Creek. Look in these areas for American Dipper, Great Blue and possibly Green Heron, Mallard, Wood Duck, Hooded Merganser, Virginia Rail, Red-winged Blackbird, Marsh Wren, and Common Yellowthroat. Cougar Mountain Park connects with Coal Creek County Park and partially adjoins May Creek Park. Land also has been acquired on Squak Mountain. Eventually, there will be a Mountains-to-Sound wildlife corridor along I-90, which will allow wildlife to wander back and forth in uninterrupted habitats.

To reach Cougar Mountain Park, take I-90 east from Seattle to Exit 11A, 150th Avenue SE. Keep right at the exit ramp, right at the stop sign, and continue about 0.5 mile south to SE Newport Way. Next, turn left for a mile, then right on 164th Avenue SE and follow it for about two miles until it becomes Lakemont Boulevard. Two miles further, turn left on Cougar Mountain Way. In another mile when the road becomes SE 60th Street after a sharp right turn, proceed and then turn right on Cougar Mountain Drive. The park gate is about a mile away. Parking is available up the hill at Radar Park.

Blue Heron Marsh

This is an ideal spot to observe an active Great Blue Heron rookery in all its raucous glory. Since 1968, a colony of herons has nested in a stand of red alder on a hillside. The marshy pond and surrounding area evolved gradually as an abandoned gravel pit slowly filled with rainwater and water from nearby Mill Creek. Cattails and other plants followed, and it grew into the area now seen.

Blue Heron Marsh is a minimalist park; no rest rooms or fancy facilities. The 0.25-mile trail is often muddy. There is a bench and interpretive sign at the viewpoint at the end of the trail; 25–30 nests usually are active. Sit there, with scope or binoculars, and watch the daily routine of the adult parent herons courting, building and tending nests, feeding young, and flying in all directions. If you come early while the parents are on eggs, and then again later when the young are demanding food, you will notice the striking difference of the noise level: nearly quiet early on, but wild and strident a few weeks later. The rookery is active from mid-February through June.

The marsh is reached from Seattle by following I-5 south to Exit 143, South 320th Street (just under 20 miles). Go east on 320th and note that after crossing Military Road, it becomes Peasley Canyon Road. Three miles from I-5, at the West Valley Highway junction, turn south, then south again into a small gravel parking lot for the marsh. The trail heads north from the parking lot (back towards Peasley Canyon Road) to the marsh; the heron rookery is across the marsh on the hillside.

Hylebos Wetlands State Park Natural Area

This special wetlands reserve covers 56 acres of native western Washington shade- and water-related plants and animals. The wetland encompasses the West Hylebos Headwaters area and includes peat, floating bog, marsh, deep sinks, sand boils, springs, streams, and floods. There is a nature trail a mile in length; also a "Trail of the Giants" with a variety of mosses, liverworts, shrubs, trees, rare fungi, and many other aquatic life forms. Bird species either seen passing through or resident number 144.

To reach this unusual preserve, travel west from I-5 on South 348th Street. After crossing Pacific Highway South, watch for a single-lane blacktop road on the south side (do not go by an electrical substation). At the site, a garage attached to a house has large wall maps and a guest register. Signing helps convince the state this is a serious site that needs more land and an interpretive center.

Green River Gorge

The Green River Gorge Conservation Area was formed in 1969 and includes about 2,500 acres, including 12 miles of the Green River; state parks now cover 1,851 acres and have 18 miles of shoreline. Historically, coal and cinnabar were mined here. The two developed state parks are the forested Kanaskat-Palmer State Park with 50 campsites, at the upstream end, and Flaming Geyser State Park, day-use only, downstream. The "geyser" designation in the name comes from the burning methane gas from old test holes bored into underlying coal seams; the flame is about 6–10 inches now, but once was quite spectacular. Kayakers and white-water rafters frequent this area of the river; it is rated Class III (expert).

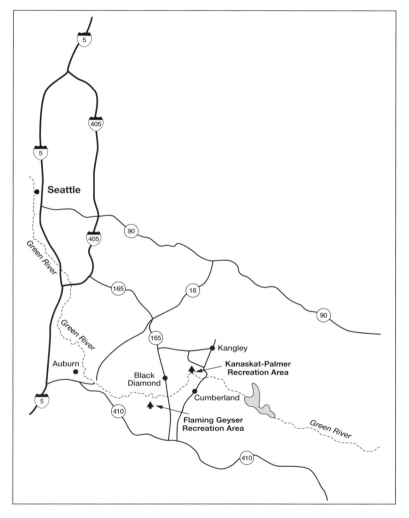

Green River Gorge

American Dipper. Dippers have a food-hunting strategy entirely different from any other North American passerine. They find most of their prey, aquatic larvae, under water, and actually can forage on stream bottoms where the current is too swift for a person to stand. Dippers can fly with their wings underwater and walk along the bottom. There are three viewing locations between Flaming Geyser State Park and Kanasket State Park where American Dippers may be seen as they fly low over the river or sing atop large boulders.

1. From I-5 take SH 18, Exit 142A, in Federal Way east approximately six miles to the Auburn-Black Diamond cut-off. At the stop sign turn right, then take another right (do not follow Flaming Geyser sign) onto Green Valley Road. Go through open farmland approximately six miles to the state park. Go to the far end of the road, then walk straight ahead, following a fisherman's path to the river. Also check shallow waters near the picnic areas and the bridge.

2. After leaving the park, continue right until the junction with SH 169, then left into Black Diamond, then right onto Green River Gorge Road until reaching the bridge and a walkway over the spectacular gorge; dippers may be seen far below.

3. One-half mile after crossing the bridge, make a sharp left turn up a steep hill then go two miles to the Cumberland intersection. Turn left on Veazir-Cumberland Road for 2.5 miles to Kanasket State Park. Dippers have nested here. There are good viewpoints along the river trails at both ends of the park.

Both state parks have a variety of mammals including deer, skunks, raccoons, weasels, flying squirrels, and small rodents. Waterfowl are abundant, changing with seasonal migrations. The mixed woods are home to most of the western lowland forest birds, plus a variety of migrants.

TACOMA

Historically, the Nisqually, Puyallup, and Steilacoom Indians coexisted peacefully around the shores of Puget Sound. By 1833, the Hudson's Bay Company had built a fort and trading post three miles north of the Nisqually River. In 1852, Nicholas Delin built a sawmill and became the city's first white settler. Since those times, Tacoma has evolved into an official "All-American City," is home to the world's largest wood-domed arena, and also is home to "Galloping Gertie," the infamous original Tacoma Narrows Bridge. The Nisqually River delta is now the site of the Nisqually National Wildlife Refuge.

Tacoma Narrows

The Narrows is a very active body of water between the city of Tacoma and northern Pierce County. It is bordered by Dalco Passage to the north and South Puget Sound to the south. The original bridge over The Narrows was built in 1940 and received its "Galloping Gertie" designation from drivers because of its undulations. Unfortunately, these movements got out of hand and after only four months in use, a 42-knot wind caused the center span to writhe and twist and then collapse into the Sound. It still lays at the bottom, serving very nicely as a reef.

The Narrows is home to a delightful array of gulls and seabirds from fall to spring. Glaucous-winged, Bonaparte's, Ring-billed, Mew, Thayer's, and possible rarities such as Little Gull might be seen. Common Murre, scoters, guillemots, mergansers, and other ducks also forage here. Best views are from the beaches and bluffs, with scope if possible, edging The Narrows.

Point Defiance Park. Point Defiance Park sits at the very northwest tip of the city. In early days it was a military reservation, but in 1905 the city received title to the land. It has evolved into a 700-acre parkland with a reconstruction of old Fort Nisqually overlooking The Narrows, beautiful landscaping with native plants, and a fine zoo and aquarium. A five-mile drive that passes through most of the wooded park and by several scenic viewpoints is worth following. The Narrows and its attendant water birds can be seen from the viewpoints. Pigeon Guillemots nest on the north bluffs in small numbers. A variety of western coniferous forest species can be found in the park. The world-class Point Defiance Zoo and Aquarium also are located here.

Glaucous-winged Gulls

Gog-le-hi-te Wetland

"Where the land and waters meet" is the translation of the Puyallup Indian name "Gog-le-hi-te." This name, bestowed on a marsh first called Lincoln Street Wetland and Mitigated Marsh, is fitting, for it is truly where the Puyallup River met an abandoned garbage landfill. It took six years and $2.8 million for the environmental conflict between the Puyallup Indian Tribe and federal, state, and county agencies to be reconciled. This now-very-fertile 9.5-acre wetland alive with birds was helped along by UW graduate students who planted 48,000 sedges. A small portion of the river levee was removed, allowing twice-daily tidal action from Commencement Bay in and out of the new marsh. Within a few short weeks, Killdeer took over the uplands and juvenile salmon were discovered feeding in the wetlands. Interpretive signs and viewing platforms were added.

Soon rarities and regulars arrived: Bar-tailed Godwit, yellowlegs, Canada Goose, goldeneyes, wigeons, Green-winged Teal, Great Blue and Green Heron, Snow Goose, Western and Horned Grebes, Double-crested Cormorant, American White Pelican, 18 duck species, Peregrine Falcon, Merlin, American Kestrel, accipiters, Thayer's

Gull, and 11 shorebird species. The species that has brought attention, however, has been the Slaty-backed Gull, which wintered and was seen until March 11, 1994. The bird list is still growing and now stands at 114 species.

To reach the Gog-le-hi-te Wetlands, take the Portland Avenue exit from I-5. Go north for 0.5 mile to Lincoln Avenue, then turn east and go 0.25 mile, crossing the Puyallup River, to the entrance. Parking is to the right.

The Nature Center at Snake Lake

The Nature Center at Snake Lake is located in the center of Tacoma. Its 54 acres of lake, forest, brambles, and marshland provide a haven for resident red foxes, raccoons, Great Blue Herons, Canada Geese, Mallards, and many more species. Two miles of self-guided nature trails and four observation shelters with wildlife feeders multiply the possible wildlife sightings. An interpretive center with helpful staff and volunteers is at the center. Thirty-three biological stations on the park's less-than-two-mile nature trail allow visitors to sample the history, flora, and fauna of the center. The park belongs to the plants and animals; be sure to stay on the trail.

A variety of plants lives here. Douglas-fir, of course, is one of the Pacific Northwest standbys; as you wander along the trail, be on the lookout for Oregon ash, black cottonwood, cascara buckthorn, bitter cherry, filbert, madrona, Pacific dogwood, and Garry oaks, which make up part of the tree ecology of the park. Salal, red huckleberry, honeysuckle, and baldhip and peafruit rose make up much of the understory. This combination of canopy and understory provide habitats for a variety of frequent and commonly seen birds: Bufflehead, Common Flicker, Downy Woodpecker, Violet-green and Barn Swallows, American Crow, Bushtit, Red-breasted Nuthatch, Bewick's Wren, American Robin, Varied Thrush, Golden and Ruby-crowned Kinglets, Cedar Waxwing, Red-winged Blackbird, Purple Finch, Rufous-sided Towhee, Dark-eyed Junco, and Fox and Song Sparrows. More unusual, but occasionally seen, are Pied-billed Grebe, teal, Canvasback, Merlin, California Quail, Solitary Sandpiper, Greater and Lesser Yellowlegs, gulls, Mourning Dove, Western Screech-Owl, Cliff Swallow, Hermit Thrush, Red-eyed Vireo, MacGillivray's War-

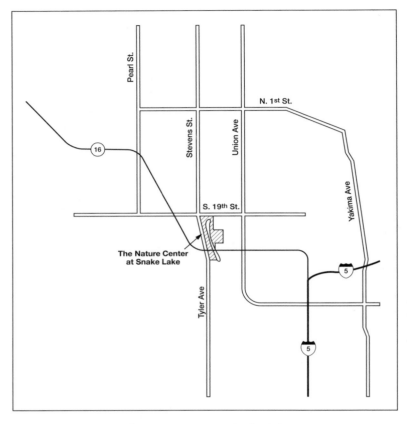

The Nature Center at Snake Lake

bler, and Lincoln's Sparrow. The Nature Center at Snake Lake is reached from I-5 by taking Exit 132 and following SH 16 west towards Bremerton. Before Cheney Stadium, take Tyler Street north; the center is on the corner of Tyler and 19th Street.

Orting

The town of Orting is located in a valley between the Carbon and Puyallup rivers. To the north and east of town is land rising to 1,000 feet, eastward is an upland plateau that has been clear-cut, but now has various stages of Douglas-fir growth. Agricultural lands lie to the south and west. As in most flatland areas, follow the farm roads that crisscross the area, and look for Common Snipe; Dunlin; Killdeer; Semipalmated Plover; Greater and Lesser Yellowlegs; Western, Least, and Solitary Sandpipers; and Short- and Long-billed Dowitchers. Winter brings raptors to the area; watch for Bald Eagles along the Puyallup River, and also Red-tailed and Rough-legged Hawks, Merlin, Northern Harrier, accipiters, and occasional American Kestrels.

Western Kingbirds have been found nesting in the area, and Green Heron, American Bittern, Belted Kingfisher, Hooded Merganser, and Brewer's Blackbirds have been found just south of the city limits on SH 162. Migrant warblers also have been seen, including MacGillivray's Warbler plus Western Bluebird and White-crowned Sparrow. Further on SH 162 is the town of Crocker where Yellow, Orange-crowned, and Wilson's Warblers are known to nest. Further east on SH 162 is South Prairie, which has a large population of nesting Lazuli Bunting and Savannah Sparrow. Nesting Black-headed Grosbeak, Cedar Waxwing, Western Tanager, Western Wood-pewee, and Northern Orioles also can be found here. Regular species usually found in the Orting area range from Downy Woodpecker; Bewick's Wren; Lincoln's, Fox, Song, and Golden-crowned Sparrows; and Northern Shrike.

The route through the Orting area can be reached by following the Valley Freeway, SH 167, south from I-405 in Renton, then turning east on SH 410, then south again on SH 162 and on to Orting, Crocker, and South Prairie.

FORT LEWIS

Fort Lewis is not all tanks and barracks. Its more than 86,000 acres are made up of 59,000 forested acres, 20,000 acres of prairie, and 4,000 acres of wetlands. These thousands of acres include 27 lakes, the Nisqually River system, nine feeder streams in excellent ecoshape, 38 miles of salmon and trout habitat, and 2.5 miles of saltwater shoreline. The Fort Lewis grounds are part of a fairly well-protected Nisqually River corridor that starts in Mount Rainier National Park, passes through Fort Lewis, and finally ends at the Nisqually

National Wildlife Refuge. The corridor is particularly helpful to those species dependent on salmon runs.

Several studies are in progress on the post, and several have been concluded. Earlier studies addressed the management of threatened, endangered, and candidate species at the post. Nest box programs have been in progress since the late 1970s and early 1980s for Western Bluebirds, Purple Martins, and Wood Ducks. More than 100 nesting pairs of Western Bluebirds now make the army post their summer home. Two new studies will address neotropical migrants and raptors. Fort Lewis also is involved in the Cornell Laboratory of Ornithology's Project Tanager and the Monitoring Avian Productivity and Survivorship Program (MAPS).

Fort Lewis, home to five active Bald Eagle nests, restricts airplane flights during nesting season and keeps military activities a proper distance away. Winter counts of Bald Eagles in the area have been very good: 168 eagles in 1992, and 156 individuals in 1993. Eight communal night roosts have been found. A study of cavity nesting species—Pileated Woodpecker, Vaux's Swift, and Purple Martin—resulted in 42 pileated detections, no swifts, and martins at 14 different sites. Another study showed no nesting Marbled Murrelets on the post.

Sage Grouse also are benefiting from the Fort Lewis Environmental and Natural Resources Division. A conservation agreement between the Army, U.S. Fish and Wildlife Service, and the Washington Department of Fish and Wildlife is being worked out for the thousands of acres in eastern Washington used for military maneuvers in the Yakama Firing Range. It is also endangered Sage Grouse habitat. Plans have been enacted to cut grazing in half, avoid brooding and nesting habitats, restrict the use of pyrotechnics on a seasonal basis, and close down one range entirely.

The environment of oak woodlands, grassland, and mixed forest has attracted Blue and Ruffed Grouse; Northern Bobwhite; White-breasted Nuthatch; Ruby-crowned Kinglet; American Pipit; Northern Shrike (winter only); Hutton's, Solitary, and Warbling Vireos; Western Meadowlark; Mourning Dove; Chipping and Vesper Sparrows; House Wren; Lazuli Bunting; and many more. Wetlands attract four species of grebe, Double-crested Cormorant, Green Heron, Great Egret, Tundra Swan, Greater White-fronted Goose, teal, Northern Shoveler, Canvasback, and others.

Double-crested Cormorant

Fort Lewis is located on I-5 midway between Tacoma and Olympia. The post is open to visitors except in restricted areas. Stop at the main gate, obtain a visitor's pass, and ask about areas open to birding.

NISQUALLY NATIONAL WILDLIFE REFUGE

The Nisqually River and Red Salmon and McAllister creeks form one of the largest remaining undisturbed estuaries in the state of Washington. In 1974, the Nisqually National Wildlife Refuge was formed to protect this part of southern Puget Sound and its rich and diverse habitats of fresh and saltwater marshes and woodlands. Mixed forests of evergreens, maples, and alders cover the hillsides above the delta and provide nesting habitats for Great Blue Heron and perching spots for hawks, falcons, and eagles. During the fall and winter, flocks of more than 20,000 American Wigeon, Green-winged Teal, Mallard, and other ducks invade the refuge wetlands. Short-eared Owl, Northern Harrier, Peregrine Falcon, and Merlin hunt the marshes fall to spring.

The Nisqually NWR covers 1,797 acres of delta where the Nisqually flows into Puget Sound. Dikes separate fresh and saltwater habitats. Ten different habitat types have been identified at the Nisqually Refuge, including mudflats, salt marshes, grassy meadows, and upland forest. The bird checklist for Nisqually is 176 species. Another 36 species are listed as accidental, and 87 species nest here.

Nisqually River Trail. The River Trail is a 0.5-mile self-guided nature trail through a riparian woodland. Forest, slough, cotton-woods, the river, damp bottomland, and an abundance of old snags make this walk rich in birds. Watch for Pied-billed Grebe, Great Blue Heron, Green-winged Teal, Northern Shoveler, Gadwall, Red-tailed Hawk, Great Horned Owl, Pileated Woodpecker, California Quail, Red-breasted Sapsucker, Rufous Hummingbird, Belted Kingfisher, Western Wood-pewee, Willow Flycatcher, Bewick's Wren, swallows, chickadees, Swainson's Thrush, Common Yellowthroat, Wilson's Warbler, Song Sparrow, and a variety of other species.

Brown Farm Dike Trail. The 5.5-mile Brown Farm Dike Trail allows visitors to view six distinct habitat types and the birds that fre-

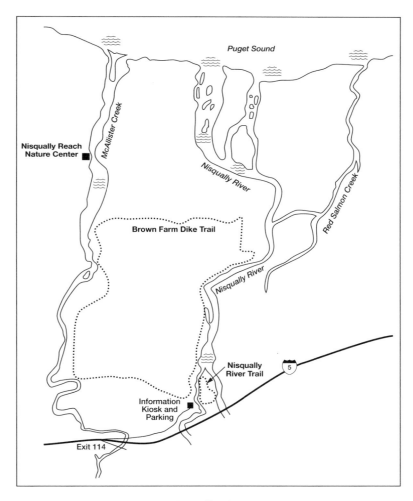

Nisqually NWR

quent them. To the north, salt marsh and open mudflats can be seen edging the tidal waters of Puget Sound. Rich nutrients such as shrimp, crabs, clams, and worms live in the mud and provide fare for the many gulls, waterfowl, and shorebirds that forage on the flats.

Scan the flats for Bonaparte's, Mew, Ring-billed, California, and Glaucous-winged Gulls, always checking for possible rarities. Parasitic Jaeger and Franklin's and Glaucous Gulls are some of the scarce species. Shorebirds to look for are Greater and Lesser Yellowlegs; Western, Least, and Baird's Sandpiper; Dunlin; Short- and Long-billed Dowitchers; plus occasional vagrants. Loons, grebes, cormorants, and a variety of waterfowl can be seen in the adjacent waters, all in season, of course.

To the south, the freshwater habitats and open grassy areas provide resting and wintering areas for huge numbers of waterfowl. Mice and voles in the meadows provide sustenance for coyotes, Red-tailed and Rough-legged Hawks, Northern Harrier, American Kestrel, and Short-eared Owl. The sedges and cattail marsh edgings provide protection to Marsh Wren, Sora, American Bittern, blackbirds, and a variety of amphibians. Belted Kingfisher, Killdeer, and Common Snipe also are seen. A variety of waterfowl is common, especially in winter. Look for specialties such as Greater White-fronted Goose, Snow Goose, and Blue-winged Teal among the flocks of Mallard, wigeons, and Northern Pintail. Also watch for occasional Peregrine Falcons and Merlins.

McAllister Creek. The dike trail also proceeds through some riparian woodland and bramble habitats. Wild rose, blackberries, and crabapples provide food for an assortment of songbirds. Winter Wren, Evening Grosbeak, Cedar Waxwing, Pacific-slope Flycatcher, Warbling Vireo, Common Yellowthroat, Wilson's Warbler, House and Purple Finches, and a mixture of other species have been recorded.

Nisqually NWR is one of the easiest to reach because it is adjacent to I-5. To reach the refuge, including the offices for the Puget Sound and Coastal Washington Refuge Complex, take Exit 114 off I-5, about seven miles east of Olympia, and go north into the refuge. Travel within the park is by foot only, and no pets are allowed. Information: Nisqually Refuge Complex Office, 100 Brown Farm Road, Olympia, WA 98506; (206) 753-9467. Ask for the excellent checklist of the wildlife of the refuge.

OLYMPIA

Olympia is Washington state's capital and a gateway to ocean beaches and the Olympic peninsula. Original settlers in the 1840s named the town Smithfield, which became the site of the first U.S. Customhouse. The name was changed to Olympia in honor of the Olympic Mountains to the northwest. Olympia is located at the extreme southern end of Puget Sound. Olympia has the tallest domed masonry state capitol building in the United States. Budd Inlet, Olympia's harbor, attracts many wintering Black Scoters, along with a good variety of other waterfowl and seabirds. Pelagic Cormorants often are seen.

Adjacent to Olympia is the small community of Tumwater, home to Olympia Beer. If you decide to take a tour of the brewery (given every day), which is located at a waterfall on the Deschutes River, check the shrubs and brambles edging the parklike grounds of the brewery; warblers and a variety of migrant passerine often are seen. Just south of Tumwater is Wolfhaven, a non-profit corporation that is working to help threatened wolf species survive. Tours are interesting, and on some weekend nights there are "howl-ins" where visitors join the wolves in expressing themselves.

Capitol Lake Park

The park surrounds most of Capitol Lake and is directly across the road from Budd Inlet. Migrating salmon can be seen in fall from the 5th Street Bridge at the north end of the lake. The big attraction, however is the huge numbers (up to a thousand, at times) of Barrow's Goldeneye that roost on the lake at night in November. Arrival time is from 3 p.m. until dark. Barrow's Goldeneye seem to prefer calmer waters than Common Goldeneye. A variety of other waterfowl also are present on the lake and in Budd Inlet.

KENNEDY CREEK ESTUARY

The Kennedy Creek Estuary is a prime migration resting area and wintering grounds for a variety of shorebirds. In the fall, Western and Least Sandpipers, Black-bellied and Semipalmated Plovers, Killdeer, Dunlin, Greater and Lesser Yellowlegs, Red Knots, Short-billed Dowitchers, and others are found here. Waterfowl are interesting, too: Canada and Greater White-fronted Goose, Green-winged Teal, Mallard, Northern Pintail, Northern Shoveler, Gadwall, American Wigeon, Greater and Lesser Scaups, White-winged and Surf Scoters, Redbreasted and Common Mergansers, Bufflehead, and Barrow's and Common Goldeneyes have been recorded. Domestic geese and otters are reputed to reside here, also. In the winter, huge numbers of Dunlin, 3,000–5,000, and Black-bellied Plovers, 400–600, have been recorded.

To reach Kennedy Creek Estuary take the Shelton exit, US 101, from Olympia. The estuary is about midway between Olympia and Shelton, roughly eight miles. Two viewing spots are suggested: the first, at milepost 356, at the intersection of US 101 and the Old Olympic Highway, gives a good overview of the estuary; to reach the second spot, follow the Old Olympic Highway to the north about 100 yards. A wide parking spot is on the left and a trail/road leads down to an open area next to the flats on the right. Waterfowl and the two small mud islands that harbor shorebirds during winter high tides are best seen from here.

MIMA MOUNDS NATURAL AREA PRESERVE

The Mima Mounds have been baffling scholars and farmers alike for more than 150 years. The Mima Mounds are, physically, six-foot-high masses that are rather evenly spaced across the prairie-type land south of Olympia. As far back as the Wilkes Expedition in 1841, the mounds were pondered. Three theories, briefly, are that they came about because of pocket gopher building skills; glacial freezing and thawing 10,000–15,000 years ago; or severe earthquakes. Still, no one is sure. The 445-acre preserve is an evolving prairie: originally grasses, camas flowers, lichens, mosses, and a variety of herbs prevailed;

now, clusters of Scotch broom and Douglas-fir have been encroaching at a rate of a quarter to almost a half mile per year.

The prairie habitat found here tends to draw a variety of interesting birds, such as Northern Bobwhite; Western Meadowlark; Chipping, Savannah, and Vesper Sparrows; Western Bluebird; and Lazuli Bunting. Several other species of land birds can be found in the tree copses. Bald Eagles and Red-tailed Hawks often perch in the Douglas-firs.

The Mima Mounds area is open all year during daylight hours. There is an interpretive sign, marked nature trails, and a paved half-mile pathway for the disabled. No motorized vehicles, horses, or pets are allowed past the parking lot. There is a small picnic area. To reach the preserve go south on I-5 from Olympia, then turn west at Exit 95 onto SH 121 to Littlerock. Go through town, turn right at Waddell Creek Road, and the entrance is on the left.

IKE KINSWA STATE PARK

Historically, fall, winter, and spring found the Lower Cowlitz Indians living in villages along the streams and rivers in this area. They spent their lives in cedar-plank houses, and fished and hunted and gathered plants for food and medicines. The park was first called Mayfield Lake State Park, but was changed to Ike Kinswa to honor an early member of the Cowlitz tribe. Two fish hatcheries, one for salmon and one for trout, are nearby.

Dead trees and snags are common within the park, and Bald Eagles perch on them in winter while Ospreys use them for nesting sites in the summer. Beavers, deer, otters, skunks, and raccoons live in the park, and resident or nesting birds include Great Blue Heron, Virginia Rail, Wood Duck, Mallard, Common Yellowthroat, Black-throated Gray Warbler, American Kestrel, Red-tailed Hawk, and a variety of others.

Ike Kinswa State Park is located 20 miles east of the junction of I-5 and US 12. It is on the north side of Mayfield Lake and has 46,000 feet of freshwater shoreline. This is a 454-acre park and is one of the few that reserves campsites. Information: Ike Kinswa State Park, 873 Harmony Road, Silver Creek, WA 98585-9706; (360) 983-3402.

RIDGEFIELD NATIONAL WILDLIFE REFUGE

Ridgefield NWR originally was established as an area for wintering waterfowl. Thousands of Canada Geese, more than 300 Tundra Swans, and a large variety of ducks visit every year. The refuge is also a stopover for migrating Lesser Sandhill Cranes. More than 300 cranes pass through in September, October, and March. There are nesting Bald Eagles and a variety of raptors, herons, and songbirds. There are 181 birds listed for the refuge, with 80 nesting species. A special aspect of the refuge is that it has a barrier-free observation blind, and most of the roads and pedestrian trails are relatively level. Kathy Arm-

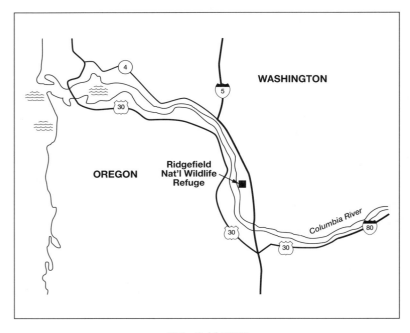

Ridgefield NWR

strong, a wildlife biologist at the refuge who uses a wheelchair and is an avid birder, finds the area especially attractive and usable.

The Ridgefield refuge covers 4,615 acres of marshes, woodlands, and grasslands. Three units along the lower Columbia River make up the complex: the Carty unit with a wildlife nature trail along the Columbia River floodplain; the Roth unit with a more level landscape forested with willows, ash, and cottonwood; and the River "S" Unit and Bachelor Island, which are diked. A variety of grass and crops are cultivated for waterfowl forage. Canoeing is an excellent way to see this refuge, especially in the north unit where there are flooded willows and a variety of canals. There are also several miles of roads and trails to explore.

Permanent residents or nesting species at the refuge are Pied-billed Grebe, Double-crested Cormorant, American Bittern, Great Blue Heron, Canada Goose, Wood Duck, Northern Pintail, Northern Shoveler, Gadwall, Blue-winged and Cinnamon Teal, Hooded Merganser, Northern Harrier, American Kestrel, American Coot, Ruffed Grouse, Common Snipe, Spotted Sandpiper, Wilson's Phalarope, Mourning Dove, Common Barn-Owl, Western Screech-Owl, Great Horned Owl, Rufous Hummingbird, Downy Woodpecker, Western Wood-pewee, Purple Martin, Scrub Jay, White-breasted Nuthatch, wrens, Yellow and MacGillivray's Warblers, and Black-headed Grosbeak.

Three subspecies of Canada Goose are found in winter at the refuge: Dusky, Cackler, and Taverner's. Trumpeter and Tundra Swans also winter here. Accidentals include Cattle Egret, American Avocet, Sharp-tailed Sandpiper, Red Phalarope, Ash-throated Flycatcher, American Tree Sparrow, Harris' Sparrow, Lapland Longspur, and Black-billed Magpie.

Oaks to Wetlands Wildlife Trail. A 1.9-mile loop trail on the Carty Unit has both wetlands and woodlands. There is one seasonal detour—from March 1 through September 30 this section of the trail goes over private land and is open; the remainder of the year it is closed, and marked so. The wetlands of the Carty Unit show a transition between the Columbia River and the uplands. The changing water level of the river alters the flow of Gee Creek and, in turn, raises and lowers the waters in the wetlands. Drought and flooding are necessary for the seasonal cycle of wetlands.

A variety of wetland inhabitants lives here, including painted turtles, beavers, bullfrogs, Great Blue Heron, Belted Kingfisher, gall wasps, American Crow, American Bittern, Green Heron, Black-crowned Night-Heron, Pied-billed Grebe, Wood Duck, Cinnamon Teal, Hooded Merganser, Marsh Wren, Tree and Violet-green Swallows, Common Yellowthroat, Wilson's Warbler, Red-winged and Brewer's Blackbirds, and Song Sparrow.

To reach Ridgefield NWR, take Exit 14 west off I-5. The refuge is about 16 miles north of the Washington/Oregon border. Information: Ridgefield National Wildlife Refuge, P.O. Box 457, 301 North Third Street, Ridgefield, WA 98642; (360) 887-4106. Brochures about the refuge and a wildlife checklist are available.

HULDA KLAGER LILAC GARDENS

If there are gardens, there are birds, and this is no exception. Ultramontane trees and flowers are everywhere in this lovely homestead. Hulda Klager came here from Germany in 1865 when she was only two, and soon became interested in plants. In 1905, she began working with lilacs. The Woodland Federated Garden Club rescued this outstanding habitat from the bulldozer after Hulda died at age 96; it subsequently became a state and national historic site. The club continues to maintain the site. Spring is best for the beautiful lilacs and the birds that gravitate to the lush gardens. A variety of songbirds make use of this interesting habitat: American Robin; Rufous and Anna's Hummingbirds; White-crowned Sparrow; Scrub Jay; Dark-eyed Junco; Pacific-slope Flycatcher; Tree, Violet-green, and Barn Swallows; Downy Woodpecker; American Crow; Cedar Waxwing; Warbling Vireo; Orange-crowned, Yellow, Yellow-rumped, Black-throated Gray, and Wilson's Warbler; American Goldfinch; House Sparrow; and House Finch all have been seen.

To reach the gardens, leave I-5 in Woodland at Pacific, which turns into Goerig. Turn west on Davidson, then south on S. Perkin Road until you come to the gardens. Information: Hulda Klager Lilac Gardens, P.O. Box 828, Woodland, WA 98674; (360) 225-8996.

American Goldfinch

COLUMBIA RIVER LEVEE ROAD

To reach the area, take SH 501 (NW River Road) out of central Vancouver. The road goes for some time through an industrial and freight area, gradually thinning out a bit. Vancouver Lake and its wetlands will appear first on the northeast. Continue following SH 501 making a right-angle turn west, then another turn north to parallel the Columbia; it is now called Lower River Road, but still is SH 501. There are several access areas along the route, the Shillapoo-Vancouver Wildlife Area, Frenchman's Bar, and Post Office Lake. The road is a diked area with Sauvie Island in Oregon and the Columbia River on the west, and Ridgefield NWR to the northeast. The road dead-ends after several miles on the dike.

Excellent views of the mighty Columbia and the Cascade Mountain range include Mount Hood, Mount St. Helens, Mount Adams, and possibly Mount Rainier. Birds should be similar to the Ridgefield NWR: huge numbers of Canada Geese, plentiful ducks, Tundra and Trumpeter Swans, and raptors in winter including Peregrine Falcon, Merlin, Rough-legged Hawk and Bald Eagle; Sandhill Cranes in migration; plus a variety of marsh and open grassland birds. Near Post Office Lake in winter and spring, Bald Eagle, Sandhill Crane, and Great Egret are often seen; Osprey summer here.

Chapter 6
Western Cascades and Crest

Rising from the lowland valleys of the Puget Trough, the great granite wall of the Cascade Mountains surpasses 14,000 feet at the summit of Mount Rainier. The Cascade crest zigzags from its northern point at the British Columbia border southwest past Mount Rainier in a line of relatively even peaks and ridges. South of Rainier the Cascades are less harsh, but the overall feeling is of height and greatness.

Five glacier-topped volcanic cones interrupt the Cascade's march southward. Mount Baker, 10,778 feet, and Glacier Peak, 10,541 feet, are in the Mount Baker-Snoqualmie National Forest. Mount Rainier at 14,412 feet is Washington's highest peak and namesake of a national park. Mount St. Helens, a lowly 8,366 feet after its eruption May 18, 1980, is the center of the Mount St. Helens National Volcanic Monument. Mount Adams, Washington's second-highest peak at 12,267 feet, is the most remote of the volcanic cones. It is the central focus of the Mount Adams Wilderness Area.

I-5, west of the Cascades, and US 97, to the east, follow the north-south alignment of the Cascades the length of the state. Five major passes go between these two routes; each has its own flavor, and four have major ski areas. Two passes, the North Cascades Highway and Chinook Pass, are closed all winter.

The eastern parts of Whatcom, Skagit, Snohomish, King, Pierce, and Lewis counties, plus all of Skamania County are in this ravine-filled region, about 20% of the state. Douglas-fir and western hemlock, western redcedar, bigleaf maple, and red alder rule these humid forests, giving way after 3,000 feet to Douglas-fir, grand fir, western white pine, and lodgepole pine. Mountain hemlock, yellow cedar, and subalpine fir are at the upper elevations.

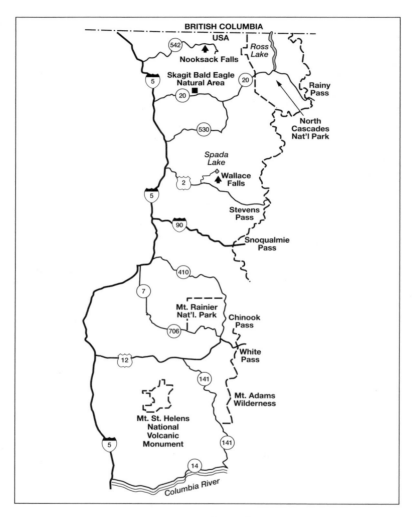

Western Cascades and Crest

Mammals include a variety of shrews and moles, several species of bats, snowshoe hare, pika, mountain beaver, yellow-bellied and hoary marmots, golden-mantled ground squirrel, northern flying squirrel, porcupine, black bear, Roosevelt elk, mule deer, and mountain goat.

MOUNT BAKER-SNOQUALMIE NATIONAL FOREST

The Mount Baker-Snoqualmie National Forest is made up of nearly 820,000 acres of both heavily forested and glaciated mountain areas, dotted with large and small lakes, meadows, and marshes. Within the national forest lie the Mount Baker National Recreation Area, the Mount Baker Wilderness Area, and parts of the Glacier Peak and Alpine Lakes Wilderness Areas. National forestland extends along the Nooksack River and the highway approach to the Shuksan and Baker area.

There are many hiking possibilities to see montane birds and beautiful scenery. Special sites on the road to Mount Shuksan and Mount Baker are Nooksack Falls, seven miles east of Glacier, with a 170-foot vertical drop; the "Grove of the Druids," a stand of 600-year-old Douglas fir found just after Mile Marker 37; and Picture Lake and Artist Point at the end of SH 542, which is the classic photographer's viewpoint of Mount Shuksan and the Baker area. Northern Goshawk, White-tailed Ptarmigan, Golden Eagle, Mountain Bluebirds, and Gray-crowned Rosy Finches are specialties in the area, especially on the higher trails.

NOOKSACK RIVER BALD EAGLES

The Nooksack River does not have an eagle preserve such as on the Skagit, but it is well worth investigating because many of Washington state's 1,500 or more Bald Eagles also visit the Nooksack during salmon spawning season. It is a short distance, as the eagle flies, between the two rivers. During several years of censusing, the Nooksack has had more eagles than the popular and more accessible Skagit. The Nooksack drains 600 square miles of land west of Mount Baker, and five species of salmon migrate up its three main tributaries. From late September until March, eagles can be seen. Counts have recorded more than 200 birds in mid-January when the eagle's staple food, the chum salmon, spawns.

Bald Eagles spend about 85% of their day perched in cottonwoods, maples, and conifers along the river and its sloughs; they feed in early morning and late afternoon. At night, the eagles disperse to one of eight or so night roosts high on the wooded slopes. These night roosts offer wind protection, wide visibility, and security from human disturbance. There are good locations for viewing eagles on the Nooksack from the roadside.

Bald Eagles

MOUNT SHUKSAN

Mount Shuksan, whose Skagit Indian name means "roaring mountain," is 9,127 feet in elevation. It is about 12 miles northeast of Mount Baker. With rugged cliffs and hanging glaciers, it is a study in contrast with Baker's snow-capped symmetry. It truly is a roaring mountain; from campsites near Lake Ann, a beginning spot for climbs, ice from Upper Curtis Glacier rumbles and roars, especially on warm days as avalanches drop down the side of the mountain. But as the ice roars, Northern Goshawks occasionally soar overhead; Gray-crowned Rosy Finches, Mountain Chickadee, and Evening Grosbeaks chatter in the trees; and, with luck, White-tailed Ptarmigan will appear near the trail or campsite.

Lake Ann Trail. The trail is 2.5 miles of forest, stream, and rocky meadow, plus a final mile of rocky, exposed scree slope to the lake, which sits in its iciness at 4,800 feet elevation. Good birding can be found in even the first two much less strenuous miles. Mountain birds and others abound: American Pipit, Mountain Bluebird, Olive-sided Flycatcher, Rufous Hummingbird, Horned Lark, Steller's Jay, Common Raven, Red Crossbill, Three-toed Woodpecker, White-crowned and Lincoln Sparrows, plus kinglets, chickadees, and nuthatches. Watch for Golden Eagle, Vaux's Swift, swallows, and possible accipiters soaring overhead and American Dipper along Swift Creek. Wildflowers are outstanding in midsummer.

The Lake Ann trailhead is reached by following SH 542 to Mount Baker Lodge, then continuing one mile to Austin Pass to a sign marking the trail and parking area. Early in the season, there is apt to be much snow; August and September are probably the best months, trail-wise. Information: Mount Baker Ranger Station, 2105 Highway 20, Sedro Woolley, WA 98284; (360) 856-5700.

MOUNT BAKER

Mount Baker was called Koma Kulshan, meaning "white, shining, steep mountain," by the early Nooksack Indians. It is the highest point in the national forest and is home to the headwaters of the Nooksack and Baker rivers. Twelve glaciers and 44 square miles of snowfields cover Mount Baker's upper slopes; Mount Baker erupted six times from 1843 to 1880, but has not rumbled since. Bird life at the highest elevations is scarce. On midsummer climbing trips, I have noted only Common Raven and Golden Eagle plus an occasional misguided passerine.

Heliotrope Ridge. This trail is on the western side of Mount Baker and, like many others in the high country, is best hiked in August and September. Wildflowers are spectacular in this alpine environment. The distance to the ridgetop is 3.25 miles, starting at 3,700 feet elevation. The trail begins in forest habitat, eventually emerging onto the moraines dotted with flowers next to Coleman Glacier. This is also the beginning of the most popular climbing route up Mount Baker. Watch for White-tailed Ptarmigan, Gray-crowned Rosy Finch, and Northern Goshawk, plus a variety of other mountain species including marmots and pika. To reach the trailhead, take SH 542 one mile past the town of Glacier to Glacier Creek Road, No. 39. Turn right and go about eight miles to the parking lot and trail sign.

Ptarmigan Ridge. This trail on the northeast side of Baker is much more open than the Heliotrope Ridge trail. The trail to Ptarmigan Ridge starts in a meadow habitat and ascends to the top of the rocky and usually snowy ridge. The scenery is spectacular, and the ridge was named for the White-tailed Ptarmigan that live here. Keep an eye out for mountain goats, too. The full length of the four-mile (one way) trail goes close to Rainbow Glacier. Watch for Golden Eagles soaring. Hike as far as you like on the ridge, all the while looking for Gray-crowned Rosy Finches, Horned Larks, Mountain Chickadees, and Mountain Bluebirds. During fall migration, raptors such as Northern Harriers often hunt the high meadows. Sharp-shinned Hawks are seen in good numbers, also.

To reach the area, take SH 542 to the Mount Baker Ski Lodge at the Heather Meadows Recreational Area. Follow the gravel Kulshan Ridge Road for about three miles upwards to the road end. (As in most cases, the road is often not open all the way until late August.) Hike a mile to the saddle between Ptarmigan Ridge and Table Mountain. At the fork in the trail, go left on Camp Kiser trail No. 683 and wander at will.

EVERETT LAKE

Located two miles from the small town of Concrete, Everett Lake recently has been found to be an extremely productive birding site. Diurnal raptors that have been seen, in season, are Turkey Vulture, Bald and Golden Eagles, Osprey, Red-tailed Hawk, Merlin, and

Sharp-shinned Hawk. Western Screech-Owl and Great Horned Owl nest in the area, and Northern Pygmy-Owl and Barred Owls also have been seen. Glaucous-winged Gull, Black and Vaux's Swifts, Common Nighthawks, and American Crow are regulars, and nesting usuals include Warbling and Red-eyed Vireos, Black-headed Grosbeak, Rufous Hummingbird, Common Yellowthroat, Black-throated Gray Warbler, plus Song, White-crowned, and other sparrows.

Spring migrants seen are Northern Rough-winged Swallow; Willow, Hammond's, and Pacific-slope Flycatchers; and Song and White-crowned Sparrows. Waterfowl recorded have been Wood Duck, Northern Shoveler, American Wigeon, Bufflehead, Hooded Merganser, goldeneyes, and probable others. To reach Everett Lake, turn north on Everett Street after crossing the Baker River, then bear west onto E. Main Street. Turn northeast onto Baker River Road, go past the utility substation, and take the second left, Road LS 1100. Continue on LS 1100 to the lake; park anywhere.

HOWARD MILLER STEELHEAD PARK

This is the closest park to the Bald Eagle Natural Area, and eagles are often present. Look for them in trees along the river and soaring high above with snow-covered Sauk Mountain in the background. At times, we have seen 20 or more eagles soaring overhead. Park facilities are wheelchair-accessible. It has all amenities plus a store within a mile; Rockport State Park, with some old growth Douglas-fir is just to the west. The campground, popular with steelhead fishermen, is set among mixed hardwoods at the edge of the Skagit River. Watch for Common Merganser, occasional goldeneyes, Belted Kingfisher, Steller's Jay, and migrant passerines, plus Cedar Waxwing, chickadees, and kinglets around the campground. The park is located at the junction of SH 20 and SH 530, just west of the bridge over the Skagit River.

SKAGIT RIVER BALD EAGLE NATURAL AREA

Upstream 60 miles from the raptor-rich Skagit Flats, between Marblemount and Rockport, more than 1,000 acres of excellent winter habitat for Bald Eagles is owned by The Nature Conservancy and the state Department of Fish and Wildlife. The U.S. Forest Service oversees the riparian habitat within the eagle preserve due to the 1978 designation of the Skagit as a Wild and Scenic River Corridor. The artist for this book, Libby Mills, is The Nature Conservancy Steward for the area. She conducts weekly censuses of the eagles and gives informational slide programs to elementary schools.

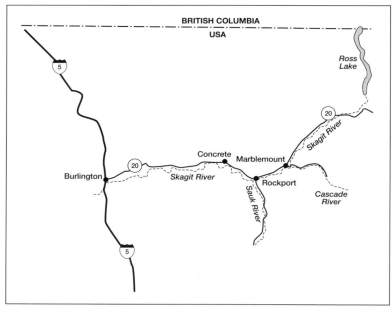

Skagit River Bald Eagle Natural Area

Bald Eagles begin returning to the Skagit preserve along with the spawning runs of chum salmon, usually in early November. Eagle numbers peak in January at between 200–300, then gradually dwindle until mid-March when most have gone to take over nesting duties elsewhere. Pink salmon, which run a bit earlier, and coho salmon are also present. The eagles can be seen in the many cottonwoods and evergreens lining the river and on the gravel bars where they feed on the salmon carcasses. Watchers should minimize movement and noise when out of their cars; pets must be on leash or, better yet, left in the car. Please report any harassment of the eagles to the Washington Department of Wildlife at (800) 562-5626.

It is recommended that eagle-watching be confined to the two following sites on SH 20. Washington Eddy (mile 99) and Sutter Creek Rest Area (mile 100) are excellent spots. An interesting interpretive sign telling about the eagles is at the Washington Eddy site. Special tours are available and can be arranged by contacting The Nature Conservancy's Washington Office in Seattle, (206) 728-9696.

NORTH CASCADES NATIONAL PARK

The North Cascades are surely North America's most rugged landscape. The Cascade Range starts near Lassen Peak in northern California. It creates a mammoth divide until it terminates in British Columbia's Manning Park. To the south, the range is a massive high plateau interspersed with tall volcanic cones; to the north, the mountains are not volcanic in origin but are composed of some of the youngest granitic rock found in Washington. These sharp pinnacles thrust themselves up in a tortuous, chaotic fashion—a beauty unparalleled. The national park officially was created in 1968 after much squabbling and ruckus. Roads are still few and far between; everything is basically anchored to the North Cascades Highway, SH 20, which opened in 1972.

Backcountry hiking, camping, and rock-climbing are favorite pursuits in the park. Mountain goats are found on the craggy cliffsides, but no sheep species. Grizzly bears probably are present in an extremely small, resident population, but any bears seen along the road will be black bear. The North Cascades area has been evaluated by the Interagency Grizzly Bear Committee as habitat capable of sustaining populations of grizzly bears; but it is doubtful, unfortunately, that the future will see more bears in the backcountry. Elk, mule deer, mountain lion, hoary marmot, pika, several species of bats, and many other mammals also are present.

Camping is allowed only at designated campgrounds within North Cascades National Park: Goodell Creek, Newhalem, Colonial Creek, Lone Fir, Klipchuck, and Early Winters. These six locations are spaced between Marblemount and Early Winters. Three trails within the park are barrier free: Happy Creek Forest Walk (Mile Post 134), Rainy Lake (Mile Post 157), and Washington Pass Overlook (Mile Post 162).

Nearly 88,000 acres of National Forest along the North Cascades Highway was named by Congress as the North Cascades Scenic Highway and is managed for recreation and scenic beauty. The North Cascades route can be combined with the Stevens Pass highway for a spectacular mountain loop trip. Sites not to miss are Diablo Lake and Dam, Ross Lake and Dam, the three-hour Skagit Tour which includes lunch, a trip up an incline railway, and a boat trip on Ross Lake (the tour is to view the Skagit hydroelectric project, but one can spot quite a few birds, too), and the Washington Pass Overlook, dominated by Liberty Bell Mountain.

Bird life gradually changes as the highway progresses from the lowland elevation of 300 feet near Marblemount on up to Rainy Pass at 4,855 feet, Washington Pass at 5,477 feet, and then down into the dry eastern side of the Cascades. Two hundred and six bird species have been recorded in the park and the adjacent Ross Lake and Lake Chelan National Recreation Areas. Habitat types are quite varied: lakes and ponds, rivers and streams, marsh, riparian, deciduous forest, both west slope and east slope coniferous forest, rocks and talus slopes, subalpine, and alpine tundra. Although birds are found in all of the habitat types, several areas are of special interest.

County-Line Ponds

The main pond, which does not freeze in winter, is quite good for observing Barrow's and Common Goldeneyes, Hooded Merganser, Ring-necked Duck, Mallard, Bufflehead, and a variety of other waterfowl. Riparian habitat along the river is host to many passerines including Common Yellowthroat, Willow Flycatcher, Nashville Warbler, Virginia Rail, and Marsh Wren; special birds here have been American Redstart and Red-eyed Vireo. Two roads give walking access to the ponds, one at the county line sign on the south side of SH 20, the other a mile west of the Goodell campground.

Goodell Creek Campground

This small campground is located where Goodell Creek pours into the Skagit River in the Ross Lake National Recreation Area. It is on SH 20 just west of Nehalem and has 22 campsites. The elevation here is just over 300 feet, and many of the usual western forest birds are here: Winter Wren, American Robin, Varied and Swainson's Thrushes, Black-capped Chickadee, Red-breasted Nuthatch, Yellow-rumped Warbler, Pileated Woodpecker, Vaux's Swift, swallows, kinglets, and Brown Creeper. Along the stream and in the Skagit River, American Dipper, Common Merganser, and Barrow's and Common Goldeneye have been seen; look up and Black Swifts can be seen high overhead, especially in late afternoon. Black-tailed deer, black bear, and mountain goats are in the area. A spectacular view as you leave the park is the Pickett Range in all its glory.

Newhalem, which is very near the campground, has a variety of habitats including a lodgepole pine stand in the national park campground and a succession of environments going up the steep hillsides. Special birds that have been seen in the area are Calliope Hummingbird; Blue Grouse; Pileated Woodpecker; Swainson's, Varied, and Hermit Thrushes; Lazuli Bunting; and Nashville and MacGillivray's Warblers.

Big Beaver Creek Research Natural Area

This Nature Conservancy Reserve extends northwest from Ross Lake and is reached by a 6.8-mile hiking trail. Sixty-nine species of birds have been recorded in this extremely versatile habitat or, I should say, habitats since 28 types of identifiable plant communities have been identified in this valley. Recorded are 268 plant species belonging to 63 families, enough to make avian residents ecstatic. Special birds are seen such as Great Gray Owl, Wood and Harlequin Ducks, Golden Eagle, and Common Loon.

Extensive marshes and ponds in the area draw a variety of interesting more usual species including Green-winged Teal, Northern Shoveler, Spotted Sandpiper, Willow Flycatcher, Common Yellowthroat, Nashville Warbler, and Gray Catbird. Gray wolves, a rarity, have been seen nearby, and the area is rich in amphibious life. This unique area can be reached by the Ross Dam Trailhead at Milepost 134 on SH 20, or by boat from Ross Dam or the Hozomeen area at the international boundary with Canada at the northern end of Ross Lake.

Ross Lake

Ross Lake, a result of the 1949-built Ross Dam, extends north for 24 miles, including a mile-and-a-half into Canada. East of the lake is the Pasayten Wilderness Area and, to the west, North Cascades National Park. The lake forms an unusual migration corridor and nesting area for many unusual species including Common Loon, Eared Grebe, Sora, White-winged Scoter, Sandhill Crane, Osprey, Golden Eagle, and Common and Caspian Terns. A variety of raptor species are present, including all three accipiters, Red-tailed Hawk, Bald Eagle, and American Kestrel.

Subalpine ridges and slopes

The ridges are excellent for hawk watching. Species seen in addition to those listed previously include Northern Harrier, Rough-legged Hawk, Merlin, and Prairie Falcon. Migrant songbirds such as Vaux's Swift, Townsend's Solitaire, American Tree Sparrow, and American Pipit also have appeared on the ridges. Summering birds that might be spotted in the higher elevations in a variety of habitats are Olive-sided Flycatcher, Hairy Woodpecker, Northern Pygmy-Owl, Band-tailed Pigeon, Common Snipe, Killdeer, Spotted Sandpiper, Blue and Spruce Grouse, Horned Lark, Clark's Nutcracker, Boreal and Mountain Chickadees, Townsend's Solitaire, Gray-crowned Rosy Finch, crossbills, and many others. The high passes through the park are, for the most part, subalpine habitat with its special birds.

A bird checklist, an excellent guide ("Welcome to North Cascades Scenic Highway"), and a brochure and map ("North Cascades") are available from the Superintendent, North Cascades National Park, 2105 Highway 20, Sedro Woolley, WA 98284; (360) 856-5700. Information also is available along the highway at Marblemount, Newhalem, Diablo, Washington Pass, Early Winters, and Winthrop.

SULTAN BASIN RECREATION AREA

The Sultan Basin lies a little more than 13 miles northwest of US 2 and the town of Sultan. Spada Lake is 4.8 miles long, covers 1,870

E.A MILLS

Clark's Nutcracker

acres, and is the focal point in the basin. It was created when Culm-back Dam was built across the Sultan River in 1965. The lake is the main source of drinking water for two-thirds of Snohomish County, therefore no swimming, camping, or gas-powered boats are allowed. The 1,800 acres surrounding the lake is owned and managed by the Snohomish County Public Utilities; much has been logged, small trees grow in some areas, 10-to-15-year-old trees in others, and old-growth timber is found in the canyon of the Sultan River. There are eight recreation sites for various use: picnicking, fishing, scenic views, and information.

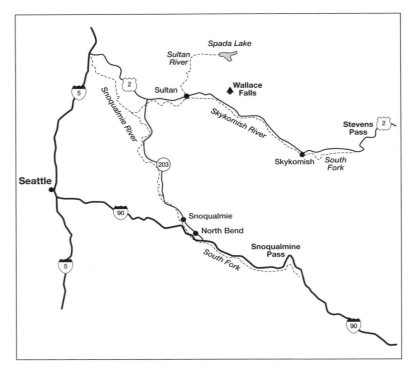

Sultan Basin

The land surrounding Spada Lake is designated as wildlife habitat. Osprey, American Kestrel, and Sharp-shinned Hawk nest here or are attempting to at this time. (Young Ospreys were trying to decide on a site during the summer of 1994; two platforms have been erected, but no choice has been made.) Bald Eagle and Turkey Vulture are seen occasionally. Marbled Murrelets have been heard flying in the vicinity of the Culmback Dam and are thought to nest in the old growth down the Sultan River (only 10% are ever actually seen). Spotted Sandpiper, Warbling Vireo, and Red-breasted Sapsucker also nest in the area. At the far eastern end of the lake, at the DNR Grieder Lake Trailhead, there are two small ponds with a pathway. A variety of warblers have been seen in this area, along with Tree Swallow, Cedar

Waxwing, and others. Spotted Sandpipers frequent the lake edge, but only Mallards seem to nest here. During migration, Western Grebe, Barrow's and Common Goldeneyes, Harlequin Duck, Bufflehead, and Ruddy Duck are here; Common Loon is seen all summer.

Otters and pika also have been seen, and deer, elk, bears, and a variety of other mammals are known to live here. This relatively unexplored area shows much promise for birders. To reach Spada Lake, go through the town of Sultan on US 2, turn north on the Sultan Basin Road, and follow signs to the basin and Spada Lake. For more information on the Sultan Basin area, contact Snohomish County P.U.D. at (800) 562-9142. Ask for the brochure "Sultan Basin Recreation Sites," which contains a map.

STEVENS PASS (4,061 FEET)

U.S. Highway 2 is two-lane except for a four-lane stretch near the summit. The highway follows the Skykomish River up much of the west side, and meets, then follows, the Wenatchee River on the east side. Stevens Pass Ski Area has a 1,700-foot drop from its peak elevation of 5,700 feet. A variety of forest birds such as Hairy Woodpecker, Varied and Hermit Thrushes, Mountain Chickadee, occasional Mountain Bluebird, and chickadees, kinglets, and nuthatches can be seen here. Mountain goats sometimes are seen, especially on the rocky slopes to the north just before the summit.

Scenery can be spectacular east of the pass, especially as the road passes through Tumwater Canyon in the fall when the vine maples, cottonwoods, and larches are a blaze of color. Great Horned Owl, Osprey, American Dipper, occasional eagles, both Vaux's and Black Swifts, and an interesting array of songbirds are seen along the river. American Redstarts have been present in cottonwoods along the stream at the Tumwater National Forest Campground, about 30 miles east of the summit. There are rest stops and various pull-outs along the way. For information about trails and the area, contact the Stevens Pass Ranger Station, P.O. Box 305, Skykomish, WA 98288; (360) 677-2414.

SNOQUALMIE PASS (3,022 FEET)

I-90 out of Seattle, which goes over Snoqualmie Pass, receives the heaviest traffic. It is a quick, well-traveled, four-lane highway that passes through scenery less dramatic than the previous two passes. Excellent vistas of clear-cut land vs. forested land are prevalent. Four ski areas are found here just 45 minutes from Seattle: Alpental, Ski Acres, Snoqualmie, and Hyak. Snow is speedily plowed and delays are not often long in winter. At the summit, both Bald and Golden Eagles can be seen, plus Osprey and Turkey Vulture in migration.

There are a variety of short hikes that can be taken in the area. Small lakes may have Barrow's Goldeneye, Hooded Merganser, or Ring-necked Duck, and grouse often are seen from the trails. Birds, in general, are similar to the Stevens Pass area and there are plenty of places to stop. The summit of Snoqualmie has places to eat, motels, and gas stations. For information on trails and the area, contact the Snoqualmie Pass Ranger Station, 42404 SE North Bend Way, North Bend, WA 98045; (206) 888-1421.

MOUNT RAINIER NATIONAL PARK

Mount Rainier is the largest single mountain system in the lower 48 states. Twenty-seven glaciers covering 35 square miles blanket this 14,412-foot dormant volcano. It is part of the "Ring of Fire"—volcanic ranges that almost surround the Pacific Ocean. The Puyallup, Yakama, Nisqually, Upper Cowlitz, and Taidnapam tribes lived for thousands of years in the shadow of this mountain they called "Tahoma." They hunted and foraged on its lower slopes, but out of respect and awe, did not climb the upper slopes. More than 2,500 people now climb Mount Rainier each year, but constantly moving glaciers and avalanches of ice, snow, and rock make the mountain extremely dangerous.

Mount Rainier is known for its alpine wildflowers beginning in June and peaking in late August. Much of the higher areas easily visited by road is subalpine; here wildlife is easier to see than in the thick forests. Birds vary from the deep forest species found at lower elevations to the subalpine and alpine species. Mount Rainier has old-growth forest that supports Spotted Owls; lucky hikers, especially in late summer, might see or hear them. Raptors and a variety of land birds often are seen on the higher slopes during fall migration.

Burrough's Mountain (Sunrise)

Burrough's Mountain trail is an excellent introduction to subalpine habitat. The trail begins at 6,400 feet at Sunrise and continues over meadows and by ravines with abundant wildflowers. Then, isolated clumps of trees gradually disappear, and you are into the higher, rocky open country. White-tailed Ptarmigan, Clark's Nutcracker, Northern Goshawk, Northern Harrier, American Kestrel, Common Raven, Mountain Bluebird, Gray-crowned Rosy Finch, American Pipit, Horned Lark, Calliope Hummingbird, and Mountain Chickadee have all been seen in late summer.

The Burrough's Mountain trail, a little more than two miles long, begins at the Sunrise Visitor Center parking area. Stay left at the junction to Frozen Lake. Hikes in the area can be terminated anywhere and you will still see plenty of resident high mountain birds and flowers. It is best to check with a ranger regarding trail conditions at any time.

Grove of the Patriarchs Self-guided Nature Trail

Western redcedar, Douglas-fir, and western hemlock up to 1,000 years old reside along this deep-woods trail. The trail is an easy, one-mile round-trip starting at the parking lot 0.1 mile west of the Stevens Canyon Entrance. Interpretive signs mark the way. Blue and Ruffed Grouse are nesting species in the park. Band-tailed Pigeon; Great Horned and Northern Saw-whet Owls; Pileated and Hairy Woodpeckers; Yellow-bellied Sapsucker; Western Wood-Pewee; Pacific-slope, Olive-sided, and Dusky Flycatchers; Tree, Violet-green, and Barn Swallows; Black and Vaux's Swifts; American Dipper; Varied and Hermit Thrushes; Warbling Vireo; Orange-crowned, Nashville, and Townsend's Warblers; and many others are seen along the trail.

Paradise

This is one of the most-visited destinations in the park, and many short, easy trails lead to wildflower meadows where Pine Grosbeaks, Red Crossbills, Gray-crowned Rosy Finches, Pine Siskin, and Gray Jays can be seen in the tree clusters. Also seen in and over the meadows are Fox, Lincoln, and Song Sparrows; Northern Harrier; accipiters; Golden Eagle; and others.

The Wonderland Trail

For the truly ambitious, there is a nearly 90-mile trail that encircles Mount Rainier going through primeval, virgin forests, across innumerable streams, around glaciers, and across snowfields. Should you undertake such a trip, with luck, almost every bird listed in the park could be found. The experience of sleeping next to moving glaciers and seeing the stars without the glow of city lights is a unique experience. Our best experience was a Northern Goshawk hunting in a 7,000-foot-high meadow with hardly a glance at us.

Other nesting species that might be seen are Harlequin Duck, Common Merganser, Cooper's Hawk, Spotted Sandpiper, Western Screech-Owl, Northern Pygmy-Owl, Rufous Hummingbird, Lewis' Woodpecker, Three-toed Woodpecker, Hammond's Flycatcher, Northern Rough-winged Swallow, Pygmy Nuthatch, Swainson's Thrush, Solitary Vireo, Yellow Warbler, Common Yellowthroat, Western Tanager, Evening Grosbeak, Dark-eyed Junco, and Chipping Sparrow.

Four visitor centers have trail information, free backcountry permits, wildlife brochures, interpretive displays, slide presentations, ranger-guided walks, evening campfire programs, and a variety of maps and books. They are the Longmire Hiker Information Center (southwest), the Henry M. Jackson Memorial Visitor Center at Paradise, the Ohanapecosh Visitor Center (southeast), and the Sunrise Visitor Center (east). The Carbon River Entrance has no visitor center, but the ranger station at Ipsut Creek has information.

Saw-whet Owl

Park Headquarters. The main park headquarters is located ten miles west of the Nisqually Entrance: Mount Rainier National Park, Tahoma Woods, Star Route, Ashford, WA 98304; (360) 569-2211.

CHINOOK PASS (5,430 FEET)

SH 410, starting at Enumclaw, can be joined from a number of highways out of the Puget Sound area. Chinook is open spring to mid-fall. There are spectacular views of Mount Rainier and also access to the park. SH 410 joins SH 12, the White Pass Highway, just west of Naches, which leads into Yakima. The Chinook Pass highway is two-lane and slower traveling, but well worth it. Crystal Mountain Ski Resort (actually a year-round resort) is a good spot for fall hawk watching. Crystal Mountain has a vertical drop of more than 3,000 feet from the 7,002-foot top of Silver Queen. It is 76 miles from Seattle, just off SH 410. A variety of mountain species can be seen.

WHITE PASS (4,500 FEET)

SH 12 out of Chehalis is two-lane and accesses this southernmost pass. In summer you can also go via SH 410. It has good views of Mount Rainier, but this is a more gentle route, scenery-wise. On the west side, the road follows the Cowlitz River part of the way. At the summit, the road parallels Rimrock Lake, then follows the Tieton River down the east slope. White Pass Ski Area, with a vertical drop of 1,500 feet, is located at the pass. In this area, watch for Golden Eagle, accipiters, Williamson's Sapsucker, Rock Wren, Lincoln's Sparrow, American Pipit, Clark's Nutcracker, and possible Three-toed Woodpecker. During migration, watch for a variety of raptors and passerines.

MOUNT ST. HELENS

When I climbed 9,677-foot Mount St. Helens years ago, there was much more of it. On May 18, 1980, with an explosive eruption that made news around the world, the summit was no more. Now, 14 years later and about 1,300 feet lower, the mountain still rumbles and spews forth ash occasionally. But now it has a brand new access road for visitors, and 120 miles or more of trails have been rebuilt. Much is growing, lakes have regenerated and are full of nutrients and life, and wildlife has returned. It is still, however, an awesome sight to see.

When the mountain blew, the landscape was devastated, but there were a few survivors. The northern pocket gopher was one and a helper for others to follow. The pocket gopher's burrowing pushed soil to the surface and made a base for seeds to germinate and for plants to return. Beetles were the first insects to return, other than underground ant colonies. Bird species that feed and nest on the ground were the first to begin new colonies. Where standing trees

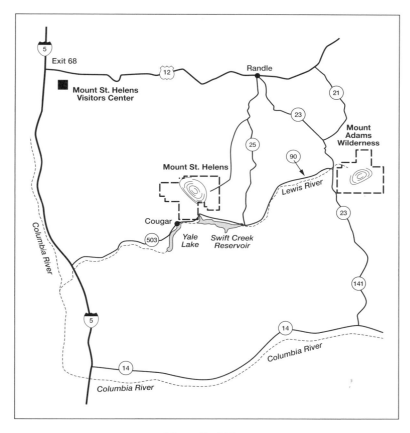

Mount St. Helens

had been left in the form of snags, Hairy Woodpecker, Red-breasted Nuthatch, and Common Flicker returned. American Kestrels began hunting the wide open area, and Osprey and Great Blue Heron returned to lakes. But bird and mammal species dependent on old-growth forests will not colonize the blast area for centuries, not until conifers again become the dominant plant species. Birds, however, visit the area in large numbers; seeds and insects are abundant.

Cougar

The Cougar Road, SH 503, climbs from lowlands into higher, drier forestland. East of Cougar about five miles, Hermit Warblers have been seen, and a little further on, when SH 503 turns to FR 90, Varied and Swainson's Thrushes, American Dipper, Three-toed Woodpecker, Brown Creeper, Hammond's and Olive-sided Flycatchers, Gray Jay, swallows, and Vaux's Swift may be seen.

Cedar Flats Northern Research Natural Area

This beautiful old-growth forest area of predominantly western redcedar looks down on the mudflows of Muddy River. An easy and short trail leads into this splendid ancient forest. Northern Goshawk, Pileated Woodpecker, Brown Creeper, Blue and Spruce Grouse, Spotted Owl, chickadees, kinglets, Hermit Thrush, American Robin, Winter Wren, and others are all possibilities.

The area is 23 miles northeast of Cougar. Follow SH 503 to Cougar; it becomes Forest Road 90 following Yale Lake. Continue along the Lewis River to the dam, then along the north shore of Swift Creek Reservoir. At the Mount St. Helens National Volcanic Monument, go left (north) on FR 25. In a little more than two miles, the trailhead will be on your left.

There are many campgrounds in the Gifford Pinchot National Forest, some of them free. The Mount St. Helens Visitor Center is located five miles east of Castle Rock on SH 504. Information: Mount St. Helens National Volcanic Monument, 3029 Spirit Lake Highway, Castle Rock, WA 98611; (360) 274-2100. The national forest office is at 6926 East 4th Plain Boulevard, Vancouver, WA 98668; (360) 750-5000.

MOUNT ADAMS

Mount Adams is the second-highest peak in the Cascades at 12,276 feet. Not as conical as many of the volcanic mountains, it was formed in stages as several successive cones erupted.

Mount Adams is 25 miles north of Trout Lake. A 46,800-acre wilderness area is located along the west slope of the mountain in the Gifford Pinchot National Forest. Mount Adams is the oldest of the Cascade volcanoes, and the only one that can claim to have had sulfur mined from its sides. There are 56 miles of hiking trails in the Mount Adams Wilderness Area that go through alpine forests, over lava flows, by glaciers, and through meadows of wildflowers. The area has been used for hundreds of years by the Indians; it borders the Yakama Indian Reservation to the east.

State Highway 141

This highway is a relatively untraveled road. It leads from White Salmon to Trout Lake, then on to the Mount Adams Recreational Area. It is a peaceful, restful drive. From the Columbia River and its hordes of colorful windsurfers, the way winds slowly up into the drier highlands. Small farms and orchards featuring Anjou pears, peaches, and varieties of apples dot the way. At Trout Lake, after getting maps and directions to huckleberry fields and bird information, follow SH 23 through the foothills to Randle. Some of the road is good gravel and, unfortunately, is closed in winter, but wonderful in summer and early fall. Spectacular views of Mount Adams and its glaciers are to the east. There is one pass to cross: Babyshoe Pass at 4,350 feet. Along the roadway, watch for black-tailed deer, Ruffed Grouse, Sandhill Crane, Osprey, Golden Eagle, Steller's Jay, Dark-eyed Junco, and migrants. At some of the small ponds, scan for Spotted Sandpiper, Common Merganser, Harlequin Duck, a variety of other waterfowl, and Great Blue Heron.

STEIGERWALD LAKE NATIONAL WILDLIFE REFUGE

Steigerwald refuge covers 627 acres of Columbia River bottomland including riparian woodland, improved pastures, and canary grass marshes. It is prime resting and wintering environment for waterfowl and especially raptors. Other marsh and water birds frequent the water edges, and songbirds forage in the riparian habitat.

Look for Canada Goose, Mallard, Common and Barrow's Goldeneyes, Canvasback, Redhead, Green-winged Teal, Northern Shoveler, and occasional Lesser Scaup. The marshy areas have American Bittern, Great Blue Heron, Green Heron, Virginia Rail, Sora, Redwinged and Yellow-headed Blackbirds, and Marsh Wren. Raptors include Turkey Vulture, Bald Eagle, Northern Harrier, Red-tailed and Rough-legged Hawks, and American Kestrel. Uncommon or vagrant species that have been seen here are Peregrine and Prairie Falcons, Wilson's Phalarope, White-faced Ibis, Western Kingbird, Acorn Woodpecker, and Say's Phoebe.

Steigerwald Lake NWR is located east of Washougal between the Columbia River and SH 14. Information: Steigerwald Lake NWR, c/o Ridgefield NWR, P.O. Box 457, 301 North Third Street, Ridgefield, WA 98642; (360) 887-4106.

Franz Lake National Wildlife Refuge

Franz Lake Refuge is just east of Steigerwald Lake refuge between SH 14 and the Columbia River. This refuge has 395 acres of large, shallow floodplain lake habitat plus another 98 acres of forested uplands in the Indian Mary Creek watershed, which flows into Franz Lake.

In addition to ducks and Canada Geese, Franz Lake and its nearby wetlands provide a wintering environment for nearly 1,000 Tundra Swans. Upland habitat within the refuge provides habitat for raptors, forest passerine birds, and large mammals. Watch for Steller's Jay; Pileated Woodpecker; Varied, Hermit, and Swainson's Thrushes; chickadees; nuthatches; kinglets; and a variety of vireos, flycatchers, warblers, and other passerines.

Black-capped Chickadee

Pierce National Wildlife Refuge

A third refuge, this one just after Franz Lake and between SH 14 and the Columbia River, has 329 acres of river bottomland with wooded habitat, riparian vegetation, and open pastureland. Birds are similar to the previous refuges, primarily Canada Geese and waterfowl, plus a variety of upland birds. One of the last remaining chum salmon runs on the Columbia River is here. The refuge can be scanned best from the trail to the top of Beacon Rock, the second-largest monolith in the world.

Pierce Island Preserve. Pierce Island is a Nature Conservancy preserve that lies in the middle of the Columbia River just off Beacon Rock. The acreage at low river tide is about 200 acres. The island is located in one of the last free-flowing stretches of the Columbia River. Pierce Island is an important floodplain habitat with a cobble-gravel shoreline. A rare plant, the endangered Persistentsepal yellowcress, grows along this pebbly shore and is one of the Conservancy's priorities in preserving the habitat. The Great Basin subspecies of Canada Goose also nests and winters here. Yellow Warblers flit among the black cottonwoods and willow and ash thickets in search of the island's original namesake, the mosquito. Greater Yellowlegs and Spotted Sandpiper have been seen on the beaches, and an assortment of waterfowl and land birds make good use of the island.

Pierce Island is open from July 15th to February 15th, and is accessible only by boat. To reach Pierce Island, take SH 14 east about 25 miles and follow signs to the boat launch site at Beacon Rock State Park.

Beacon Rock State Park

Birds are similar to those found in the three preceding national wildlife refuges. The park does have year-round camping with 14 miles of hiking trails leading both inland and up Beacon Rock, which overlooks the Columbia River Gorge. Sturgeon fishing in the Columbia is popular. There are 35 campsites, and there are boat launch facilities. Some facilities are wheelchair-accessible. Beacon Rock SP is 35 miles east of Vancouver on SH 14. Information: Beacon Rock State Park, State Highway 14, Skamania, WA 98648; (509) 427-8265.

Chapter 7
Eastern Cascades

 The Eastern Cascades mark the gradual departure from the cool, wet, green side of the state to the beginning of a drier, more open, pastel-hued landscape. The temperatures are warmer in the summer and colder in the winter.

The region's western border follows the crest of the Cascade Mountain range. To the east, it abuts the Okanogan and Columbia rivers to approximately Vantage, where it then edges the foothills of the Cascades to the Oregon border. Parts of Okanogan, Chelan, Kittitas, Yakima, and Klickitat counties are in this region, which covers about 12% of the state.

From the crest of the Cascades, the more open, parklike subalpine forests of Pacific silver fir and mountain hemlock predominate. Azaleas, beargrass, and meadows lush with hundreds of species of wildflowers blaze with color in the spring and summer. Typical bird life includes Clark's Nutcracker, Blue Grouse, Hermit Thrush, Townsend's Solitaire, Olive-sided Flycatcher, McGillivray's Warbler, and Fox Sparrow.

A drier climate in the lee of the Cascades has resulted in a stretch of ponderosa pine found as widely spread individual trees or as part of dense stands of Douglas-fir up to 3,200 feet elevation. Northern Goshawk, Steller's and Gray Jays, Varied Thrush, and Winter Wren are typical. The Eastern Cascades continue down until they meet the bunchgrass prairies of the Columbia Plateau.

HART'S PASS

In the 1890s, Colonel W. Thomas Hart, a hardy entrepreneur who knew of the gold strike in the mountains, had a narrow-gauge road built from Robinson Creek and through the pass to the mines, no

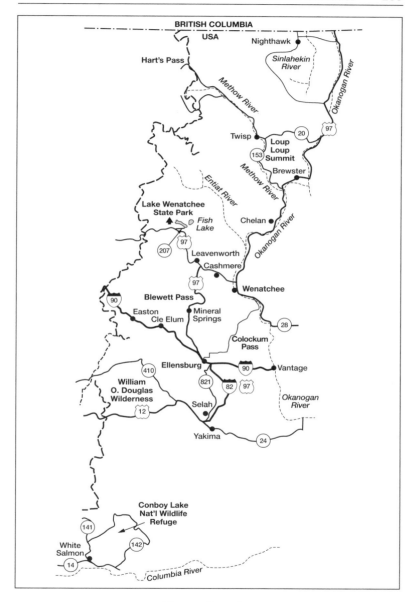

Eastern Cascades

mean feat in any day. At that time, a single shipment of ore, carried on horses, was worth $35,000 in gold. In 1903, the new road was widened to 36 inches, and doesn't seem a lot wider now. It was rebuilt by the Forest Service in 1935 following most of the original route; it is one lane with turnouts and good gravel. It is steep, but well worth the drive (no RVs or trailers allowed). Drivers should not bird-watch! This 6,197-foot pass is in beautiful high country with eagles, grouse, and a variety of high-mountain species. The Pacific Crest Trail passes through, and you can walk into Canada in a long day. Hart's Pass sits at the edge of the 500,000-acre Pasayten Wilderness Area, which has more than 500 miles of high-country trails.

At the top of Hart's Pass, the road divides: to the right is the road to Slate Peak, at 7,500 feet the highest automobile road in Washington and site of fall hawk watches and raptor banding stations at various times; to the left, the road leads to Meadows Campground. Sharp-shinned Hawks are the most numerous, but Red-tailed Hawks, Northern Harriers, Golden Eagles, and American Kestrel also are seen in good numbers. In recent years, Merlin and Prairie Falcon numbers have increased. Geese, ducks, and a variety of land birds also are seen during migration.

The Pacific Crest Trail heads north along the ridgeline and is easy going. You can meander up to ridge tops or down to meadowed ravines. The trail section starts at the parking lot at the first switch-back on the Slate Peak road. Watch for possible boreal species such as Boreal Owl and Chickadee, Spruce Grouse, Bohemian Waxwing, Common Raven, Harlequin Duck, White-winged Crossbill, Black-backed Woodpecker, American Pipit, and Horned Lark. Hoary marmots and pika are common; black bear sometimes are seen.

Two campgrounds are at Hart's Pass, one just across from the guard station with five tent sites; and one a mile up the road to the left, Meadows Campground, with 14 tent sites, tables, firepits, and toilets. Neither has piped water, so bring your own. We camp at Meadows Campground where Clark's Nutcracker, Three-toed Woodpecker, Northern Pygmy-Owl, Hermit Thrush, Mountain Chickadee, American Robin, Townsend's Solitaire, and Fox and White-crowned Sparrows have been seen. Once in mid-October, we heard flock after flock of Canada Geese migrating by all through the night.

Bohemian Waxwing

To reach Hart's Pass, follow the North Cascades Highway to Mazama, 16 miles northwest of Winthrop. Drive up the glacier-carved Methow valley past the Mazama store and post office, and continue into the mountains. Part of the way up, there is a salt lick to the left where mule deer and mountain goats occasionally are seen. The drive is 18.5 miles from Mazama to Hart's Pass, and the road is well-signed. Information: Winthrop Ranger District, Box 579, Winthrop, WA 98862; (509) 996-2266.

METHOW RIVER VALLEY

The North Cascades Highway is paralleled by the tranquil Methow River as it descends the dry eastern slopes of the mountains. It then meanders alongside SH 153 until finally joining the Columbia River at the town of Pateros. There are many fine birding spots and a variety of habitats along the Methow River.

Methow Habitat Management Area

This area lies west of the town of Twisp, which was once a major fish-drying station. The Indian name "Twips" meant yellow-jackets, which were common and inflicted their stings upon the fish dryers. The Twisp River Road west out of Twisp on SH 153 leads into the Methow HMA as do several other roads off SH 153. The area's 20,437 acres are prime winter range for north-central Washington's mule deer herds. Two units, the Big Buck and the Chilwist Units, are part of the Methow HMA. Much of the land is open sage and bitterbrush at lower elevations, and semi-open yellow pine forests in the higher country. Merriam's Turkey, the largest North American upland game bird and one of six races, or subspecies, is found here. Other interesting birds are Ruffed, Spruce, and Blue Grouse; Ring-necked Pheasant; Bald Eagle (wintering); Mourning Dove; California Quail; Mallard; Lewis' Woodpecker; Eastern Kingbird; Mountain Bluebird; Red-eyed Vireo; Veery; Cassin's Finch; and Gray Jay. Large mammals in the area include cougar, black bear, deer, and elk.

Alta Lake State Park

Alta Lake State Park's 177 acres is in a dry pine forest at an elevation of 1,163 feet. The park is next to Alta Lake where you can swim, boat, and water ski. Common Merganser, scaup, Ring-necked Duck, and Mallard share the lake at times. Overhead, Common Nighthawks, Black and Vaux's Swift, and swallows can be seen. Western Wood-Pewee, Cassin's Finch, Gray Jay, Yellow-rumped Warbler, chickadees, and nuthatches can be seen near the camp area. There are trails from the park and you can see Black-billed Magpie, Yellow-headed Blackbird, Western and sometimes Eastern Kingbirds, Chukar, White-

Mountain Bluebird

throated Swift, Olive-sided Flycatcher, Gray Catbird, Western Tanager, Black-headed Grosbeak, and Western Bluebird.

The park has 184 campsites, plus 16 sites with full hookups; some facilities are wheelchair-accessible. To reach the park, turn off SH 153 at Alta Lake Road. Drive southwest on Alta Lake Road for two miles to the park. Information: Alta Lake State Park, Star Route 40, Pateros, WA 98846; (509) 923-2473.

NIGHTHAWK

Not far east of the Pasayten Wilderness Area and a couple of miles from the Canadian border is the town of Nighthawk, Washington's exemplar ghost town. The town was named for a prominent mine which, in turn, was named for the bird with the rasping, booming sound heard throughout the valley. Nighthawk, in its heyday, was a transshipping center; it is now all private land, and a few people still live in the town's historic buildings. Visitors are not encouraged. It has been photographed, birded, and ogled, but from a distance.

Nighthawk is about two blocks long bordering the Similkameen River about ten miles west of Oroville. The highway just north of the river and town offers good views of the historic buildings and the cliffs behind it. Golden Eagles, American Kestrels, and Prairie Falcons live in the area. Common Nighthawks still are heard overhead in summer, but not in the numbers there once must have been. Common Flicker, Black-billed Magpie, Red-tailed Hawk, California Quail, yellowlegs, Spotted Sandpiper, bluebirds, Black-headed Grosbeak, swallows, Lazuli Bunting, and Vesper and Grasshopper Sparrows have been seen.

SINLAHEKIN HABITAT MANAGEMENT AREA

This important winter habitat for the entire Sinlahekin Valley mule deer herd covers 14,035 acres of sparsely timbered grasslands covering rolling hills. The slopes of the eastern Cascades border the valley. Other mammals also resident are white-tailed deer, bighorn sheep, black bear, badger, porcupine, skunk, beaver, pine squirrel, and a variety of smaller mammals. Mallard, Ring-necked Duck, Lesser Scaup, Common Goldeneye, Ruddy Duck, Hooded and Common Mergansers, Red-necked Grebe, all three accipiters, Gray Partridge, Chukar, California Quail, Ring-billed Gull, Black-chinned and Calliope Hummingbirds, White-throated Swift, Hammond's and Dusky Flycatchers, Pygmy Nuthatch, Marsh Wren, Veery, Orange-crowned and Nashville Warblers, Yellow-breasted Chat, Northern Oriole, Pine Grosbeak, Cassin's Finch, Red Crossbill, and Evening Grosbeak are some to look for. The Sinlahekin HMA is located along Sinlahekin Creek south of Nighthawk and Palmer Lake on Sinlahekin Road; it extends as far as Fish Lake.

LOUP LOUP

Douglas-fir and western larch fill the landscape of this old mining area. Trappers from the Hudson Bay Company found the area rich in furs, hence "loup," French for "wolf." At an elevation of 4,200 feet, Loup Loup is fine habitat for birds of the pine forests; its altitude also adds to the variety of bird species. Loup Loup has a bit of a reputation for owls: Barred Owl, Great Horned Owl, and Northern Pygmy-Owl are resident. Spruce Grouse, Northern Goshawk, Mountain Bluebird, Red-breasted and Pygmy Nuthatches, Mountain and Boreal Chickadees, Williamson's Sapsucker, Calliope Hummingbird, Hammond's Flycatcher, Cassin's Finch, Red Crossbill, and Ruby-crowned Kinglet also have been seen in the area. A wet meadow area on the lower side of the campground has had Common Snipe and Spotted Sandpiper.

Loup Loup has 25 campsites with water. The campground is 12.5 miles east of Twisp on SH 20. Information: Twisp Ranger District, P.O. Box 188, Twisp, WA 98856; (509) 997-2131.

LAKE CHELAN

One end of this fjord-like lake nestles next to the remoteness of the North Cascades National Park in the shadow of 8,000-foot peaks, while 56 miles to the southeast the lake sprawls by the busy resort town of Chelan. No roads lead to the head of this narrow, 1,500-foot-deep waterway. A passenger boat, *Lady of the Lake II*, takes tourists and residents back and forth to the tiny, rugged settlement of Stehekin once a day from April 15 to October 15. Trips are fewer the rest of the year, but still popular.

Overnight accommodations, campgrounds, and meals are available in Stehekin year-round. Everything, including the boat trip, should be reserved ahead of time no matter what time of year. Upon arrival, National Park rangers can give advice on hikes, birds, and camping. A shuttle bus travels the 23-mile road up the Stehekin River valley, and lets visitors on and off along the route. Summer birding can be interesting.

Coon Lake

There are several starting points, but the easiest way is to catch the shuttle and begin above the Tumwater Bridge. Let the bus cover most of the elevation for you. The trail to Coon Lake is an easy one-mile hike through pine and cedar forests. Listen for Common Raven and Northern Pygmy-Owl. Along the trail, watch for accipiters, Blue Grouse, Common Flicker, Three-toed Woodpecker, Calliope Hummingbird, Western Wood-Pewee, Steller's and Gray Jays, Western Tanager, Hermit Thrush, Mountain Chickadee, Red-breasted Nuthatch, Yellow-rumped Warbler, Dark-eyed Junco, Cassin's Finch, and Red Crossbill.

Before you reach the lake, there is a marshy area near the end of the road. Look for blackbirds, Common Snipe, American Dipper, and Sora, and overhead for Red-tailed Hawk, swallows, swifts, and Common Nighthawk. The lake is about a mile in length, and there often are waterfowl such as Common Merganser, Harlequin Duck, Lesser Scaup, Mallard, and others. Mule deer and beaver have been seen here, too. From Coon Lake, you can return via the same trail, or continue on for a longer, more strenuous hike. This is just one suggestion for getting out in this isolated country to see interesting birds. Obtain a trail map from the ranger and discuss the many options.

CHELAN BUTTE HABITAT MANAGEMENT AREA

One of the biggest populations of Chukar and California Quail in north-central Washington is found on Chelan Butte. The habitat consists of flat ridges, steep, grassy slopes, and deep canyons. The view from the top is magnificent. Lake Chelan stretches to the far mountains, and the Columbia River winds its way to desert and wheatfields.

Golden Eagles often are seen, and the butte has been used for hawk watches. Prairie Falcon, American Kestrel, Red-tailed and Swainson's Hawks, Sharp-shinned and Cooper's Hawks, Northern Harrier, Osprey, Turkey Vulture, and Northern Goshawk all have been recorded.

Three-toed, Lewis', and White-headed Woodpeckers; White-throated Swift; kingbirds; Clark's Nutcracker; Say's Phoebe; Pygmy, White-breasted, and Red-breasted Nuthatches; Gray Catbird; and Pine Grosbeak all have been seen here, along with a variety of migrants. Chelan Butte is reached via the Chelan Butte Fire Lookout road at the south end of Chelan off US 97.

WENATCHEE NATIONAL FOREST

The Wenatchee National Forest covers 2.2 million acres of the eastern slope of the Cascade Range from Lake Chelan in the north to the Yakama Indian Reservation in the south. Approximately 40% of the forest is occupied by seven different wilderness areas. Habitats range from the alpine zone at higher elevations down through ponderosa pine, Douglas-fir, and true fir zones to the grass-shrub zones along the lower eastern edge of the forest. Weather is variable, and temperatures range from the high 90s in July and August to winter lows that average 25°. Snowfall is 30–35 inches a year.

Three hundred ninety-six species of mammals, birds, reptiles, and amphibians live in this extensive range. Relatively common here, but rare other places, are Northern Goshawk, Spotted Owl, and mountain goat. Occasionally seen are species such as grizzly bear, gray wolf, Canadian lynx, fisher, marten, Bald Eagle, and Peregrine and Prairie Falcons. Because of the forest's elevation, from 1,000 to 8,000 feet, wildflowers are abundant, blooming from March to late November.

Entiat and Chelan Mountains

Between Lake Chelan on the north and the Wenatchee River to the south, the Entiat and Chelan mountains gradually descend into a wonderful habitat of open foothills and deep ravines. The Entiat and Swakane Habitat Management Areas lie in this environment. The Columbia River borders the areas on their eastern edges so that from US 97 huge numbers of ducks and geese can be seen, especially during migration. Wildflowers on the canyon sides are spectacular. This is an important winter habitat for a very large mule deer herd. Both areas are accessible from US 97 on the west side of the Columbia River. The roads are fairly good gravel/dirt, except when very wet.

Entiat Habitat Management Area. The Entiat's 9,675 acres—steep, western yellow pine forests that gradually turn to grassland and basalt benches—is a vital wintering area for mule deer. Porcupines, yellow pine chipmunks, and badgers also live here. California Quail and Chukar are abundant, and many species such as American Dipper, Gray Jay, sapsuckers, Mountain Bluebird, Yellow-breasted Chat, Veery, Evening Grosbeak, and others can be found. Roads leading west from US 97 or north from the Ardenvoir Road go into the Entiat. As I write, this eastern part of Washington is being devastated by forest fires. Past Entiat fires have left even more glorious fields of wildflowers and a multitude of woodpecker snags for the coming years. What these areas will be like in the near future is uncertain.

Swakane Habitat Management Area. Swakane has the most outstanding wildflowers of the area. The canyon is home to two endangered plant species and a small herd of bighorn sheep. The sheep are sometimes on the northern hillside about three miles into the management area. Driving into the canyon, the dry, grassy areas and basalt cliffs give way to steep, timbered slopes where black bear and cougar can be found. Northern Goshawk, American Kestrel, Blue Grouse, Chukar, California Quail, Clark's Nutcracker, White-headed and Three-toed Woodpeckers, Calliope Hummingbird, Mountain Bluebird, Gray Catbird, Hermit and Varied Thrushes, Townsend's and Yellow-rumped Warblers, and many others are seen here. Continue on to the ridge top and down through Nahahum Canyon to emerge at the town of Cashmere on US 2. To reach Swakane Canyon, turn west from US 97 about a mile past Rocky Reach Dam.

LAKE WENATCHEE

Lake Wenatchee is a deep, glacial lake about five miles long and a mile wide. Two rivers, the White River at the northwest end of the lake and the Wenatchee River at the southeast, are scenic areas best seen from a canoe or raft. Both are popular with waterfowl, kingfishers, swallows, and many other species. The land around the lake is mostly forested, and there are many small lakes and streams. A variety of campgrounds are near Lake Wenatchee, but the state park is the largest.

Lake Wenatchee State Park. This 489-acre park has 12,623 feet of lakefront. Swimming, boating, fishing, and hiking are popular. Deer, bear, coyotes, squirrels, raccoons, chipmunks, and a variety of amphibians are found in the park. Birds to look for are Canada

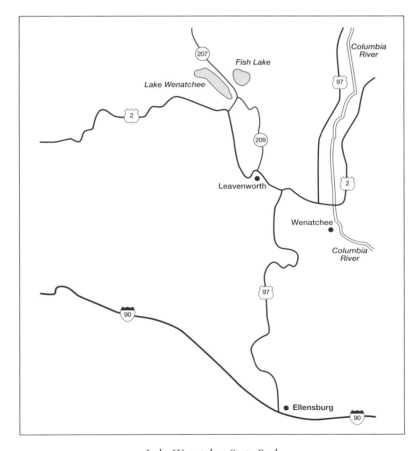

Lake Wenatchee State Park

Goose, Common Merganser, Mallard, Bald Eagle, Osprey, American Crow, Belted Kingfisher, Ruffed Grouse, White-headed Woodpecker, Veery, and Townsend's Solitaire.

Lake Wenatchee SP has 197 fairly well-separated campsites (no trailer hookups) and is open spring through fall. This is bear country, so keep all food in the car when away from camp. Canoe and horse rentals are available. To reach Lake Wenatchee, turn north from US 2 at Coles Corner onto SH 207. Coles Corner is about 100 miles from Seattle and 15 miles from Leavenworth. The park is five miles from US 2. Information: Lake Wenatchee Ranger Station, 22976 Highway 207, Leavenworth, WA 98826; (509) 763-3103.

FISH LAKE

Fish Lake is only two miles from Lake Wenatchee, but its birding possibilities, especially from a canoe or kayak, are excellent. Several small inlets feed into this shallow, 500- to 600-acre lake. A 150-acre marsh at the west end of the lake enhances the birding. The "floating bog" marsh is being considered for a research natural area, so please do not walk in this area, as there are sensitive plants here, including insectivorous sundews. While on the lake, watch for Common Loon, Canada Goose, Wood Duck, Canvasback, Green-winged and Blue-winged Teal, Common Goldeneye, Bufflehead, Great Blue Heron, and Belted Kingfisher. Overhead, scan for Violet-green Swallow, swifts, Osprey, Red-tailed Hawk, Bald Eagle, American Kestrel, and Turkey Vulture.

Plant life in the area is basically a dry, mixed ponderosa pine and Douglas-fir in the uplands, with some grand fir in the moister areas. Ocean spray, spirea, Oregon grape, and serviceberry provide understory. The trails around the lake may yield accipiters; Barred, Great Horned, and Northern Saw-whet Owls; Pileated Woodpecker; Rufous and Calliope Hummingbirds; Evening and Black-headed Grosbeaks; Red-winged Blackbird; Red-naped Sapsucker; Mountain Chickadee; Veery; Townsend's, Nashville, MacGillivray's, and Yellow-rumped Warblers; Purple and Cassin's Finch; and Pine Siskin. Obtain information about Fish Lake from the Lake Wenatchee Ranger Station.

Pileated Woodpecker

WENATCHEE CONFLUENCE STATE PARK

This state park is quite new, established in 1990. It is situated at the point where the Wenatchee River flows into the Columbia River. The park is divided into two sections by the Wenatchee River: the 97-acre north section is the campground and recreation area, and the 100-acre south section is wildlife habitat with trails. Bald and Golden Eagles, Osprey, Great Blue Heron, a variety of waterfowl, Common Yellowthroat, blackbirds, Marsh Wren, Lazuli Bunting, American Goldfinch, and a variety of other songbirds have been seen. This is an on-the-beaten-path park adjacent to the apple town of Wenatchee. The park has 51 full-hookup sites, a footbridge to the wildlife area, and 4.5 miles of trails. Information: Wenatchee Confluence State Park, 333 Olds Station Road, Wenatchee, WA 98801.

I-90 CORRIDOR

I-90 is the fast way to get across the state, but interesting birds still can be seen. With luck, in mid-October you can see multitudes of Rough-legged Hawks settling down in late afternoon to glean voles from the fields. We once counted nearly 200 hawks in fields adjacent to the freeway just west of Ellensburg. Osprey nests are not uncommon from Cle Elum to Ellensburg, often close to the highway. Often, Canada Geese use the nests in early March and April, and Osprey take over after arriving in early April. At the southern side of the highway at the west end of Ellensburg, a Great Blue Heron rookery is visible in trees across the river.

Many ponds, both large and small, can be seen from the freeway. Scan these ponds for a variety of interesting waterfowl including Ruddy Duck, Canvasback, Redhead, Ring-necked Duck, scaup, teal, and others. Yellow-headed Blackbird and Marsh Wren are often in the cattail marshes around the lakes. During migration, and especially in winter, watch for raptors; Prairie Falcons and American Kestrels in very early spring and fall; and Rough-legged and Red-tailed Hawks and Bald Eagles in winter.

LAKE EASTON STATE PARK

Lake Easton lies over Snoqualmie Pass from Seattle near I-90, and about 15 miles west of Cle Elum. It is a 247-acre reservoir about a mile long and half-mile wide owned by the U.S. Bureau of Land Reclamation. Its water is used for irrigation purposes via a network of canals in the central area of eastern Washington. Wildlife such as foxes, raccoons, squirrels, and chipmunks are abundant in the park; deer and elk occasionally visit. Mushroom-hunting in the fall is good. A pair of Osprey nest every year at the west end of the lake, and Bald Eagles occasionally are seen. We have seen Northern Goshawk, Cooper's Hawk, Red-tailed Hawk, Common Raven, Northern Pygmy-Owl, Northern Flicker, Pileated Woodpecker, Western Wood-Pewee, Steller's Jay, American Dipper, Violet-green Swallow, Western Tanager, Hermit Thrush, Yellow-rumped Warbler, Dark-eyed Junco, Cassin's Finch, and Red Crossbill in the area.

There are many trails for birding. Lake Easton is open all year and has two camping areas with a total of 145 sites; 45 have full hookups.

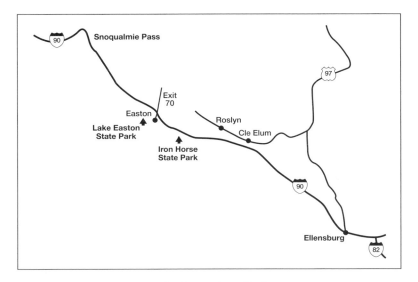

Lake Easton State Park

Information: Lake Easton State Park, P.O. Box 26, Easton, WA 98925; (509) 656-2230.

CLE ELUM AREA

Cle Elum is a gorgeous eastern slope habitat in between high-elevation conifers and the sagebrush desert. It is a land of ponderosa pine, sweeping grasslands, lakes, raptors, and coyotes, with a generous variety of everything else. The weather is cold and windy in winter and hot and breezy in the summer; spring and fall birding is wonderful. Cle Elum is a small ranching town that has some great Mexican food and lattés, and the famous Cle Elum Bakery (First and Peoh Avenue).

Roslyn

Roslyn's claim to fame is not just being the outdoor setting for television's "Northern Exposure," but its ethnic history of coal mining, i.e., its cemeteries—all 26 of them. The 26 cemeteries are on 15 acres fenced to separate the ethnic and fraternal origins. Because this is a bird book, I won't digress, but the cemetery is fascinating, and it's where good birds are!

The Roslyn Cemetery sits on a hillside forested with silver fir, western white pine, Douglas-fir, and a variety of other species. Spring and fall are especially good when flocks of songbirds invade the trees and raptors are overhead. We have seen Red-tailed Hawk; Turkey Vulture; Osprey; Nashville, MacGillivray's, Yellow-rumped, Yellow, and Orange-crowned Warblers; Lazuli Bunting; Evening and Black-headed Grosbeaks; Red-breasted Nuthatch; Golden-crowned and Ruby-crowned Kinglets; Pileated Woodpecker; Cedar Waxwing; Steller's Jay; Chestnut-backed and Mountain Chickadees; American Robin; Varied Thrush; American Crow; Common Raven; Chipping and Song Sparrows; and Ruffed Grouse. Roslyn is located two miles west of Cle Elum on SH 103. Pick up a brochure on cemetery history and a map at the Roslyn City Hall, or follow the signs—it's just a few blocks from the town center.

BLEWETT PASS

Blewett Pass, 4,071 feet, is at the summit of the Wenatchee Mountains. It was named for Edward Blewett, who operated a gold mine and ore mill in the area. Blewett Pass is the "old" highway, replaced by Swauk Pass (US 97) as the main north-south highway in the area, but it is a delightful, narrow, winding road through forests and rocky, open land. Owls are sought after here, and Great Horned, Northern Saw-whet, Flammulated, and Spotted Owls and Northern Pygmy-Owl have been seen, along with Ruffed Grouse, Red-naped and Williamson's Sapsuckers, Cassin's Finch, Red Crossbill, and Nashville and Yellow-rumped Warblers. Blewett Pass—it is also FR 7320—is signed as such from US 97 at about three miles north of Mineral Springs Campground and again at about eight miles past Swauk Pass; both turns are to the west.

RED TOP

Several groups regularly use Red Top Mountain for a hawk-watch site with good results. The drive up is scenic, the half-mile hike up Teanaway Ridge is easy but steep, and the view and birds are great. A mixed forest of Engelmann spruce, grand fir, and Douglas-fir gradually becomes sparse and the terrain more rocky with wind-twisted trees. The unused Forest Service lookout on the summit provides views over forests supporting one of the highest densities of Spotted Owls in the Pacific Northwest.

On our official hawk watches for the Hawk Migration Association, we have seen all three accipiters; both eagles; Northern Harrier; Turkey Vulture; Osprey; Red-tailed, Rough-legged, and Swainson's Hawks; Peregrine and Prairie Falcons; Merlin; American Kestrel; Blue Grouse; Williamson's Sapsucker; Hairy and Three-toed Woodpeckers; Mountain and Western Bluebirds; Say's Phoebe; Western Wood-Pewee; Olive-sided Flycatcher; White-throated Swift; Barn, Tree, and Violet-green Swallows; Common Raven; Clark's Nutcracker; Nashville, Townsend's, and MacGillivray's Warblers; White-crowned Sparrow; and many others. Great flocks of Townsend's Solitaires have been seen on the slopes in September stopping to feed on their way south.

Red Top Mountain is 5,361 feet in elevation. Magnificent, close views of Mount Stuart can be had from the top, and there are trails going north along the ridge where you can look for birds or explore the agate beds, a popular destination for rock hounds. Table Mountain, to the east, has similar bird species and habitats on a larger scale. There are a variety of campgrounds in the surrounding area. Red Top is reached from US 97 just north of Mineral Springs Resort. Turn west on FR 9802 (Blue Creek), a good gravel road, and follow signs to the top.

TEANAWAY RIVER VALLEY

The Teanaway River Valley lies about four miles east of Cle Elum, a north turn off US 97. The upper tributaries of the Teanaway River drain a huge mountainous area with many peaks over 6,000 feet; the three main branches then flow south until they meet the Yakima River. The glacier-carved valley floor is farmed, a small sawmill operates here, and there are many cabins hidden away on the hillsides. Elk and deer browse in the fields in the winter, and Bald Eagles, Northern Harriers, and Red-tailed and Rough-legged Hawks are seen. The land is in the Wenatchee National Forest, and includes dry forest, high meadows, steep open ridges, and rocky outcroppings.

There are multitudes of trails to try where you can see Western Tanager; Mountain and Western Bluebirds; Lazuli Bunting; Common Nighthawk; a variety of owls; White-headed, Three-toed, Hairy, and Pileated Woodpeckers; Varied and Hermit Thrushes; Vaux's Swift; swallows; Gray Catbird; Nashville Warbler; and Northern Oriole. The damper areas along the river have American Dipper, Common Yellowthroat, Red-winged Blackbird, Marsh Wren, Great Blue Heron, and Yellow-rumped Warbler. Turkey Vultures often are seen in migration.

Just before the turn to the Teanaway Valley, there is a road to the right leading to the 700-acre Hidden Valley Ranch. This is an out-of-this-world, relaxing place to stay while you are birding; you don't even have to leave the ranch to bird. Golden and Bald Eagles, Red-tailed Hawk, Great Horned Owl, Northern Pygmy-Owl, bluebirds, tanagers, warblers, and every other bird mentioned in the area all can be found here. Hidden Valley Ranch is a working guest ranch, open all year, with unsurpassed food and hospitality. Rustic cabins have small decks looking over the lovely valley. In the past, the University of

Great Blue Heron

Washington has used this as a base for its field excursions in the area. Information: Hidden Valley Ranch, HC 61, Box 2060, Cle Elum, WA 98922; (509) 857-2322, ext. 2344.

THE COLOCKUM HABITAT MANAGEMENT AREA

Colockum Pass, 5,373 feet, was originally a major route for native Indians who traveled on foot. Later, it became a steep, dusty, hardly passable stagecoach route from Ellensburg to Wenatchee; in places it seems not to have changed much. The management area covers 92,000 acres; part is forested land, the rest is extensive rolling sagebrush hills that drop off to steep cliffs above the Columbia River. For the purpose of this book, the road is meant as an access into good, easy hiking country—birds are possible anywhere.

The usual eastern slope timberland and dry grassland species such as White-headed and Three-toed Woodpeckers; Townsend's Solitaire; Nashville Warbler; Pygmy Nuthatch; Northern Pygmy-Owl; Great Horned Owl; accipiters; grouse; Grasshopper, Vesper, and Chipping Sparrows; and many others can be seen. Chukar, California Quail, the Rio Grande Turkey, Ruffed and Sage Grouse, Ring-necked Pheasant, and Mourning Dove also are residents. The road is passable during summer when it is dry, but is not advised as a through trip at other times except in a four-wheel-drive vehicle.

A strip of land along the Columbia is level and planted with grains, which, combined with the numerous bays, make it ideal waterfowl habitat. Canada Goose, Mallard, Northern Pintail, Ring-necked Duck, goldeneyes, teal, scaup, Northern Shoveler, and Common Merganser have been seen.

The Colockum HMA is famous for Rocky Mountain elk; it also has herds of mule deer, bighorn sheep, and pronghorn antelope. Black bear are common. The Colockum and the nearby Whiskey Dick Habitat Management Area comprise the largest amount of desert-type land in state ownership. Another HMA, just to the south of Colockum but administered through the L.T. Murray HMA, is the Quilomene. It has a similar habitat and bird species. To reach the Colockum HMA, take the Kittitas Highway east, then turn north on No. 81 Road. Turn east again on Erickson Road, and north on Colockum Road.

L.T. MURRAY AND OAK CREEK HABITAT MANAGEMENT AREAS

The L.T. Murray HMA extends south from I-90 between Cle Elum and Ellensburg, while the adjacent Oak Creek HMA spreads further south, east to the Yakima River, and west past the Naches River. The two areas blanket 200,000 acres of typical eastern slope timberland and grassy rangeland. Wonderful canyon land with a mix of woods, brush, water, and open country is found throughout both areas. Many interesting species of birds are to be found.

Bighorn sheep, Rocky Mountain elk, and Chukar are key management species. In fact, Oak Creek's big winter attractions are elk and bighorn sheep feeding stations just off the White Pass Highway at the headquarters. Look here for Clark's Nutcracker, Common Ravens, and forest passerines. There are any number of interesting drives throughout this huge management area. A few examples follow, but for more information contact the Washington State Department of Fish and Wildlife, Region 3, 1701 South 24th Avenue, Yakima, WA 98902; (509) 575-2740.

Taneum Canyon (LTM)

To reach Taneum Canyon, go nine miles east of Cle Elum on I-90 and turn south at the Elk Heights exit (Exit 93). Head south on Thorp Prairie Road, then right on Taneum Road. Follow this for about 2.5 miles to reach the beginning of the L.T. Murray, and next to Taneum Creek. Common Snipe nest in the grass and pastureland just past an irrigation canal. The road follows Taneum Creek, soon narrowing to a riparian habitat on the left and a steep, rocky, open area to the right. American Kestrel, Red-tailed Hawk, an occasional Prairie Falcon, California Quail, Lazuli Bunting, and Chipping Sparrow have been seen in the open habitat. Streamside, many riparian birds such as Willow Flycatcher, American Dipper, Northern Oriole, Evening Grosbeak, Pine Siskin, Cassin's Finch, Veery, and Swainson's Thrush are found.

About three miles into the canyon is the Taneum National Forest campground, which has a grove of old-growth ponderosa pine. Possibilities here are White-headed Woodpecker, Pacific-slope Flycatcher, Red-breasted Nuthatch, Brown Creeper, Chestnut-backed Chickadee, Golden-crowned Kinglet, Hermit Thrush, and Red Crossbill. The campground has 24 sites and water; some facilities are wheelchair-accessible. Information: Cle Elum Ranger District, West 2nd Street, Cle Elum, WA 98922; (509) 674-4411.

Robinson Canyon (LTM)

Robinson Canyon, with its spectacular lava cliffs, follows a finger of the L.T. Murray. Access the area from Exit 101 on I-90 (Thorp exit). Go south a little less than two miles, west for a half mile, then right up

Robinson Gulch. Watch for Prairie Falcon, Red-tailed Hawk, American Kestrel, California Quail, Blue Grouse, Chukar, Loggerhead Shrike, Sage Thrasher, and Brewer's Sparrow. A variety of owls has been seen here, including Northern Pygmy-Owl and Northern Saw-whet, Flammulated, and Great Horned Owls. Common Poorwills can be seen at night. Birds of the ponderosa pine forests such as accipiters, Gray Catbird, Downy Woodpecker, Yellow Warbler, Gray and Least Flycatchers, Yellow-breasted Chat, Dark-eyed Junco, and American Robin often are seen while traveling through Robinson Canyon.

Manashtash Ridge (LTM)

I-82, from Ellensburg to Yakima, passes over the Manashtash Ridge, an easy and usually productive fall hawk-watch site. Near the top on the west side, there is an overlook to Ellensburg, the surrounding farmlands, and the mountains to the north. Large numbers of American Kestrels, interspersed with Prairie Falcons, have been seen in early fall, and a variety of others including Osprey, Northern Harrier, Red-tailed Hawk, and a few Golden Eagles have been seen.

Oak Creek Canyon (OC)

To reach Oak Creek Canyon, go two miles south on US 12 from the intersection of US 12 and SH 410, then west into the management area along Oak Creek. Flycatchers and woodpeckers are interesting and common through here. Watch for Golden Eagle, Turkey Vulture, accipiters, Chukar, Rock and Canyon Wrens, Western Tanager, Common Poorwill, Northern Oriole, Black-headed Grosbeak, Western Wood-Pewee, Red-eyed Vireo, White-breasted Nuthatch, Lewis' Woodpecker, Veery, Vesper and Chipping Sparrows, and a host of others. Overhead, a variety of swallows and swifts can be seen in summer. This is one of the few places in Washington where our native western gray squirrel is found.

Wenas Creek (OC)

Wenas Creek can be visited two ways: from the north via Umtanum Road, and from the south via the Wenas-Naches Road. Umtanum Road from Ellensburg has a lot to offer, and goes through Western

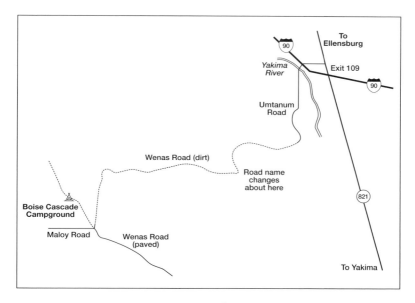

Wenas Creek Area

and Mountain Bluebird territory as it climbs from the valley floor. Golden Eagles often are seen soaring over the ridges, and a variety of other raptors are seen. Along the road in the dry pine forests, watch for Mountain Chickadee, White-headed Woodpecker, nuthatches, sapsuckers, and *Epidonax* flycatchers. Ring-necked pheasant, California Quail, Common Poorwill, and occasional Chukars are seen.

Umtanum Road, a former stagecoach road bordered by pines and aspens, goes over Ellensburg Pass on Umtanum Ridge, then south down to pavement at just about 20 miles. At the pavement, go 0.2 mile, turn right and go just under two miles, then left on Dry Creek Road to Wenas Campground. The bird list for this area is impressive. The Seattle Audubon Society has held annual campouts here in May for many years. The previously listed dryland species, plus Western Wood-Pewee, American Redstart, Vesper and Brewer's Sparrows, Western Screech-Owl, Flammulated and Great Horned Owl, Eastern Kingbird, Warbling Vireo, Downy Woodpecker, American Goldfinch, and many, many more, have been recorded here.

YAKIMA RIVER CANYON

Spectacular basalt cliffs look down on the scenic Yakima River Canyon. Several unique vegetation zones are found in the canyon: shrub-steppe, riparian, basalt cliffs, and talus slopes with rocky out-croppings. The canyon has the densest nesting area for birds of prey in the state. The cliffs ring with the early spring courtship rituals of Red-tailed Hawk, American Kestrel, Prairie Falcon, and Golden Eagle. Nearby, Northern Harrier, Osprey, and Ferruginous and Swainson's Hawks nest, and there is a possibility of others.

The Bureau of Land Management and The Nature Conservancy have enacted protection for 400 acres of cliff and native grassland habitat in Yakima Canyon. The Conservancy's preserve contains cliffs where the endangered basalt daisy grows, and a riparian habitat containing cottonwoods and willows, plus a small island. More than 200 species of birds nest in the canyon. Along with diurnal raptors, the basalt cliffs are used by Common Merganser, Rock Dove, Great Horned Owl, White-throated Swift, Violet-green and Cliff Swallows, Common Raven, and Canyon Wren.

The dwindling shrub-steppe habitat is utilized by Gray Partridge, California Quail, Horned Lark, Mountain Bluebird, Loggerhead Shrike, Brewer's Sparrow, Vesper Sparrow, and Western Meadowlark, plus rarities such as Long-billed Curlew, Sage Thrasher, and Sage Sparrow. Riparian and marshy surroundings support a vast mixture of species including Ruffed Grouse, Virginia Rail, Spotted Sandpiper, Western Screech-Owl, Downy Woodpecker, Willow Flycatcher, White-breasted Nuthatch, Marsh Wren, Gray Catbird, Cedar Waxwing, Warbling Vireo, Yellow-breasted Chat, Black-headed Grosbeak, and Fox Sparrow. Countless waterfowl, gulls, cranes, swallows, sparrows, and others use this diverse and interesting canyon.

The Yakima River Canyon Area is administered by the BLM Wenatchee Resource Area Office at 1133 N. Western Avenue, Wenatchee, WA 98801; (509) 662-4223. A Yakima River Canyon Bird List is available through both the Spokane and Wenatchee BLM offices.

VANTAGE

In 1914, the first ferry service at this site crossed the Columbia River. After two subsequent bridges of varying capacity, the present bridge was built and opened in 1961. Various waterfowl can be seen in the river and small bays, and the cliffs are home to swallows, swifts, and owls. High on the eastern ridgeline prance 16 life-size ponies, the artwork of David Govedare. From the eastern overlook off I-90, you can walk up the narrow trail to see the horses close up, and also scan the hillside and sky for Golden Eagles, quail, and a variety of songbirds.

Old Vantage Highway

The dry slopes of this area are covered with a mix of rabbitbrush, sagebrush, and greasewood dotted with a few patches of pines. Common Ravens and Red-tailed Hawks course the hillsides or placidly decorate the tops of utility poles. At the western end of the highway, before it starts its descent to the Columbia, we have seen Sage Thrasher; Long-billed Curlew; Western Meadowlark; and Brewer's, Sage, and Vesper Sparrows. Burrowing Owls once nested here, but have not been seen in recent years. Great Horned Owls nest in rocky outcroppings in the canyon, along with Rock Wrens. Shrikes are not uncommon; Loggerhead in summer, Northern in winter.

Ginkgo-Wanapum State Park

This area is a National Natural Landmark containing one of the world's most unique fossil forests. More than 200 trees entombed and petrified in molten lava have been identified. There are an interpretive trail, interpretive center, and museum to explore. The museum is on a cliff overlooking the Columbia River, a good vantage point from which to scan for raptors, migrant Sandhill Cranes, and waterfowl. For a change, you can look down on the abundant White-throated Swifts and Violet-green Swallows that nest on the cliffs. The ginkgo trees in the park attract a variety of interesting passerines including Northern Oriole, Lazuli Bunting, Rock Wren, hummingbirds, flycatchers, and warblers. Below the museum is a boat landing with a tiny cattail marsh that attracts migrant songbirds. The interpretive center is a mile up the Old Vantage Highway. A trail goes through this interesting habitat. There is no shade, so wear a hat, take water, and, of course, watch for rattlesnakes.

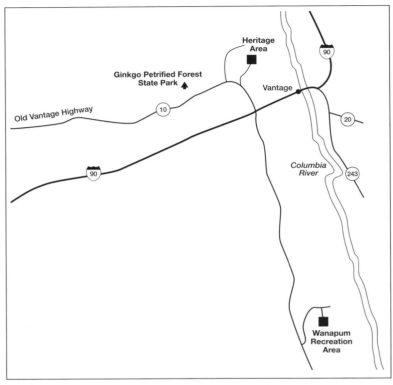

Ginkgo-Wanapum State Park

The campground part of the park is about three miles south of Vantage on the road along the river. Watch for Chukar along the road; near the road south of the park, Black-throated Sparrows have been seen in small numbers. A colony of Bank Swallows can be seen near the park boat launch. The park has 50 campsites with full hookups and all amenities. The park is between the Columbia River and Wanapum Lake. Information: Ginkgo-Wanapum State Park, Vantage, WA 98950; (509) 856-2700.

Chapter 8
Okanogan Highlands

Traveling through the Okanogan Highlands is like taking a step backward in time. The region is historical, virtually undiscovered by most tourists, and a mecca for those interested in backroad travel, high-plateau birding, mining, and a wonderful laid-back ambience.

This is high country—a land of ponderosa pine, Douglas-fir, and larch forests interspersed with extensive mountain meadows. The Selkirk Mountains, an extension of the Rockies, jut into the state near Metaline Falls. Granite and folded sedimentary rock are found throughout the region. A few higher peaks in the 6,000- to 7,000-foot range are found, but most of the region is gentle, rolling hill country. Rainfall is 15–25″ a year. Much of the wildlife is related to both the Cascade and Rocky mountains. Nowhere else in Washington can you find woodland caribou, moose, grizzly bear, and Great Gray Owls.

About 8% of the state is included in this region, taking in most of Okanogan, Ferry, Stevens, and Pend Oreille counties. The Colville, Okanogan, and Kanisku national forests, plus the Colville Indian Reservation, cover most of this remote area. The northern boundary is British Columbia, with Idaho to the east, the Columbia Basin to the south, and the Okanogan River to the west.

There are no large cities, but the towns of Omak, Tonasket, Republic, and Kettle Falls are more than adequate for anyone's needs. North-south routes include US 97 to the west, and, continuing eastward, SH 21, US 395, SH 25, and SH 31 are all good two-lane highways. Traffic is usually light. There is only one main east-west route, SH 20, which heads east out of Tonasket and snakes its way to Newport at the Idaho border.

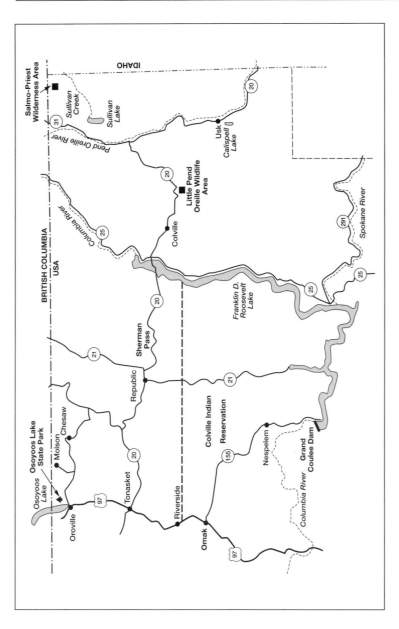

Okanogan Highlands

THE HIGH ROAD: OROVILLE TO BONAPARTE LAKE

As a collector of back roads, I find this route one of the best in the northeastern part of the state. It is fine raptor and songbird habitat, and many interesting migrants from the Okanagan Valley in British Columbia pass through. These grassy highlands were elevated above the reach of the Columbia Plateau lava flows. You can begin at Oroville, following signs east out of town toward Sidley, Lost Lakes, and Molson. At about 6.5 miles, turn north on Nine Mile Road and follow it almost 11 miles, past Sidley Lakes and along the Canadian border, to Old Molson.

The whole area has possibilities for Long-billed Curlew, Spruce and Blue Grouse, Black-backed and Three-toed Woodpeckers, White-winged Crossbill, Mountain Bluebird, Townsend's Solitaire, Lincoln and Fox Sparrows, and, in winter, Snow Bunting and Horned Lark. Golden Eagle, Northern Harrier, Red-tailed Hawk, American Kestrel, and Sharp-shinned Hawk are not uncommon. Great Gray Owl, Boreal Owl, and Northern Hawk-Owl are rarities, but possible in this part of the state.

Sidley Lakes are just before Molson along the south side of the road. Mallard, Blue-winged Teal, Northern Shoveler, Ruddy Duck, Red-winged and Brewer's Blackbirds, Belted Kingfisher, Virginia Rail, Sora, Willow Flycatcher, and Common Yellowthroat have been seen. The habitat around the lakes also could have Gray Catbird, Veery, Cedar Waxwing, and Pine Siskin.

Old Molson is worth a stop. There are rest rooms of a sort, a museum, and the remnants of a thriving mining town. Scan the fields for Savannah, Chipping, Brewer's, and Lark Sparrows. Violet-green Swallow, Common Nighthawk, Common Poorwill, Swainson's Hawk, American Goldfinch, and Ring-necked Pheasant can be seen, too. From Old Molson, continue toward Mary Anne Creek and Chesaw on the Molson-Summit Road. At 8.1 miles stay left on the Oroville-Toroda Creek Road and continue a mile to Chesaw. Chesaw is another community that was once a lively mining town, but no more.

Continue east, then south on the Oroville-Toroda Creek Road, eventually following the north fork of Beaver Creek. Common Raven, Northern Saw-whet Owl, Great Horned Owl, Mourning Dove, Tree Swallow, Spotted Sandpiper, Olive-sided Flycatcher, Western Wood-

Brewer's Blackbird

Pewee, kingbirds, Western Meadowlark, all three chickadees and nuthatches, Mountain Bluebird, House Wren, and Warbling Vireo can be seen. At Beaver Creek Campground, near the intersection of the Oroville-Toroda Creek Road and Bonaparte Lake Road, turn south on the Bonaparte Lake Road.

Bonaparte Lake is about three miles from the intersection, and there is a Forest Service campground at the southern end with 29 campsites. Scan the lake for Osprey, Canada Goose, Common Merganser, Mallard, teal, Redhead, Ruddy Duck, Pied-billed Grebe, American Coot, and others. Sora, Virginia Rail, Red-winged Blackbird, Common Snipe, Spotted Sandpiper, and Marsh Wren are also here. Continuing south on Bonaparte Lake Road for a little more than five miles will put you on SH 20 about halfway between Tonasket and Republic.

CURLEW LAKE STATE PARK

Two Osprey nests can be seen at this pleasant 130-acre campground. A high berm separates the lake and camp, but by climbing the berm or, better yet, camping at one of the berm-top sites, you can see both Osprey nests well, plus whatever is in the lake. American Kestrel, California Quail, Great Horned Owl, Cedar Waxwing, Common Raven, kingbirds, Brewer's and Red-winged Blackbirds, Mourning Dove, Violet-green Swallow, and a variety of songbirds are at the park. On the lake, Red-necked and Pied-billed Grebes, Canada Goose, Mallard, Common Merganser, goldeneyes, Northern Shoveler, and Ruddy Duck have been seen. At the north end of the lake, Bobolink have been reported.

Curlew Lake State Park is distinguished by having a Curlew at the top of its flagpole. The park, located in the middle of a gold-mining area, has 82 campsites, 18 with full hookups. Some facilities are wheelchair-accessible, and the park has all amenities. Curlew Lake is five miles north of Republic on SH 21. Information: Curlew Lake State Park, 974 Curlew Lake Street, Republic, WA 99166; (509) 775-3592.

COLVILLE NATIONAL FOREST

This National Forest of more than a million acres sits in Washington's far northeast corner, bordered by Canada and Idaho. Terrain is more gentle than to the west; mountains reach a maximum elevation of 7,309 feet at Gypsy Peak. Like many national forests, the Colville is divided into many parts across the northeastern tier of the state. Forests are predominately Douglas-fir and western hemlock, with some ponderosa pine, western larch, western white pine, grand fir, and lodgepole pine. Local native plants vary as to elevation.

Wildlife is quite diverse and includes endangered woodland caribou and grizzly bear. Great Gray Owls have been seen in the area of Sherman Pass, along with Boreal Owl and Northern Hawk-Owl. Eagles, all three accipiters, Northern Harrier, Red-tailed Hawk, Osprey, and other owls frequent these high forests. There are 25 campgrounds in the forest and more than 300 miles of hiking trails; most are sparsely traveled.

For information, including three brochures—"Birds of the Colville National Forest," "Reptiles and Amphibians of the Colville National Forest," and "Mammals of the Colville National Forest"—and a Colville National Forest Map, contact the U.S. Forest Service, Colville National Forest, 765 South Main, Federal Building, Colville, WA 99114; (509) 684-3711.

SHERMAN PASS

Sherman Pass at 5,575 feet is the state's highest mountain pass and is centrally located in the Colville National Forest. Several areas are part of the Sherman Pass National Scenic Byway.

White Mountain Fire

This is the site of a 20,000-acre forest fire ignited by a lightning strike in 1988. The subsequent open, upper elevation areas now provide chances to find large groups of Mountain Bluebirds as they stage for migration in early September. Abundant snags and regenerating forest furnish habitat for woodpeckers and other open-country birds. Scan the burn area for possible Williamson's Sapsucker; White-headed, Black-backed, and Three-toed Woodpeckers; Common Flicker; California Quail; Ruffed Grouse; and Savannah, Grasshopper, Chipping, Vesper's, and Brewer's Sparrows. The White Mountain Fire area can be seen at the crest of Sherman Pass on SH 20.

Bangs Mountain Auto Tour

This scenic, self-guided auto tour follows Canyon Creek for about two miles, then heads up Donaldson Draw until it reaches the Bangs Mountain Scenic Vista in another two miles. There are spectacular views of the Columbia River from the top. During the spring and early summer, you can find booming Blue Grouse, drumming Ruffed Grouse, and gobbling Wild Turkeys. The auto tour heads south off SH 20 just before the Canyon Creek Campground.

Sherman Creek Habitat Management Area

This 7,508-acre refuge for white-tailed and mule deer, Ring-necked Pheasant, and grouse is located in the foothills between Roosevelt Lake and the Kettle Mountains. Black bear, wolverine, red fox, lynx, bobcat, coyote, several bats, Columbian ground squirrel, and occasional moose are a few mammalian residents that might be seen. This area is bunchgrass with scattered groves of ponderosa pine, which rise to heavier stands of Douglas-fir above 3,500 feet. Bald and Golden Eagles; Merriam's Turkey; Ruffed, Blue, and Spruce Grouse; Canada Goose; Tundra Swan; American Kestrel; Cooper's Hawk; Three-toed and Lewis' Woodpeckers; Violet-green Swallow; Mountain Chickadee; kinglets; nuthatches; finches; crossbills; Cedar Waxwing; Steller's Jay; and Clark's Nutcracker are found here.

FRANKLIN D. ROOSEVELT LAKE

Franklin D. Roosevelt Lake, which stretches for more than 130 miles from Grand Coulee Dam into British Columbia, floods almost 100,000 acres. Coulee Dam National Recreational Area's 660 miles of shoreline stretches along the reservoir, and is dotted with campgrounds and boat launching facilities. A variety of habitats lie in the area: rolling hills and rocky outcroppings with ponderosa pine, grasses and sage, and mixed conifer forest. Due to its location on a secondary flyway, the lake attracts many migrating waterfowl. Watch for Canada Goose; Mallard; Green-winged, Blue-winged, and Cinnamon Teal; Northern Pintail; American Wigeon; Northern Shoveler; Redhead;

Ring-necked Duck; Common and Barrow's Goldeneyes; Lesser Scaup; Common Merganser; and Ruddy Duck.

Raptors, both diurnal and nocturnal, are fairly common in this area. Northern Goshawk; Cooper's and Sharp-shinned Hawks; Red-tailed, Rough-legged, and Swainson's Hawks; Northern Harrier; Bald and Golden Eagles; American Kestrel; Prairie Falcon; Great Horned Owl; Western Screech-Owl; Northern Pygmy-Owl; and Barred Owl are seen. A melange of land birds can be seen, including six species of swallows; Steller's and Gray Jays; American Dipper; Eastern and Western Kingbirds; Orange-crowned, Nashville, Yellow, Yellow-rumped, and MacGillivray's Warblers; Solitary and Red-eyed Vireos; and many more.

Two free ferries, the Keller and the Gifford, cross Lake Roosevelt; both are on the Colville Indian Reservation. Watch for waterfowl, nesting Ospreys, and marsh birds.

For information on the many campgrounds and to obtain a check-list of wildlife within the Coulee Dam National Recreation Area, contact the Kettle Falls Ranger District, Route 1, Box 537, Kettle Falls, WA 99141, or phone the Coulee Dam National Recreation Area at (509) 633-9441.

BIG MEADOW LAKE

Big Meadow Lake is one of several areas being developed as a Watchable Wildlife Site. When finished, the area will be signed for easy location, and will provide rest rooms and some handicapped access. Birding should be very good, as the area provides open, forested, riparian, and aquatic habitats. There is a wildlife viewing platform at the west end of the lake. Scan the lake for Canada Goose, Northern Pintail, teal, goldeneyes, Bufflehead, Redhead, and Ring-necked Duck. Osprey nest in the area, and a variety of other raptors can be seen. Northern Oriole, Evening Grosbeak, Lazuli Bunting, American Goldfinch, plus warblers and sparrows, also can be seen in the area.

Mammals such as beaver, white-tailed and mule deer, and moose are here. There is a U.S. Forest Service campground at the lake. Big Meadow Lake is located west of Ione. Take Smackout Pass Road west, then Meadow Road (FSR 2695) to the lake.

PEND OREILLE AREA

Pend Oreille (pond o-REY) is a name given the local Indians by French-Canadian fur traders, meaning "hanging ears." Evidently, the earlier natives wore ear ornaments that stretched the ear lobes to some extent. Pend Oreille is also a county, a river, and a land of rolling pine forests. Wildflowers, Rocky Mountain wildlife types, and a host of birds are in the area. Two wildlife habitat management areas, the large Little Pend Oreille HMA, and the smaller Leclerc Creek HMA, are located here.

Little Pend Oreille Habitat Management Area

The Little Pend Oreille HMA, 4,155 acres, is about 80% mountainous yellow pine forest managed to benefit white-tailed deer. It is bordered partly by the Little Pend Oreille River on the north, the Colville National Forest to the south, and the Kaniksu National Forest on the east. There are nearly 200 miles of roads and trails, seven campgrounds, two lakes, and 62 miles of trout streams for visitors to enjoy. Black bear, mink, beaver, muskrat, and several species of bats also are found here. Rocky Mountain species that come into this area include red squirrel, Columbian ground squirrel, red-tailed chipmunk, and western jumping mouse. The area is a transition zone between many eastern and western species. Bald and Golden Eagles, Red-tailed Hawk, accipiters, Great Blue Heron, Common Merganser, Barrow's Goldeneye, grouse, Common Snipe, Barred and Flammulated Owls, swallows, Vaux's swift, Common Yellowthroat, and a variety of other land birds can be found.

Two lakes are in the area, Bayley and McDowell. The Little Pend Oreille is located just south of SH 20 and about 14 miles east of Colville. There is a Little Pend Oreille Information Site at Gillette Lake, about six miles further east. There are also several lakes with campgrounds in this area.

Leclerc Creek Habitat Management Area

The Leclerc Creek HMA's 893 acres are divided into a few scattered plots along the shore of the Pend Oreille River. It is an impor-

Barrow's Goldeneye

tant nucleus for future procurement of critical wildlife habitat in the Pend Oreille River Valley. There is good birding for evergreen, mixed forest, waterside brush, and open meadows species. The area is managed primarily for Ruffed Grouse, mule deer, and black bear, plus trout and spiny ray fishing. Nesting Hooded Merganser, Mallard, Ring-necked Duck, and Green-winged Teal are found here. Great Blue Heron, Tundra Swan, Golden and Bald Eagles, Osprey, grebes, and a variety of shorebirds also use the area. In the upland habitats are Blue, Spruce, and Ruffed Grouse; Common Snipe; Northern Waterthrush; Pileated, Three-toed, and Hairy Woodpeckers; American Kestrel; and accipiters; plus warblers, crossbills, and finches.

Leclerc Creek HMA is on SH 31, north from Cusick or south from Ione, or you can drive along Leclerc Creek Road on the east side of the river. There are small signs designating the state lands and river access.

SULLIVAN LAKE

Sullivan Lake is the largest lake in the Colville National Forest at 3.5 miles in length, and lies at 2,583 feet in elevation. Bighorn sheep are seen in the area on Hall Mountain, east of the lake, and in the Maitlen Creek Research Natural Area. Surrounding forests contain pines and rather large stands of aspens and cottonwoods. There are plenty of open meadows and small streams. Common Loon are on this deep, clear, blue lake, plus many other species, but viewing is probably best in the off-season when campers are few. Several rarities have been sighted in the area.

Sullivan Creek is at the north end of the lake and flows east along FR 22 to Salmo Mountain. This is one of the few areas in the national forest where Harlequin Ducks are recorded with reliability. There is documented nesting data for this location. Riparian woodland birds are numerous here, such as Northern Oriole; American Redstart; Northern Waterthrush; Yellow, Nashville, Wilson's, and Yellow-rumped Warblers; Red-eyed Vireo; and occasional Yellow-breasted Chat. In the campgrounds, Winter Wren, Song Sparrow, Swainson's Thrush, nuthatches, chickadees, kinglets, and Cedar Waxwing might be seen. American Dipper is here, too.

Sullivan Lake Trail #504

This easy, hikers-only trail with an elevation gain of only 320 feet skirts the eastern shore of Sullivan Lake. It starts in shady creekside areas, then traverses open, rocky slopes and passes through both evergreen and alder forests between Sullivan Lake Campground and Noisy Creek Campground. Hall Mountain, with its prolific herd of bighorn sheep, looms behind the trail and over the lake; occasionally, sheep are near the trail. Instead of the four-mile return hike, you can go one way, perhaps hitching a return ride back with a fellow birder from the opposite campground. The trailhead is adjacent to Sullivan Lake Campground off FR 22.

Along the trail, watch for pika, marmots, deer, and bear, and on the lake, watch for Western and Pied-billed Grebes, Northern Pintail, teal, Redhead, Ring-necked Duck, goldeneyes, and Ruddy Duck. Forested areas yield Steller's and Gray Jays, Pileated Woodpecker, Brown Creeper, Varied and Hermit Thrushes, vireos, warblers, Fox Sparrow, and more. Raptors, Ring-billed Gull, Common Nighthawk, Vaux's Swift, and swallows can be seen overhead.

SALMO-PRIEST WILDERNESS AREA

The Salmo-Priest Wilderness Area, in the far northeastern corner of the state, is bordered by Canada on the north, Idaho on the east, and the Colville and Kaniksu national forests to the south and west. Gypsy Peak, the highest mountain in eastern Washington, is located in this huge, roadless area that covers a big part of the Selkirk Mountain Range. The area is very heavily forested except for high mountain ridges. The Salmo Research Natural Area, with nearly 1,400 acres, was created to protect wildlife species such as grizzly bear, lynx, gray wolf, and caribou. Bald and Golden Eagles are seen here, as are Spruce, Blue, and Ruffed Grouse. Several bird species—such as White-winged Crossbill, Pine Grosbeak, and Boreal Chickadee—reach the limits of their range in this area. A great variety of birds and mammals live in this remote setting.

To get some idea of what the country is like, take forest roads from the Sullivan Lake area into a long "peninsula" extending between two arms of the wilderness area. Forest Road 22/2220, which extends for more than 15 miles up this peninsula, finally ends at Salmo Mountain at 6,828 feet elevation, which is on the border of the very northern section of the wilderness. Stopping along the way to search for a variety of birds can be interesting.

CALISPELL LAKE

Calispell Lake is a special delight in mid-March when more than 4,500 Tundra Swans, 10,000 geese, and more than 20,000 ducks con-

gregate to rest on their way to northern breeding grounds. The surrounding fields are filled with foraging ducks and geese. Late in summer, there are huge Osprey concentrations. Early wintertime is also
good for waterfowl. Calispell Lake is about two miles long, fed by
Calispell Creek, which starts west of Grayback Mountain, passes
through the lake, and joins the Pend Oreille River at Cusick. The area
has acres of wetlands around the lake, and many species of waterfowl
can be seen. To reach Calispell Lake, go west of Usk on Bowman
Road (west of SH 20), then south on McKinzie Road. You will come
to the lake in a mile, and there are roads encircling the lake that also
go by the fields.

McLOUGHLIN CANYON

To reach McLoughlin Canyon, turn east on Janis Road from US 97
four miles south of Tonasket. The narrow canyon soon begins and is
an easily approached version of some of the more remote canyons.
Rugged rocky cliffs and outcroppings, brushy areas, and pine-forested
slopes provided a good spot for the only battle between Indians and
the white man in north-central Washington. The canyon also provides
habitat for interesting bird species. Look for American Kestrel, Red-
tailed Hawk, Gray Partridge, California Quail, grouse, Rock and
Mourning Doves, Northern Pygmy-Owl, Long-eared Owl, Great
Horned Owl, White-throated and Vaux's Swifts, hummingbirds, Red-
naped Sapsucker, Downy Woodpecker, Willow Flycatcher, Tree Swallow, Gray Jay, Black-billed Magpie, Black-capped and Mountain
Chickadees, House Wren, Sage Thrasher, Warbling Vireo, Yellow and
MacGillivray's Warblers, Chipping Sparrow, and American Goldfinch.

CRAWFISH LAKE

Every October, we wind our way out of Riverside on Highway 97
and up the Tunk Creek Road to Crawfish Lake. Our plan is to inter-
cept a peak Rough-legged Hawk migration through the Okanogan
highlands. The route leads from farmlands along the Okanogan River
up through rolling, rocky, high plateau country. Tunk Road is edged
with more than 100 Mountain Bluebird boxes, and the bright flash of

Black-billed Magpie

the male's azure plumage is common in the summertime. Wild sun-flowers and lupine add more color to the roadside.

Crawfish Lake, located in the Okanogan National Forest at an ele-vation of 4,475 feet, straddles the northern boundary of the Colville Confederated Tribal lands. The southern half of the lake is in the reservation; the northern half is bordered by a comfortable, free national forest campground complete with nesting Ospreys. During fall trips, we have been lulled to sleep (and awakened!) by a family of Barred Owls calling back and forth.

Besides Osprey and Barred Owls, there are many songbirds, Ruffed and Blue Grouse, ducks, and other birds. On one trip, a Sharp-shinned Hawk hunted in the campground for more than an hour. Another time, a Northern Goshawk was present. Waterbirds spotted on the lake have been Common Loon, Redhead, Barrow's Goldeneye, Ruddy Duck, Common Merganser, Mallard, and Great Blue Heron. In the fall, the campground has Dark-eyed Juncos, American Robins, and the usual resident forest birds including Varied Thrush. While traveling nearby roads, we have seen Great Horned Owl, Black-billed Magpie, California Quail, Northern Harrier, Northern Pygmy-Owl, Ring-necked Pheasant, Mourning Dove, Boreal Chickadee, and others.

In 1992 we made an early August trip, and the campground was full of young juncos, Yellow-rumped Warblers, and Mountain Chickadees. Other species seen were Williamson's Sapsucker, Western Tanager, Wilson's Warbler, Clark's Nutcracker, Pine Siskin, Brown Creeper, Red-breasted Nuthatch, Common Raven, and Ospreys (still in the nest). Close to the campground were Red-tailed Hawks, Pileated Woodpecker, Common Flicker, Western Meadowlark, Cedar Waxwings, both Eastern and Western Kingbirds, and Brewer's and Red-winged Blackbirds.

There is a small herd of Rocky Mountain elk nearby that spends much of its time on the reservation side of Crawfish Lake. The surrounding forest of predominantly western larch, lodgepole pine, and western white pine is good habitat for the solitary and nocturnal Canada lynx, which preys almost entirely on snowshoe hare. Deer, cougar, porcupine, black bear, flying squirrels, and many other small mammals also are found nearby. Of Washington's 16 bat species, we saw little brown Myotis and hoary bats near the lake.

The campground has 15 single-family sites, four multi-family sites and a picnic area. All sites have picnic tables and fire grills. Because the campground is situated in fairly dense forest, some of the campsites have a bit of privacy, something hard to find in most state and public parks. There are toilets, but there is no piped drinking water. Water is available about a mile up the road at a spring, but it is suggested that you bring your own. The campground can accommodate campers up to 31 feet long. If you fish the northern half of the lake, only a Washington State Fishing License is necessary, but to fish the entire lake, you need a tribal permit from the Tribal Council in Nespelem. A boat launch is located at the lake, and there are plenty of places to pull a small boat out near many of the campsites.

Crawfish Lake is 15 miles northeast of Omak. From Omak, continue north on 97 for seven miles to Riverside, head east on the Tunk Creek Road (County Road 9320) for 17 miles, then 1.5 miles south on FR 30, and, finally, southeast for 400 yards on FR Road 30100 to the campground. Or you can head 8.5 miles north from Disautel on State Route 155 (between Omak and Nespelem). All these roads are paved or good gravel, and they are signed.

TUNK AND AENEAS VALLEYS

The high country of the Tunk and Aeneas Valleys is a wonderful spot for viewing all sorts of raptors in the fall. Golden Eagle, Prairie and Peregrine Falcons, Red-tailed and Rough-legged Hawks, American Kestrel, an occasional Swainson's Hawk, Sharp-shinned and Cooper's Hawks, Northern Harrier, Turkey Vulture, and Osprey all pass by eventually, some quite often. Sandhill Cranes, Black-crowned Night Herons, Canada Geese, and many songbirds are also migrants. In mid-August, we were fortunate to see a group of nearly 30 Common Nighthawks heading south. Coyotes and deer also can be seen in daylight hours.

Any of the roads heading north off the Tunk Creek Road (while on your way to Crawfish Lake) are good for viewing migrants. The Aeneas Valley can be reached from Crawfish Lake by turning right when leaving the campground entrance and following Forest Road 30 (sometimes called Peterson Road)—*watch for wild log trucks!*—for about nine miles until reaching the Aeneas Valley Road. Turning left will take you through the valley and, after about nine miles, you will reach State Route 20. Turn left and continue for about 13 miles, and you will come to Tonasket. There are several "recreation" areas along the valley road, mostly man-made lakes with water from the Sanpoil River. Songbirds and waterfowl are common during migration.

COLVILLE INDIAN RESERVATION

The Colville Indian Reservation covers 1.3 million acres of north-central Washington state. More than 7,700 individuals are members of the Colville Confederated Tribes. Chief Joseph, the leader of the Nez Perce, and Chief Moses, leader of the Wenatchee and Sinkiuse, both lie buried near Nespelem, where tribal headquarters is located. The reservation is bordered by the Columbia and Okanogan rivers and the Colville National Forest. Outstanding birding can be found on the reservation. American Kestrel, Blue Grouse, Virginia Rail, Spotted Sandpiper, Long-billed Curlew, Common Snipe, Calliope Hummingbird, Common Nighthawk, Clark's Nutcracker, Dusky and Hammond's Flycatchers, Hairy and Lewis' Woodpeckers, Northern Oriole, Nashville and Orange-crowned Warblers, Rock Wren, Cassin's Finch, Lazuli Bunting, and Chipping and Song Sparrows were only some species seen on a recent Breeding Bird Survey on the Owhi Watershed within the reservation.

Reservations are not public lands; visitors are allowed to drive paved and unpaved roads, but not to hunt, camp, picnic, cut wood, or collect specimens of any kind. To bird at spots on the reservation other than the main highways, stop at tribal headquarters and obtain a permit. SH 21 splits the reservation north to south from south of Republic to Roosevelt Lake. SH 155 starts at Omak and goes east, then south through the reservation to end at Grand Coulee Dam. Information: Colville Confederated Tribes, P.O. Box 150, Nespelem, WA 99155; (509) 634-4711.

Omak Lake

Omak Lake is narrow—eight miles long—and on the Colville Indian Reservation. Historically, the Indians called the lake Omache, meaning "good medicine," as it was thought to have medicinal qualities. There is no outlet for the lake save for evaporation since there is not enough rainfall to keep the basin full. Consequently, salt and sodium carbonate provide a bitter, soapy taste, enough to deter fish from living here. Birds, however, abound along the lake's riparian and dry, brushy habitats. Look for California Quail, Mourning Dove, Great Horned Owl, Long-eared Owl, Vaux's Swift, Calliope and Rufous

Hummingbirds, Downy Woodpecker, Northern Flicker, Western Wood-Pewee, Say's Phoebe, Hammonds and Dusky Flycatchers, kingbirds, swallows, Steller's Jay, Common Raven, Black-capped and Mountain Chickadees, Golden and Ruby-crowned Kinglets, Hermit Thrush, and a variety of warblers and sparrows.

Omak Lake is about six miles south of the town of Omak. Between the lake and the Okanogan River about 10–15 miles to the west lie a multitude of small lakes, ponds, and wetlands. Roads go to some of the areas, and a variety of waterfowl can be seen, including Common Merganser, Wood Duck, Bufflehead, Canada Goose, Mallard, and Ring-necked Duck. Great Blue Heron, Common Snipe, Virginia Rail, and a variety of raptors also have been seen. Geology is varied in the area, and at the lake spectacular rock formations soar upward from the water.

Chapter 9
Columbia Plateau

The massive Columbia Plateau encompasses 30% of the land area in the state. Great glaciers of ice ages past carved out this giant basin. The Columbia River's meanderings further eroded the landscape, and the great Spokane Floods from thousands of years ago also left their mark. At least four million years of concentrated lava activity created the 200,000-square-mile plateau that covers central and southeastern Washington, most of eastern Oregon, northeastern California, and a far west strip of Idaho. It is one of the largest basalt flows in the world.

The Columbia Plateau is also a very fertile land. Asparagus, hops, and barley are important crops, and wine grapes from the Yakima valley are world-class. But wheat is the state's leading crop, and nearly all of it grows on this alluvial plateau. Gigantic blocks of black basalt, called glacial erratics, can be seen throughout the wheat lands. These erratics, resembling huge haystacks, broke off from the northern edge of the Columbia Plateau and were carried south by the advancing ice sheet to be left hit-and-miss across the landscape.

The driest and warmest region of the state, the Columbia Plateau is distinguished by a shrub-steppe plant community and countless acres of marshes, ponds, and lakes created from the Columbia Plateau Project irrigation waters. These "potholes"—the area surrounding Moses Lake is a fine example—create abundant habitats for ducks, American Avocets, gulls, terns, and many other migratory species. Mule deer and coyotes are abundant, and Golden Eagles and Prairie Falcons are not uncommon in this high desert country.

Douglas, Grant, Lincoln, Spokane, Adams, Whitman, Franklin, Benton, and parts of Pend Oreille, Stevens, Ferry, Kittitas, Yakima, and Klickitat counties make up the Columbia Plateau.

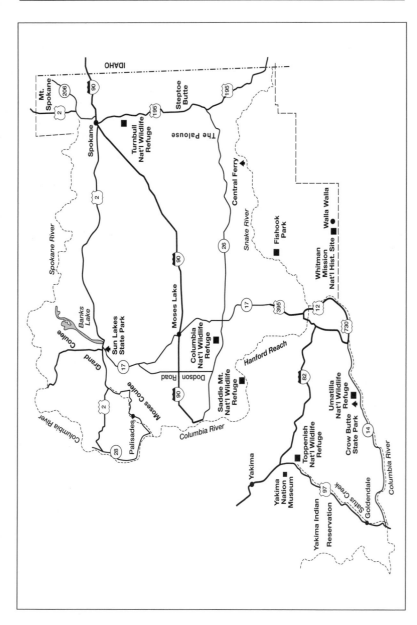

Columbia Plateau

The Columbia River, containing one-third of the potential water power of the United States, is one of the most valuable resources of the region. The Grand Coulee Dam on the Columbia River is the most massive dam in the world; it is taller than a 46-story building and more than 12 city blocks long. One-hundred-fifty-mile-long Franklin D. Roosevelt Lake, created by Coulee Dam, is the state's largest and extends north into British Columbia. Irrigation projects along the Coulee Dam and many other dams on the Columbia support a $3 billion agriculture industry.

CENTRAL FERRY CANYON

This beautiful canyon is a Columbian Sharp-tailed Grouse habitat management area. At one time, tens of thousands of Sharptails ranged across eastern Washington—the most abundant game bird in the northwest. Now, fewer than a thousand are found. The Sharptail is found primarily in bunch-grass habitat, sometimes in yellow-pine areas. This elegant grouse has a yen for nesting in farm fields and, unfortunately, this has added to its decline. The Sharptail, like the Sage Grouse, has a rather riotous mating "dance," usually in the early hours near dawn.

Other species found in the Central Ferry Canyon in summer are Red-tailed Hawk, American Kestrel, Common Raven, Common Nighthawk, Grasshopper Sparrow, Horned Lark, Burrowing Owl, Sage Thrasher, and Lark Sparrow. In winter, a variety of raptors can be seen plus Northern Shrike and, occasionally, Snow Buntings.

To reach Central Ferry Canyon from Brewster, take US 97 across the Columbia River Bridge going south, turn west on Cranes Road for a little more than two miles, then head south on Central Ferry Road. At about 11 miles (you are now on the plateau), continue on Dyer Hill Road for a few more miles (the road makes several right-angle turns across the plateau) until you reach Bridgeport Hill Road. Follow this road south until reaching SH 172. To reach US 2, follow SH 172 west five miles, then south for 14 miles.

BRIDGEPORT STATE PARK

This is a nice state park to use as a base for exploring the Columbia River and the surrounding mesas and farmlands. Bridgeport State

Park lies along the shore of 51-mile-long Rufus Woods Lake Reservoir. Chief Joseph Dam, two miles downstream, stretches a mile across the river and rises 236 feet from bedrock; it is the third-highest dam on the Columbia. Canada Goose, Common Merganser, scaup, Northern Pintail, American Wigeon, and a variety of other waterfowl can be seen. The park also has 825 acres of lawn and shade trees surrounded by natural habitat where California Quail, Gray Partridge, Chukar, Horned Lark, Western Kingbird, Rock Wren, Northern Oriole, a variety of songbirds, marmots, coyotes, mule deer, and rattlesnakes live. In winter, Bohemian Waxwings are regular, and Common Redpoll and Snow Bunting may be seen.

Bridgeport State Park has 30 campsites, 20 with hookups, and all amenities plus an adjacent nine-hole golf course. The park lies three miles northeast of Bridgeport off SH 17. Information: Bridgeport State Park, P.O. Box 846, Bridgeport, WA 98813; (509) 686-7231.

U.S. HIGHWAY 2

The section of US 2 east of the Cascades should be named "the birder's highway." The volume of traffic is relatively low, there is plenty of room to pull off on the road edge, and the view is unobstructed. This is wheat country. During the spring and fall migrations, thousands of ducks, geese, raptors, Sandhill Cranes, and songbirds pass above the high, rolling countryside.

The farm roads are great for exploring. They run in a crisscross, grid-type pattern of north-south and east-west. Most are good gravel even though clearly marked "Primitive Road." These roads are excellent for birding, but after heavy rains—*beware!* Winter road edges can yield Gray-crowned Rosy Finches, Snow Buntings, the ubiquitous Horned Lark, Gray Partridge, plus raptors and Common Ravens.

People density is low, and the towns along this route are small, but adequate, for food, gas, and other amenities. Almost every small town has a park—many with large, old trees. Not only do these parks offer a glimpse of the local passerine population, they are usually good rest stops, especially in the hot summer.

US 2 and US 97 leave East Wenatchee together and head north along the Columbia River through apple, cherry, and peach groves. At the town of Orondo, elevation 765 feet, US 2 heads east and begins a

Sandhill Crane

climb through Corbaley and Pine Canyons before reaching the Waterville Plateau, elevation 2,812 feet. At a pullout about a third of the way up, there are two large deciduous trees planted by Louis F. Yonko in 1955 "with the hope that weary travelers could enjoy their shade and tranquility." Their shade is a good spot from which to look out across the winding, open canyon land for Golden Eagle, Great Horned Owl, Common Nighthawk, Sage Thrasher, Canyon Wren, and a variety of sparrows.

St. Andrews

St. Andrews, for birding purposes, is two roads on the high plateau just west of Banks Lake. It is a reliable area to see migrating Sandhill

Cranes in April and the fall. Many flocks of hundreds of birds pass through, keeping together with their wild calls and sometimes settling in the fields. Driving these roads and other farm roads in the area can be extremely rewarding for raptors and also migrant songbirds. We have seen Ferruginous and Swainson's Hawks, Golden Eagle, Sage Grouse, Loggerhead Shrike, and many others. Long-eared Owls are known to nest in the riparian areas. St. Andrews South Road (heading north!) is just about four miles west of Banks Lakes on US 2.

GRAND COULEE

The *American Heritage Dictionary* defines a coulee as "a deep gulch or ravine formed by rainstorms or melting snow." Washington's Grand Coulee is recognized as the most outstanding example of glacial and flood drainage in the world.

Grand Coulee is actually two coulees, the Upper and Lower, which are joined at Dry Falls. Blocked by thousands of feet of ice 10,000 years ago, the Columbia River's course was pushed westward at the Big Bend. Floodwater from the glacial Lakes Missoula and Columbia pushed the waters of the river ever higher until it flowed onto the lava plateau at the head of the Upper Grand Coulee and began its work of scouring out the huge canyons and ravines we see today. Centuries later, the river returned to its regular channel, leaving the coulees dry.

Dry Falls Interpretive Center

Dry Falls represents the skeleton of one of the largest waterfalls in geological history. In prehistoric times, the Columbia River fell over 350 feet from the Upper Grand Coulee as it wound its way to the Pacific Ocean. It was once 3.5 miles wide and created the chasm of the Lower Grand Coulee, now partially filled with water from Banks Lake. The interpretive center has an excellent exhibit that explains the phenomena of the river, the coulees, and the high country called the Columbia Plateau.

The lookout from Dry Falls is expansive. White-throated Swifts are often at eye level as they dip and turn on the clifftop air currents. Raptors are found on or above the cliffs, and swallows, doves, and quail inhabit the rocky surroundings.

Sun Lakes State Park

Sun Lakes State Park is just south of the Dry Falls Interpretive Center. Sun Lakes is actually ten lakes of varying sizes—some large, such as Park Lake across from the campgrounds, and some small, such as Mirror Lake behind the campground. The 4,000-acre park has excellent birding and is one of the best spots to see huge creches of Canada Goose goslings. Geese nest around the lake, on the hilly areas, and on the high cliffs to the east. In April, the young are mostly past the small downy stage and are gathered into large groups, or creches. The geese stay on the east side of the lake on the lawns under the large willows. Yellow-bellied marmots also have young here and can be seen just across the road to the east around the houses.

Sun Lakes is a busier campground than many others mentioned, but it is quite pleasant and is ideally sited for investigating the Grand Coulee and its many species of birds. The area is a good representation of what might be found at many of the parks and lakes in this part of the state. Spring and fall are best for birds and for less campground bustle. The park is located in the coulee and is surrounded by cliffs with nesting Red-tailed Hawk, American Kestrel, Rock Dove, Great Horned Owl, White-throated Swift, Gray-crowned Rosy Finch, and Cliff Swallow. Rock Wren, California Quail, and Lazuli Bunting are usually in the brushy, rocky areas around the base of the cliffs. In April, Sandhill Cranes often are seen migrating overhead by the hundreds.

On Park Lake, scan for Common Loon, Western and Pied-billed Grebes, goldeneyes, Bufflehead, Redhead, Mallard, Franklin's and Ring-billed Gulls, Black and Caspian Terns, Lesser Scaup, and American Coot. Great Blue Heron, Black-crowned Night-Heron, Virginia Rail, Sora, Red-winged and Yellow-headed Blackbirds, and Marsh Wren can be found in the cattail and brushy edgings. Overhead, Violet-green, Barn, and Tree Swallows cavort.

Just past the campground is a well-signed road that turns east to Deep Lake and Camp Delaney, an environmental learning center for groups; both are within a mile or two of the campground. The road to Deep Lake winds by some small lakes, then cliffs on the south and, finally, open sagebrush country. Watch for a variety of species including Northern Harrier, Golden Eagle, Prairie Falcon, Western Meadowlark, Long-billed Curlew, Mountain Bluebird, Mourning Dove,

Common Nighthawk, Loggerhead Shrike (Northern Shrike in winter), Common Raven, Black-billed Magpie, Ring-necked Pheasant, Killdeer, American Robin, Western Tanager, and many more.

The road to Camp Delaney continues across the sagebrush flat for half a mile. Park at the barred gate and walk the road a short distance to the camp. Delaney Spring and its small shallow lake sometimes has ducks and marsh birds. Northern Orioles nest in the trees near the lake. A variety of desert birds are here, plus riparian species and raptors, including Golden Eagle and Prairie Falcon, which nest on nearby cliffs.

Sun Lakes State Park is located seven miles south of Coulee City on SH 17. There are 193 campsites—18 with full hookups—in the state park campground; some facilities are wheelchair-accessible. There also is a concession-run Sun Lakes Park Resort within the park, which has 112 campsites with full hookups plus rather rustic, air-conditioned cabins along the lakefront. All amenities are here including a small store, tackle shop, and horses for riding. Information: Sun Lakes State Park, Star Route 1, P.O. Box 136, Coulee City, WA 99115; (509) 632-5583.

BANKS LAKE

Banks Lake is a 30-mile-long, man-made reservoir. Water is pumped 280 feet uphill from Lake Roosevelt behind Grand Coulee Dam before flowing into Banks Lake. The water then continues from the equalizing reservoir, through Dry Falls Dam and into the main canal, and, finally, across 500,000 acres of farmlands. SH 155 borders the eastern edge and provides access to many recreational activities. Birding, hiking, and camping are excellent, and trout, perch, walleye, crappie, large- and small-mouth bass, kokanee, and whitefish are what fishermen seek—even through winter's ice—in this 24,900-acre water paradise.

The extensive grassy fields stretching between SH 155 and Banks Lake as you travel north from Coulee City can offer good views of Northern Harriers, perhaps transferring prey from male to female in flight during the spring nesting season. American White Pelicans, Redheads, Canada Geese, and grebes can be found at the edges of the small bays.

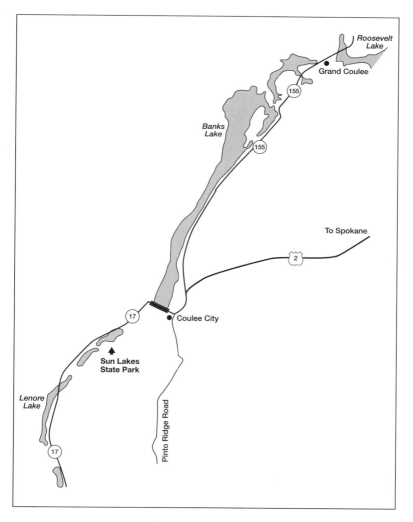

Banks Lake/Sun Lake Area

At 7.7 miles from the intersection of US 2/SH 155 is a sign, "Banks Lake-Bureau of Reclamation," which is a pullout above the lake. Here, look high on the cliffs and over the shore for an active and noisy colony of White-throated Swifts in spring and summer.

Coulee City

Coulee City, the oldest platted town in Grant County, is located on US 2 on the floor of the Grand Coulee and at the southern tip of Banks Lake. Agriculture and recreation go hand in hand in Coulee City: several million bushels of Big Bend wheat (of the Columbia River, not Texas) are shipped from Coulee City annually, and three state parks are within a 15-mile radius.

Coulee City Community Park is at the north edge of town on Banks Lake. In spring and summer, Ring-billed Gulls congregate under the park sprinklers and nest on nearby islands along with California Gulls. Clark's Grebe, Canada Goose, Killdeer, American Robin, Mallard, Brewer's and Red-winged Blackbirds, and Northern Orioles are also at the park. A mile or so east on US 2, Northern Harriers and Swainson's Hawks often are seen.

US 2 passes over Dry Falls Dam at the western edge of Coulee City. Look north to the lake for grebes, gulls, loons, and waterfowl, and south to a potholed wetland for teal, phalaropes, and a variety of other birds.

Steamboat Rock State Park

About midway in Banks Lake, an extensive grassy peninsula ending in the massive monolith of Steamboat Rock curves into the lake. The state park, one of Washington's newest and nearly always full in summer (reservation definitely required), covers most of the area. The park's 900 acres support 100 campsites with full hookups, five tent-only sites, 12 boat-in sites, and 21 planned new sites. There are also boat launches and everything else a primitive camp doesn't have.

Trails up Steamboat Rock lead to 640 acres of summit plateau with trails, wildlife, and excellent views of the lakes and surrounding countryside. The whole Grand Coulee area is in the Pacific Flyway, and waterfowl are especially numerous during migration. Information:

Steamboat Rock State Park, P.O. Box 370, Electric City, WA 99123-0370; (509) 633-1304.

Northrup Canyon

This lovely canyon covers 3,120 acres and contains the only natural forest in Grant County. Here you are surrounded by high basalt cliffs and can see and hear the calls, in spring and summer, of Mourning Dove, Black-billed Magpie, Northern Flicker, Rock Wren, truly wild Rock Doves, American Kestrel, Northern Oriole, Western Wood-Pee-wee, Common Nighthawk, and many others.

Northrup Canyon is the juxtaposition of history, ecology, and geology. The run-down buildings of a 19th-century farm are near a modern park ranger dwelling; the evergreen forests intermingle with stage-brush-steppe habitat, and the lava flows are not as old as the basalt cliffs that lie on a bed of granite. It is a miniature Grand Coulee and one of the few such canyons not on private land.

For the adventuresome, a hike to Northrup Lake, a 5.5-mile round-trip, will be rewarding. There are a variety of habitats, starting at 1,925 feet and continuing on to the crest of the canyon at 2,389 feet, where you might see Golden Eagle, Red-tailed Hawk, warblers, vireos, Western Tanager, Lazuli Bunting, Lark Sparrow, and others.

Northrup Canyon is located 2.4 miles north of the main entrance to Steamboat Rock State Park. Turn east across from the park boat launch road near milepost 19 and drive .5 mile to a gate. Because the canyon is part of Steamboat Rock State Park, a free permit must be obtained at the main park entrance before hiking.

Spring Canyon

Spring Canyon is located on a hillside overlooking Lake Roosevelt in a bunchgrass prairie community, part of the Upper Sonoran Life Zone. This is a land of temperature extremes: very cold in winter, and hot and dry in summer. The sandy soil does not hold rain, so plants must quickly absorb moisture as it passes through. Bunchgrass, a perennial with dense basal tussocks, once covered much of eastern Washington. Giant wild rye, needlegrass, spiked wheatgrass, and Indian ricegrass are a few of the examples that can be found on the

Bunchgrass Prairie Nature Trail at Spring Canyon Park. Sagebrush, antelope brush, horsebrush, arrow-leaf balsam root, evening primrose, and northern prickly pear cactus are all part of the habitat for Red-tailed Hawks, Great Horned Owls, Northern Oriole, Black-billed Magpie, and swallows. The northern Pacific rattlesnake also is found here, along with other desert reptiles, small mammals, and deer.

Spring Canyon, a National Park Service campground with 78 campsites, has a boat launch, a sandy beach, and a picnic area. To reach Spring Canyon from the intersection of SH 155 and SH 174 in the town of Grand Coulee, follow SH 155 about three miles east to the park sign, turn and continue two more miles to the park.

Grand Coulee Dam

The Columbia River is the longest river in the Northwest. It flows 1,243 miles from its source in Columbia Lake, British Columbia, to its estuary linking the boundaries of Oregon and Washington at the Pacific Ocean. Eleven dams harness the Columbia's awesome power: Bonneville Dam, nearest the Pacific, to Grand Coulee Dam, the largest and most northerly.

The lakes, marshes, ponds, and wetlands created by the dams have beckoned to many species of birds not found here before. Ducks, geese, swans, grebes, loons, and many other water-oriented birds find nesting, loafing, and wintering habitat along the Columbia. Riparian habitats support songbirds, and the high cliffs provide nesting spots for hawks, owls, and other cliff-nesting species.

For a "Grand Coulee Dam Area Visitor's Guide" write to the Grand Coulee Dam Area Chamber of Commerce, Box 760, Grand Coulee, WA 99133-0760, (509) 633-3074. For information about the Coulee Dam National Recreation Area, write to Superintendent, Coulee Dam National Recreation Area, P.O. Box 37, Coulee Dam, WA 99116; (509) 633-9441.

WILSON CREEK

Wilson Creek and its canyon and surrounding uplands is an excellent example of shrub-steppe habitat. When the canyon bottom is a large lake, usually during a wet spring, the birding is excellent. Large concentrations of waterfowl such as Northern Pintail, Cinnamon Teal, American Wigeon, Gadwall, Mallard, Redhead, and several species of gulls can be found. Raptors such as American Kestrel, Red-tailed Hawk, and Great Horned, Burrowing, and Short-eared Owls are seen, and Ferruginous Hawks nest here.

Also look for Black-crowned Night-Heron; Gray Partridge; Long-billed Curlew; California Quail; Loggerhead Shrike; Downy Wood-pecker; Northern Flicker; Warbling, Red-eyed, and Solitary Vireos; Hermit Thrush; Brewer's, Fox, Grasshopper, Savannah, Song, and Vesper Sparrows; and Lazuli Bunting. An unusually high density of Yellow-breasted Chats, 12 individuals, was recorded recently. Sage and Sharp-tailed Grouse are rarities. There is a barrier-free trail from the parking lot to the overlook that goes through the shrub-steppe habitat. To reach the Wilson Creek area, take Lewis Bridge Road south off US 2 about a mile past Almira and continue about four miles. Or, from Govan, just off US 2, take the Govan Road south to the parking lot. A checklist, "A Guide to the Birds of Lincoln County," is available from the Washington State Department of Fish and Wildlife, N8702 Division Street, Spokane, WA 99218-1199; (509) 456-4082.

CRESTON

An interesting backroad loop off US 2 starts just at the eastern edge of Creston. Turn north on Lincoln Road, an excellent gravel road that eventually becomes well-paved. After about a mile, ponderosa pines start appearing and the countryside becomes rolling hills. Kingbirds and kestrels are everywhere in the spring and early summer. The road winds down a small creekbed profusely endowed with cow parsnip and wild rose. It is a perfect habitat for Long-eared Owl, warblers, vireos, and towhees. At 7.3 miles, turn right on Bachelor Road (going straight brings you to a dead end at the town of Lincoln on Roosevelt Lake—FDR, as the locals call it). Continue onto Bachelor Road. Here, snuggled in a deep canyon, you pass the very modern JR Ostrich Farm with its many elegant inhabitants. Golden Eagles, red-tails, and kestrels sometimes can be spotted along the ridge tops.

At one time Sage Grouse were more common, but disappearing sage brush habitat has made this species far less reliable. Dense sage-brush is needed year-round for food, nesting, and cover; farming has eliminated much of this habitat. The mating style of some grouse species (Sage and Sharp-tailed in Washington) draws together males once a year to a traditional site, a "lek." There, the male grouse postures in front of females, calling with a popping or booming sound while strutting in a ritualized dance. Brightly colored air sacs in their necks help entice the female. The female chooses her partner, mates, then leaves to tackle motherhood without assistance.

HAWK CREEK

Hawk Creek and Indian Creek come together to form Hawk Falls, which empties into a canyon flooded by the Columbia River and is called—Hawk Bay, of course. It is a serene setting with the north side of the lake arid steppe and the south side of the lake forested in ponderosa pine. There are hiking trails, sandy beaches, primitive camping, and good fishing. Beware of poison ivy around the lake. Steppe wildflowers including sticky geranium and larkspur are common. Cliff swallows nest near the falls, and American Goldfinch, Black-billed Magpie, and Western Tanager are on the drier side of the bay.

From Creston, continue on US 2 for two miles, turn left at the "Fort Spokane 18" sign for 11.7 miles, then left into Hawk Creek Campground. If you are coming from the east on US 2, turn right on SH 25. At the "Seven Bays Marina" sign, turn left for 6.2 miles to the campground.

Fort Spokane

Fort Spokane is situated on a high bluff at the junction of the Columbia and Spokane rivers. Fort Spokane was established in 1880 as an Army post to keep peace between local Indian reservations and the growing number of settlers to the south. The Fort was transferred to the Indian Bureau in 1899 and was run for 30 years as an Indian boarding school, tuberculosis sanitorium, and hospital. Today, all but four of the original 45 buildings are gone, leaving the parade grounds and all else to the birds and visitors. Look for Sharp-shinned Hawk in the wooded areas, and also Violet-green and Barn Swallows, Mourning Dove, American Kestrel, Killdeer, Burrowing Owl, Common Nighthawk, kingbirds, Common Raven, White and Red-breasted

Nuthatches, Orange-crowned and Yellow-rumped Warblers, Western Meadowlark, Brewer's Blackbird, Western Tanager, Black-headed Grosbeak, Pine Siskin, Savannah, White-crowned, Song and Chipping Sparrow.

From Davenport on US 2, turn north on SH 25 for 18 miles. The fort is administered by the National Park Service as a National Historic Site. The park has 67 campsites; some facilities are wheelchair-accessible. Information: Fort Spokane, Star Route, Box 30, Davenport, WA 99122; or phone the Coulee Dam NRA (509) 633-9441.

CHANNELED SCABLANDS

Channeled Scablands is not a particularly pleasant-sounding name for a land lush in its own right with birds and other wildlife, but it is a fitting description. Scablands are sage and grasslands intersected by lava canyons and rocky outcroppings; the scoured basalt landscape was formed by the great Spokane Flood, which washed away topsoils during the last ice age. Burrowing Owls and Northern Harriers forage at the canyon rims, while farmers plant hay and feed in the coulee bottoms. Common Nighthawk; Western Meadowlark; both Eastern and Western Kingbirds; Ruddy Duck; Blue-winged, Cinnamon, and Green-winged Teal; American Coot; Red-tailed and Ferruginous Hawks; Long-billed Curlew; and American Kestrel all make their home in this rather forbidding landscape. The scablands are 14 miles northwest of Davenport or about five miles southeast of Creston on US 2. Turn off at Telford South Road and drive through the area for a few miles. Eventually, the Bureau of Land Management will distribute a bird guide for this area.

SPOKANE

Spokane (Spo-CAN) is the largest city between Seattle and Minneapolis and is Washington's second-largest. Historically, this area was a crossroads for trading with native Americans. The first commercial enterprise in Washington state began in 1810 when Canadian fur traders opened a post on the Spokane River. Years later, Spokane was host to the 1974 World's Fair and, as a result, now has a lovely Riverfront Park and a variety of museums and cultural centers. Fine birding can be found within the city; Spokane rarities include Cattle Egret and Common Redpoll. Riverside State Park, where the Spokane River has carved a gorge through old lava flows, is just outside the city. Many other good birding areas are within easy drives of the city, and Turnbull National Wildlife Refuge is only 15 miles away. A checklist, "A Guide to the Birds of Spokane County," is available from the Washington Department of Fish and Wildlife, N8702 Division Street, Spokane, WA 99218-1199; (509) 456-4082.

Riverside State Park

Riverside State Park is set in a narrow valley along the Little Spokane River. In spring and during migrations, the park is alive with songbirds that frequent the cottonwoods and brushy areas along the river. Some species to look for would be Common Poorwill; Gray Catbird; Varied, Hermit, and Swainson's Thrushes; Mountain Bluebird; Cedar Waxwing; Solitary and Warbling Vireo; Yellow, Nashville, Yellow-rumped, Townsend's, MacGillivray's, and Wilson's Warblers; Yellow-breasted Chat; Common Yellowthroat; American Redstart; Northern Oriole; Western Tanager; Black-headed Grosbeak; Lazuli Bunting; Cassin's Finch; Pine Grosbeak; Rufous-sided Towhee; and a variety of others.

In winter, Bald Eagles hunt the river and are seen especially at the confluence of the Little Spokane and Spokane rivers. Waterfowl are found all along both rivers. Other permanent residents of the area are Western Screech-Owl; Northern Pygmy-Owl; Northern Saw-whet Owl; Belted Kingfisher; White-headed and Three-toed Woodpeckers; Gray and Steller's Jays; Clark's Nutcracker; Black-capped and Mountain Chickadees; Red-breasted, White-breasted, and Pygmy Nuthatches; and Winter, Canyon, and Rock Wrens.

Riverside State Park has 101 campsites with most amenities. The park has an interpretive center, riding stable, boat launch, and hiking trails. To reach the park, drive six miles northwest on Riverside Park Drive to the intersection of SH 291, where the park entrance is located. Information: Riverside State Park, N. 4427 Aubrey L. White Parkway, Spokane 99205; (509) 456-3964. For specific directions to all sites within the park, contact the park ranger on duty.

Deep Creek Canyon. Deep Creek runs through Riverside State Park to the southwest. It is home to a variety of bird species. Known nesting species include Common Merganser; Osprey; Spotted Sandpiper; Mourning Dove; Great Horned Owl; Downy Woodpecker; Northern Flicker; Western Wood-Pewee; Willow, Dusky, and Cordilleran Flycatchers; Violet-green Swallow; Common Raven; Rock and Canyon Wrens; Veery; Yellow Warbler; Pine Siskin; and many others.

Little Spokane River Natural Area. The Natural Area roughly parallels Rutter Parkway and takes in 7.3 river miles within its 1,353 acres. It is adjacent to and managed as part of Riverside State Park under a joint interagency agreement with Spokane County Parks. The best way to see the area is by canoe or kayak down the gentle Little Spokane River. A Great Blue Heron rookery is in tall cottonwoods by the river—travel quietly from February through August. Beaver, muskrat, porcupine, raccoon, coyote, marmot, white-tailed deer, and other mammals also live here.

A 1.7-mile hiking trail meanders along near the river to the north. Watch for Bufflehead; Northern Harrier; Canada Goose; Ring-necked Pheasant; Great Blue Heron; Greater Yellowlegs; Western Meadowlark; Common Nighthawk; Black-chinned, Rufous, and Calliope Hummingbirds; accipiters; six species of swallows; and a variety of flycatchers, vireos, warblers, and sparrows. The trailheads are at Indian Painted Rocks parking area and at the Highway 291 parking area.

Nine Mile Reservoir. Waterfowl and screech-owl boxes placed along Nine Mile Reservoir next to the Natural Area in 1990, in addition to earlier boxes located in the Little Spokane Natural Area, enhance nesting opportunities for a diversity of cavity-nesting species. Usage has been fairly high, and species using these boxes have included Wood Duck, Hooded Merganser, one unidentified duck, Northern Flicker, small unidentified owls, one unidentified song bird, flying squirrels, red squirrels, one raccoon, and three hives of honey bees.

Dishman Hills Reserve

A Nature Conservancy Reserve, the Dishman Hills are atop some of the oldest geological formations in the state. After the last ice age

15,000 years ago, the Missoula Flood carved its granite hills and created scablands. Two separate habitats eventually evolved: the lower slopes of ponderosa pine, Douglas-fir, and grasslands; and a forest of larch, grand fir, and western hemlock along the creek on the east side of Tower Mountain. A variety of rare and endangered plants and animals survive here. Most of the birds that nest in high forests can be seen here. The preserve totals more than 530 acres with units owned by various groups. Fifty-two butterfly species live here, rubber boas frequent the grasses, and a variety of birds are present. The preserve is open year-round. To reach Dishman Hills, take I-90 east from downtown Spokane. At the Argonne Road exit go south to Sprague Avenue, then turn right and drive a quarter mile to Sargent Road. Turn left and continue on Sargent Road to the Camp Caro parking lot. There is a foot trail from the parking lot.

MOUNT SPOKANE

The view from the top of 5,878-foot Mount Spokane encompasses Idaho, Oregon, Montana, and British Columbia. There are skiing, hiking, and horseback riding available in the area and a state park nearby. Mount Kit Carson, 5,180 feet, also is close, and birding in this area is great. Accipiters, Turkey Vulture, American Kestrel, Gray Partridge, Ring-necked Pheasant, Blue and Ruffed Grouse, Mourning Dove, Western Screech-Owl, Great Horned and Northern Saw-whet Owls, Common Poorwill, White-headed Woodpecker, Olive-sided and Hammond's Flycatchers, Horned Lark, Gray Jay, Common Raven, Chestnut-backed Chickadee, Wilson's Warbler, Pine Grosbeak, Pine Siskin, and Cassin's Finch are possible. A Great Gray Owl was recorded in 1984.

Mount Spokane State Park is south of the peak and has 14 campsites and limited amenities. There are a variety of signed hiking trails, riding stables, and tennis courts. Mount Spokane SP is 30 miles northeast of Spokane on SH 206. Information: Mount Spokane State Park, Route 1b, Box 336, Mead, WA 99021; (509) 456-4169.

REARDON SLOUGH

This is the top shorebird location in the region. This ex-sewage lagoon was renamed Audubon Lake by the Department of Fish and

Wildlife. I'm told it was better in its sewage days, but it still is an excellent spot for Greater and Lesser Yellowlegs; dowitchers; Baird's, Solitary, and Pectoral Sandpipers; all small peeps; Wilson's and Red-necked Phalaropes; and plovers. The waterfowl is interesting, and Eurasian Wigeons are regular every spring. A small lake one mile north is also good birding. Great Horned Owls nested in trees along the shore until a farmer "cleaned up" the grove. To reach Reardon Slough (Audubon Lake), go about 18 miles west of Spokane on US 2, then turn north on SH 231. It is just out of town, and is accessible on the west side through the rodeo grounds and a fertilizer plant, and on the east side by permission. Much can be seen from parking along the road.

FISHTRAP (MILLER RANCH)

The Bureau of Land Management bought the historic 8,000-acre Miller Ranch in 1993. A variety of habitats—wetland, pond and lake, brushy edge, both evergreen and deciduous forest, riparian, shrub-steppe, and grassland—combine to make this an outstanding birding destination. The ranch property lies between the Burlington-Northern railroad tracks and Fishtrap and Hog Lakes just off I-90. At present, only the old county road, running north-south through the property, is open to automobiles; all other access is by foot or on horseback. Bird-watching, hiking, fishing, and hunting are available. Camping is by permit only. As of mid-1993, a comprehensive management plan was being formulated, and a bird list and further information eventually will be available.

Nine species of raptors are found at Fishtrap, including both eagles and Ferruginous and Swainson's Hawks. Fishtrap Lake and various ponds host Common Loon, Canada Goose, Gadwall, Northern Pintail, Redhead, Canvasback, Ruddy Duck, and many others. Long-billed Curlew, Gray Partridge, Northern Shrike, and Savannah, Grasshopper, and Vesper Sparrows frequent the open fields and grasslands. Varied and Swainson's Thrushes, Brown Creeper, Pygmy Nuthatch, Common Raven, and Great Horned Owls frequent the forests. Violet-green, Bank, Cliff, and Rough-winged Swallows can be found in Hog Canyon and near the lakes, and the brushy areas sometimes yield Lazuli Buntings, California Quail, and Ruffed Grouse. A Sharp-tailed Grouse lek is also on the Fishtrap property.

To reach Fishtrap (Miller Ranch) Headquarters, go 3.6 miles south of the Fishtrap Interchange, off I-90, on the Old Sprague Highway. There is a sign at the road going into the ranch headquarters. For further information and for camping permits, contact the BLM in Spokane at East 4217 Main, Spokane, WA 99202; (509) 353-2570.

TURNBULL NATIONAL WILDLIFE REFUGE

Turnbull NWR has 27 square miles of rough scabrock, pine and aspen forests, and grasslands of blue bunch wheat grass and reed canary grass. Mixed into this fairly open country are about 20 small lakes and more than 100 ponds. Turnbull is very dependent upon water as its prime responsibility is to breeding and migratory waterfowl in eastern Washington. Several of the lakes are managed primarily for diving ducks such as Lesser Scaup, Redhead, and Canvasback. Waterfowl number between 5,000 and 6,000 adults during the summer, and local birds slowly begin accumulating in August. A peak is reached in October when numbers swell to as many as 50,000 birds. A second peak is in November when northern migrants pass through.

Mallards are most abundant on the refuge. Redhead, Blue-winged, and Cinnamon Teal, American Wigeon, Ruddy Duck, and Lesser Scaup also are regulars. Gadwall, Green-winged Teal, Ring-necked Duck, Northern Pintail, Northern Shoveler, Wood Duck, and Hooded Merganser nest at Turnbull. Other prolific breeders on the refuge are American Coot, Pied-billed and Eared Grebes, Killdeer, Spotted Sandpiper, and Black Tern. At Stubblefield Lake, shorebirds are regular fall migrants. Upland game birds and a variety of songbirds also are found here. A total of 216 species has been recorded at Turnbull Refuge, including 16 accidentals.

A five-mile auto tour of the refuge is a good way to see many of the birds in good weather. There are also hiking trails. Go to the headquarters first and pick up literature, a map, and information on areas open for visiting on the refuge. Turnbull NWR is reached by taking I-90 west from Spokane for about ten miles from city center, then turning south on SH 904 at Four Lakes. Continue about three miles to Cheney, then take the Cheney-Plaza Road south for four miles and turn left at the refuge sign. The headquarters is two miles east. Information: Refuge Manager, Turnbull National Wildlife Refuge, Route 3, Box 385,

Eared Grebe

Cheney, WA 99004; (509) 235-4723. Two brochures of interest are a checklist, "Birds of the Turnbull National Wildlife Refuge, Washington," and "Common Wildlife of the Turnbull NWR."

THE PALOUSE

The Palouse is named for the native Americans who dug camas roots and grazed their horses on its rolling hills. These hills now undulate with mile after mile of wheat fields blowing in the ever-present wind. The Palouse is a lovely, serene landscape covering 4,000 square miles in southeast Washington. In winter, like much open country, it is host to many raptors. In summer, sparrows and other songbirds, curlews, and a medley of other species call it home.

Steptoe Butte

Steptoe Butte is the highest point in the Palouse at 3,612 feet. The farmland seen from its top is probably some of the most photographed in the country. The butte is a mountain of Precambrian rock poking through layers of much more recent basalt lava. The term "steptoe" has been adopted worldwide by geologists to designate this type of land form. Steptoe Butte is named after Lt. Col. Edward J. Steptoe, who fought and was defeated in the Battle of Te-Hots-Nim-Me against marauding Palouse Indians in 1857.

The 4.5-mile road to the top spirals the mountain and gives views of a variety of habitats. Watch for many sparrows including Chipping, Brewer's, Vesper, Lark, Savannah, Fox, Lincoln's, Song, and possible Clay-colored. Red-tailed, Swainson's, and Ferruginous Hawks sometimes can be seen soaring on high. Steptoe Butte is a day-use state park (no drinking water) with a picnic area.

Kamiak Butte

Kamiak Butte is another in a series of isolated buttes left over from the northern Rockies that marks the edge of the old North American continent. Kamiak rises 3,360 feet from the surrounding Palouse wheat fields. The Pine Ridge hiking trail leads 3.5 miles to the summit through ponderosa pine, Douglas-fir, and western larch. Watch (and listen) for Great Horned Owl, Northern Pygmy-Owl, Mourning Dove, Red-naped Sapsucker, woodpeckers, Olive-sided and Cordilleran Flycatchers, Western Wood-Pewee, all three nuthatches, Calliope Hummingbird, Red Crossbill, and many others.

The Kamiak Butte County Park is a very nice park with camping. Black-headed Grosbeak and Lazuli Bunting are common. A Hooded Warbler in 1985 and other rarities also have been seen, along with a variety of more common songbirds. Kamiak Butte is located ten miles north of Pullman on SH 27. Information: Whitman County Parks Department, (509) 397-6238.

Rose Creek Preserve

The Nature Conservancy's 22-acre Rose Creek Preserve contains one of the finest black hawthorn-cow parsnip riparian areas left in the Palouse. The hawthorns reach a height of 15 feet or higher, and the understory of cow parsnips sometimes reaches six feet, creating a pocket wildlife sanctuary. Rose Creek runs through the preserve and creates a complex habitat attracting more than 100 species of birds and supporting more than 250 species of vascular plants. Mammals profit here also; shrews and voles provide prey for patrolling Red-tailed Hawks, and coyote, porcupine, and white-tailed deer forage in the preserve. Habitat loss and degeneration in the Palouse has had a severe negative effect on much wildlife; preserves such as Rose Hill help in a small way to counteract this loss.

There is a marked trail (no pets here, please) leading from the parking area. Long-eared Owls roost in the compact hawthorn thickets as Gray Catbirds scuttle in the underbrush. As you are walking, watch for Black-chinned and Calliope Hummingbirds, Yellow-bellied Sapsucker, Downy Woodpecker, Willow Flycatcher, chickadees, nuthatches, kinglets, Veery, Northern Oriole, Yellow and MacGillivray's Warblers, American Redstart, Vesper, Song and Chipping Sparrows, Western Meadowlark, Red Crossbill, Pine Siskin, American Goldfinch, plus many others. To reach the Rose Hill Preserve, go north from Pullman on SH 27 and turn left on the Albion-Pullman Road. In Albion, turn right on Main Street (which becomes Old Albion Road, gravel) and proceed 2.8 miles. Turn left on Four Mile Road and continue, bearing left, for 0.5 mile to the preserve on the right.

Palouse Falls State Park

Palouse Falls drops a torrent of water nearly 200 feet into the deep chasm carved centuries ago by the great Spokane Floods. This green island in the middle of dry, open shrub-steppe habitat draws an abundance of interesting birds. Northern Orioles, American Robin, warblers, and swallows nest in this 83-acre park. The land surrounding the park is excellent for raptors including Golden Eagle, Swainson's and Red-tailed Hawks, American Kestrel, Prairie Falcon, and Great Horned Owl, some of which nest in the canyon. Long-billed Curlew,

Western Meadowlark, Common Raven, Black-billed Magpie, and a variety of desert-type songbirds also can be found.

The whole area is excellent for wildlife viewing; check especially around the park, along the gravel road leading in from SH 261, and downstream from the falls. There are ten primitive campsites and rest rooms here. A larger and fancier park, Lyons Ferry, is six miles south on SH 261. Palouse Falls State Park is 23 miles southeast of Washtucna. Follow SH 260 southwest, then turn southeast on SH 261. Continue until the state park sign appears and go 2.5 miles east to the park.

WALLA WALLA COUNTY

Walla Walla County is sandwiched between the Blue Mountains to the east, Oregon to the south, and the Columbia and Snake rivers to the west and north. Its 1,265 square miles encompasses a variety of habitats on which 277 species have been recorded. Many vagrant birds show up at the confluence of the Snake, Columbia, and Walla Walla rivers. Pacific Loon, White-faced Ibis, Trumpeter Swan, Brant, Oldsquaw, Whimbrel, Red Knot, Red Phalarope, Parasitic Jaeger, and Glaucous and Sabine's Gulls all have been recorded in the wetlands in the area. In the shrub-steppe habitat to the east, Long-billed Curlew, Sage Thrasher, Gray Partridge, and Brewer's Sparrow are regulars; where there is bunchgrass, Grasshopper Sparrows sometimes are found. Wintering Bohemian Waxwings and visiting Blue Jays occasionally are seen in the city of Walla Walla. As in most areas of open winter habitat, raptors are plentiful and varied.

Walla Walla River Delta

Birders living in the southeastern Washington area have found the Walla Walla River Delta to be a gold mine for shorebirds, waterfowl, and a variety of other species. April to May and August to September seem to be the best months for migration observations, with the third week in September by far the most productive. Western Sandpiper, Killdeer, and Long-billed Dowitcher are most prevalent, with good showings also by Red-necked Phalarope; Common Snipe; Baird's, Pectoral, and Least Sandpipers; Spotted Sandpiper; Black-bellied Plover; Greater and Lesser Yellowlegs; and American Avocet. Less frequent are Lesser Golden-Plover and Semipalmated Plover, Whimbrel, Marbled Godwit, Ruddy Turnstone, Red Knot, Sanderling, Semipalmated Sandpiper, Dunlin, Stilt Sandpiper, Short-billed Dowitcher, and Red Phalarope.

Other species that have been seen along the delta are Red-necked and Clark's Grebes; American Bittern; American Black Duck; Surf and White-winged Scoters; Northern Goshawk; Ferruginous Hawk; American White Pelican; Franklin's, Western, and Bonaparte's Gulls; Black, Caspian, and Forster's Terns; Merlin; Osprey; Peregrine Falcon; plus passerines such as Tri-colored Blackbird; Yellow-rumped and Orange-crowned Warblers; Northern Waterthrush; and House and Bewick's Wrens.

To reach this outstanding shorebird site, take SH 12 south from Pasco to Milepost 307 in Walla Walla County. Turn west south of the milepost and north of the guard rail. Park at the railroad tracks and walk to the water's edge on a narrow trail. It is necessary to wade across to the mudflats, which puts you on the North Delta. The first 100 feet is the most difficult and the deepest, about knee deep.

Fish Hook Park

Fish Hook Park is one of several on the Snake River managed by the Army Corps of Engineers. This park is noted for its owls. From November until March several species of owls take up residence, including Common Barn-Owl, Long-eared Owl, Great Horned Owl, Western Screech-Owl, and Northern Saw-whet Owl. Trees and shrubbery are thick and provide good winter protection, plus prey is usually plentiful. The road is barred after the park is closed in September, but you can walk in and carefully look about. Avoid playing tapes or making noise near the roost areas. Waterfowl on the river also can be interesting, with Canada Geese, Mallard, Trumpeter Swan, Redhead, scaup, Canvasback, and many other species.

Fish Hook Park has 35 tent sites and 41 drive-up sites, boat launch facilities and dock. Some facilities are wheelchair-accessible. It is open from April to September. Information: Army Corps of Engineers, P.O. Box 2427, Tri-Cities, WA 99302; (509) 547-7781. To reach the park, go east out of Pasco on US 12, cross the Snake River, and

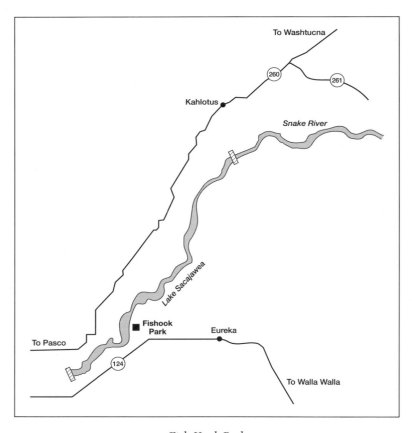

Fish Hook Park

turn east on SH 124. Continue a little more than 14 miles, then go north on Fish Hook Road for four miles to the park.

Badger Island

Badger Island, in the Columbia River 8.7 miles south of the mouth of the Snake River and 4.1 miles north of the Walla Walla River mouth, is the one spot in Washington where American White Pelicans can be seen year-round. Numbers are small, but the birds are often on the northeast side as this area offers more shelter from the winds. To observe the pelicans, pull out on the west side of SH 12 just south of Milepost 303 and look west across the tracks.

McNARY NATIONAL WILDLIFE REFUGE

McNary NWR includes 3,629 acres divided into three units: McNary, Strawberry Island in the Snake River, and the Hanford Islands in the Columbia River. Up to 100,000 migrating waterfowl rest and feed at McNary, including Tundra Swans, Snow Geese, and several species of ducks. Nesting at the refuge are Canada Geese; Northern Pintail; Mallard; Northern Wigeon; Gadwall; Northern Shoveler; Green-winged, Cinnamon, and Blue-winged Teal; Wood Duck; Redhead; Canvasback; and Lesser Scaup. American Avocet, Long-billed Curlew, Yellow-headed Blackbird, and Burrowing Owls also nest here. The islands are home to colonial nesting species such as Ring-billed and California Gulls and Forster's Tern.

Raptors seen on the refuge include Northern Harrier, American Kestrel, Sharp-shinned and Cooper's Hawks, and Red-tailed Hawk. Songbirds are often in the vicinity of Burbank Slough's western end and the interpretive trail where there is more cover. The Hanford Island Unit is closed July 1 to January 1. To reach the refuge, take US 395 southeast from Pasco, cross the Snake River, and continue to the refuge entrance. An area brochure regarding the refuge is available. Information: McNary National Wildlife Refuge, c/o Umatilla NWR, Post Office Building, 6th and I Streets, P.O. Box 239, Umatilla, OR 97882; (503) 922-3232.

JUNIPER FOREST MANAGEMENT AREA
(JUNIPER DUNES WILDERNESS)

A combination of the most extensive natural groves of western junipers (*Juniperus occidentalis*) and the largest active sand dunes in the state are what make the Juniper Dunes Wilderness unique. The area contains 7,000 to 8,000 fenced acres within the Management Area. The ancient juniper groves—historically regarded as 6,000 to 8,000 years old—are at the northernmost limits of their range; the sand dunes range up to 130 feet high and 1,200 feet wide. Many of the dunes are unstabilized, but the forested dunes are secured by bit-terbrush, sagebrush, and bluegrass.

This wild semi-desert area is a remnant ecosystem containing about 17,120 acres of the original 250,000 acres that once extended to the Columbia and Snake rivers. The unstabilized dunes are thought to have migrated here from the river areas with the push of southeaster-ly winds. Mule deer, bobcat, coyote, and badger, plus many reptiles and small mammals, reside in the dunes.

Songbirds and raptors are special here. On one early March trip, we counted more than 40 migrating Mountain Bluebirds flitting about in the grassy areas at the base of one of the dunes. Ferruginous, Swainson's, and Red-tailed Hawks nest here, as do Great-horned, Long-eared, and Short-eared Owls. Long-billed Curlews and Dusky Flycatchers are spring nesters, and Horned Larks, Gray Partridge, American Kestrel, Black-billed Magpie, plus pheasants, ravens, and crows are found all year. Summer passerines include Say's Phoebe, Violet-green Swallow, Western Kingbird, MacGillivray's Warbler, and Lark and Sage Sparrows.

Spring and fall are the best times to visit. Prospective visitors to the area must contact the BLM's Border Resource Area Office in Spokane prior to planning a visit for the latest access information and for a permit. The address is 4217 Main Avenue, Spokane, WA 99202; (509) 353-2570.

UMATILLA NATIONAL WILDLIFE REFUGE

The Umatilla NWR has five units that stretch along 18 miles of the Columbia River between Oregon and Washington. Two are in Ore-gon. The Paterson, Ridge, and Whitcomb units are in Washington, and the Ridge and Whitcomb units contain Telegraph, Blalock, Sand Dune, Straight Six, and Long Walk islands. The refuge habitat includes 16,500 acres of water, 1,100 acres of planted crops, 11,070 acres of wheat grass-sagebrush desert, and 700 acres of marsh. All species of western waterfowl are seen during spring migration. The Great Basin Canada Goose, Long-billed Curlew, Burrowing Owl, and many others nest on the refuge.

In winter, Bald Eagles are attracted by the large waterfowl concen-trations. Horned Lark, Snow Bunting, Lapland Longspur, and others also can be found in winter, along with a variety of raptors. The refuge lists 185 recorded species and 69 nesting species. The Umatilla NWR is located near Paterson on SH 14; there are several access points. A refuge brochure and map are available. Information: Umatilla NWR, 6th and I Streets, P.O. Box 239, Umatilla, OR 97882; (503) 922-3232.

Crow Butte State Park

Crow Butte State Park shares Whitcomb Island in Lake Umatilla, created by the construction of the John Day Dam, with the Umatilla NWR. The habitat is mostly semi-arid sagebrush land, but the park has green lawns and a variety of plantings that attract many species of land birds including kingbirds, Northern Oriole, Black-headed Grosbeak, and Killdeer. The causeway to the island crosses a large, shallow

Killdeer Chick

part of the lake where interesting waders, gulls, and shorebirds often are seen; swallows nest under the bridge. Sand dunes opposite the campground are where Savannah Sparrows can be found. The shoreline on the south side of the dunes is undeveloped, and there are small bays and inlets that often harbor waterfowl.

Crow Butte is a great base for trips in this part of the state because there are few other parks nearby. The off-season (it is open all year) is especially quiet and is an excellent time to enjoy the many migrants. This state park has 50 campsites with full hookups plus most amenities. Crow Butte is 14 miles west of McNary Dam on SH 14. Information: Crow Butte State Park, P.O. Box 277, Paterson, WA 99345; (509) 875-2644.

BICKLETON

There are bluebird "trails"—numbers of bluebird houses along a route—all across the country, but Bickleton has been dubbed the "Bluebird Capital of the World" due to the efforts of Jess and Elva Brinkerhoff to "provide homes for every bluebird that came to Bickleton." At the peak of the birdhouse building-and-placing phase, the mid-1970s, the trail covered 325 square miles along 200 miles of dusty backroads and contained 1,500 bird houses—all with blue roofs and almost all occupied, mostly by Mountain Bluebirds. A Washington State University study at the time discovered that bluebirds chose the blue-roofed houses over plain ones almost every time. Now, there are roughly 800 houses in the area, mostly occupied, and the Brinkerhoffs have received prestigious awards for the conservation efforts.

Bickleton is located on the Goldendale-Bickleton Road about halfway between Mabton (just out of Yakima) and the Columbia River. This is an interesting road in its own right, with a variety of desert species. Continue to Goldendale to visit America's Stonehenge and the Maryhill Museum. Golden Eagles and Prairie Falcons often are seen in this area.

YAKAMA INDIAN NATION

The Yakama Reservation covers more than a million acres; it is the largest reservation in the state. This vast landscape provides a home or resting spot for many of Washington's avian species. Several wildlife refuges and habitat management areas are on reservation land. The Yakama Nation Cultural Center, located on ancestral grounds near Toppenish, more than justifies a side trip from birding. Information: Yakama National Cultural Center, P.O. Box 151, Dept. B, Toppenish, WA 98948; (509) 865-2800. And yes, there are two spellings: Yakama for the native Americans, and Yakima for the town and river.

TOPPENISH NATIONAL WILDLIFE REFUGE

The Toppenish NWR includes three units along the Yakima River and Toppenish Creek, all within the Yakama Indian Reservation. Toppenish is a small reservation—1,763 acres. Still, more than 30,000 ducks and geese spend winter and spring here. Toppenish is also a major migration stop for shorebirds traveling the inland route. Shrub-steppe habitat with its sage, basalt cliffs, and grasslands is found on the nearby slopes of Toppenish Ridge and through the Horse Heaven Hills. Very much a declining habitat in Washington, shrub-steppe supports rarer species such as Long-billed Curlew, Sage Sparrow, and Sage Thrasher. Riparian habitat and marshlands also are found here.

The local bird checklist of 233 species includes Bufflehead, Northern Shoveler, Wood Duck, teal, goldeneyes, Swainson's Hawk, Virginia Rail, Common Snipe, Lesser Yellowlegs, Wilson's Phalarope, Burrowing and Short-eared Owls, Common Nighthawk, Marsh Wren, Loggerhead Shrike, Yellow-headed and Red-winged Blackbirds, American Goldfinch, and Savannah, Vesper and Sage Sparrows. Nesting species number about 108 on the refuge, including a nesting population of Bobolinks located on Lateral C between Toppenish Creek and Yost Road. During the fall, herons, egrets, gulls, and terns are common, and in the winter there are sometimes fair numbers of Bald Eagles, Prairie Falcons, and other raptors present.

Headquarters for the refuge is six miles south of Toppenish on US 97; go to the refuge sign, then continue one mile west from the sign. A bird checklist and refuge brochure with a map are available. Information: Toppenish NWR, Route 1, Box 1300, Toppenish, WA 98948; (509) 865-2405.

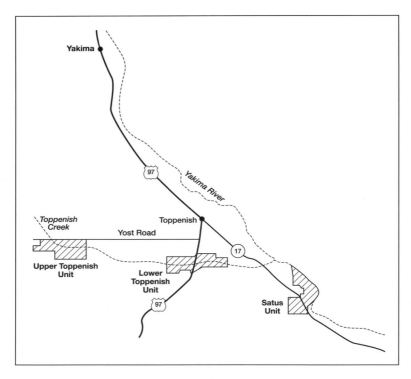

Toppenish NWR

FORT SIMCOE STATE PARK

"Mool-Mool" was the name the Yakama people called the site Fort Simcoe was built on in 1865. It had been a special stopping place for native peoples traveling from the Yakima Valley to Celilo Falls on the Columbia River. Fort Simcoe is known in the birding community as having one of the largest populations of Lewis' Woodpecker in the Pacific Northwest. The huge Garry oaks that natives used to camp under are perfect nesting habitat for the woodpecker named for Meriweather Lewis. A variety of other birds can be found here, too. Fort Simcoe is a day-use park located 30 miles west of Toppenish on

SH 220. An interpretive center depicts the fur trading post, and there is a nice picnic area.

THE HANFORD REACH OF THE COLUMBIA RIVER

The Hanford Reach is the last free-flowing, non-tidal segment of the Columbia River in the United States. It extends from one mile downstream of Priest Rapids Dam, approximately 51 miles to the McNary Pool north of Richland. Parts of the Reach are being considered for designation as a National Wild and Scenic River and National Wildlife Refuge. At least 184 bird species have been recorded along the Hanford Reach, with at least 74 nesting species.

Colonial nesting species that have established meaningful colonies here include Forster's Tern, Ring-billed and California Gulls, and Great Blue Heron. Black-crowned Night-Herons were former nesters and may return. American White Pelicans are increasing, and though they do not nest in Washington, there is suitable habitat. Canada Geese nest on many of the small islands in the Reach. Surrounding lakes seem to be more productive for duck nesting sites; along the Reach, Mallard, Gadwall, teal, and Common Merganser use available cover on islands and along the shoreline for nesting.

Increases in autumn-spawning Chinook salmon carcasses have expanded the Bald Eagle winter population from six in the 1960s to 55 in the late 1980s. About 28 pairs of Swainson's Hawks nest in the area surrounding the Reach, but leave for their wintering grounds in Argentina in early fall. The shrub-steppe habitat near the Reach supports eight nesting pairs of Ferruginous Hawks, a threatened species in Washington and a Federal candidate species. Long-billed Curlew, Sage Grouse, and Peregrine Falcon are three species of special concern at this site.

As of this writing, the management of the Hanford Reach has not been decided, but even now it is an interesting place to bird. The Hanford Reach area can be approached from the north by turning south off I-90 at Vantage onto SH 243. Continue on SH 243 until the Vernita Bridge at SH 24. Cross the bridge and go 1.7 miles south, then west on Midway Substation Road. The pavement ends and the road becomes very rough, but continues west to the Priest Rapids Dam. Stop anywhere and scan the cliffs for raptors, Cliff and Violet-green Swallows, White-throated Swift, Canyon and Rock Wrens, and Northern Oriole; the brushy areas for warblers and other songbirds; and the river and marshy areas for a variety of wetland species.

CRAB CREEK HABITAT MANAGEMENT AREA

Fine waterfowl and upland game bird habitat is found at the Crab Creek HMA and its Priest Rapids Unit on the Columbia River. The Crab Creek area is typical eastern Washington desert country with sagebrush, basalt cliffs, rolling hills, and an abundance of cattail marshes. It is said that Lower Crab Creek, which flows through the area, is one of the finest brown trout streams in the state. There is good birding all along the roadside. The high cliffs just south of the road have nesting Red-tailed Hawk, Prairie Falcon, American Kestrel, owls, Rock Dove, Common Raven, and a variety of others. Throughout the valley look for Ring-necked Pheasant; California Quail; Lazuli Bunting; Rock and Canyon Wrens; Ash-throated Fly-catcher; Western and Eastern Kingbirds; Common Nighthawk; Mourning Dove; Northern Rough-winged, Bank, Cliff, and Barn Swallows; Sage Thrasher; Loggerhead Shrike; American Goldfinch; and Brewer's, Vesper, and Song Sparrows. Also, watch for Scaled Quail, an introduced species, at the western end of the valley.

Seepage from the Potholes Reservoir and return flows from irrigated farming on the higher lands have created numerous sloughs and lakes and turned Lower Crab Creek into an all-year watercourse. Lenice, Merry, and Nunnally lakes are excellent for rainbow trout, plus American Avocet; Black-necked Stilt; Yellow-headed, Brewer's, and Red-winged Blackbirds; Marsh Wren; Common Snipe; Virginia Rail; Sora; Yellow-breasted Chat are seen here.

A triangular area near Corfu bordered by SH 26, Corfu Road, and Crab Creek Road is usually excellent. The northwest corner has trees that attract songbirds and is the best area in the Columbia NWR for migrants. Corfu Road has raptors and good views of geese in the spring. Crab Creek Road has shrub-steppe that may have Sandhill Crane (spring and fall), Long-billed Curlew, Burrowing and Short-eared Owls, Chukar, American Tree and White-crowned Sparrows, and American Kestrel. About a mile west of the Adams County line is a good area for shorebirds in the saline wetland on the north side. Sandhill Crane have day and night roosts along Crab Creek in this

ELIZABETH A. MILLS
- 1977 -

American Avocet

area. Feeding areas are mostly between SH 26 and McMannamon Road, often in corn stubble, but also in alfalfa. One favorite spot is in corn stubble behind the Sunny Royal Slope Dairy. The best way to locate them is to listen for their call.

The Crab Creek HMA road is located just past the town of Beverly on SH 243 (about six miles south of Vantage on the east side of the Columbia). Turn east and continue up the valley; the road is paved part way. Continue on through the valley, then turn north at Red Rock Coulee to come out at Royal City on SH 26; or continue on Crab Creek Road through the town of Corfu, finally joining SH 26. Coming from Othello in the east on SH 26, go a little more than 14 miles, then turn south to Corfu and Lower Crab Creek.

The Priest Rapids Unit is primarily pasture grassland and is used heavily by Canada Geese year-round. Many species of ducks also can be seen here. The Priest Rapids Unit is about eight miles south of Beverly on SH 243, west of Mattawa on Buckshot Road.

OTHELLO SETTLEMENT PONDS

The Othello sewage treatment ponds at the west end of Cunningham Road are good for waterfowl and gulls all year. Walking access is allowed to the city sewage treatment ponds on west Cunningham Road. The large settlement ponds have cattail marsh on the south edges; White-faced Ibis was seen here in 1988. Possibilities at the ponds include Great Blue and Black-crowned Night-Heron, Sora, Virginia Rail, Yellow-headed Blackbird, Wood Duck, Redhead, Lesser Scaup, Ring-necked Duck, Ruddy Duck, teal, Northern Shoveler, large numbers of Bank Swallows, Cliff and Barn Swallows, American Pipit, Common Nighthawk, and many others.

The Scabrock feedlot and potato ponds are excellent in the spring and fall for shorebirds, including rarities such as Hudsonian Godwit, Stilt Sandpiper, Semipalmated and Baird's Sandpipers, and waterfowl. McCain Foods allows birders to drive up on the dike of the potato settlement ponds. Wetlands along McManamon Road just north of the potato ponds are good in spring and summer for shorebirds and waterfowl. August shorebird counts in the Othello area usually exceed 1,000; in 1992 the peak count of 1,564 birds was on August 14, but the August 25 count, while a bit lower, had the rarer plains-associated species. Phalaropes were also more abundant on the later count.

COLUMBIA NATIONAL WILDLIFE REFUGE

The Columbia NWR was established in 1944 along with the Columbia Basin Irrigation Project. The refuge is in the heart of the channeled scablands, a dry sagebrush area, but seepage from the Irrigation Project, marshes, wet meadows, sloughs, streams, and lakes now provide habitat for many additional species of wildlife. The shrub-steppe habitat still is prominent as are basalt cliffs and croplands, all of which support a diverse and abundant number of species. More than 280 species of wildlife—208 bird species—have been recorded on the refuge's 23,100 acres.

In the fall, waterfowl populations peak at more than 100,000 birds. Major concentration areas on the refuge are closed to the public during fall and winter to provide undisturbed sanctuary. An overlook at the south end of Byers Road north of Royal Lake, however, is a good spot to view some large concentrations in winter. Canada Goose, Mallard, Blue-winged and Cinnamon Teal, Ruddy Duck, Redhead, and American Coot are principal waterfowl nesters on the refuge.

The basalt cliffs and ledges throughout the refuge are home to Great Horned and Common Barn-Owls, Common Raven, Red-tailed Hawk, American Kestrel, Cliff Swallow, Say's Phoebe, and others. At the Drumheller Channels on the north end of the refuge is a magnificent complex of basins, buttes, and once-used cataracts. Open sage-scrub country provides nesting for Long-billed Curlew, Burrowing Owl, Gray Partridge, Sage Thrasher, Sage and Grasshopper Sparrows, and many others. A five-mile, self-guided auto tour is great for getting a feel for the area, and a 22-mile loop drive gives a complete overview and includes the Royal Lake overlook.

To reach the Columbia NWR from I-90 at Moses Lake, take SH 17 southeast about 2.5 miles, then turn south five miles on Sullivan Road. Go across the bridge and turn right, and the refuge sign will be on the left. The headquarters for the refuge is in Othello, and it is best to have maps and brochures to facilitate seeing the area. The best information is in "Wildlife," a checklist of all bird, mammal, reptile, amphibian, and fish species; "Columbia Basin Recreation Areas," which has an excellent map showing all of the Habitat Management Areas, refuges, and parks along the Columbia from Grand Coulee to McNary; and "Columbia National Wildlife Refuge." Information:

Refuge Manager, Columbia National Wildlife Refuge, 44 South 8th Avenue, P.O. Drawer F, Othello, WA 99344; (509) 488-2668.

POTHOLES HABITAT MANAGEMENT AREA

The area south of I-90, and to a lesser extent north, has many management areas, recreation areas, and refuges. The Potholes Habitat Management Area is just north of the Columbia NWR. Just to the south (between Potholes and the NWR) is the Seep Lakes HMA, to the west is the Desert HMA, to the northwest is the Winchester Wasteway HMA, and just a few miles north is the Gloyd Seeps HMA. These areas provide prime habitat for an abundance of birds. Obtain the map of the whole area to sort it all out; even those of us living here are sometimes confused (listed under Columbia NWR-"Columbia Basin Recreation Areas").

The potholes came about as a result of lava flows millions of years ago that covered much of eastern Washington with basalt rock. Glaciers during the ice age, then floods, eroded this rock, forming dark, coarse sand. West winds moved the sand around, depositing it here as sand dunes. The building of O'Sullivan Dam raised the water table, filling many potholes to create the pothole lakes we see today. As Catherine Secor, a park ranger at Potholes State Park, stated, "All through the sand dunes of the Potholes Reservoir, in late August through late September, there will be many pelicans. If one goes canoeing through the dunes, you may sneak around a dune and find a beach covered with ducks, Great Blue Herons, pelicans, and Great Egrets. It is truly a sight to be seen."

The north end of the Potholes Reservoir has good birding. An island rookery of Great Egrets, Black-crowned Night-Herons, Great Blue Herons, and Double-crested Cormorants can be seen by taking Exit 169 (Hiawatha Road—one exit east of Dodson Road) from I-90. Go east on the frontage road about 2.5 miles, then turn south. Keep right until the dike; the birds can be seen from here. American Avocet, Black-necked Stilt, Wilson's Phalarope, Killdeer, Spotted Sandpiper, and others also nest in the Potholes area. In late August, American White Pelican, Greater and Lesser Yellowlegs, Solitary Sandpiper, Least Sandpiper, dowitchers, and possible godwits might be seen.

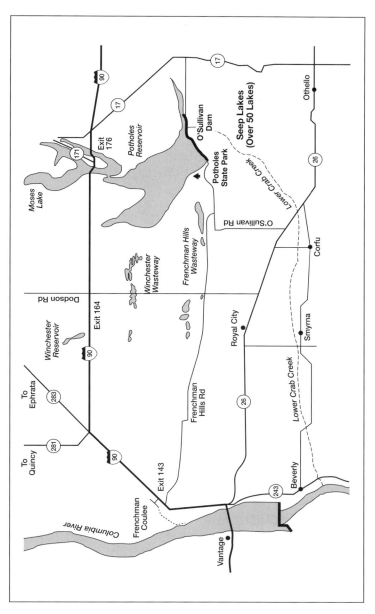

Potholes Reservoir/Dodson Road Area

All of these habitat management areas have much desert-type habitat. Watch for Red-tailed, Ferruginous, and Swainson's Hawks; American Kestrel; Short-eared and Burrowing Owls; Common Raven; Common Nighthawk; Black-billed Magpie; Horned Lark; Sage Thrasher; Western Meadowlark; Loggerhead Shrike; and Sage and Lark Sparrows.

Two state parks are nearby; Potholes State Park has camping and all amenities. Information: Royal Star Route, Othello, WA 99344; (509) 765-7271. Moses Lake State Park, a satellite of Potholes SP, is a day-use park and a good spot to compare Clark's and Western Grebes. Both nest in the area, and in spring, their elaborate "water dances" often can be seen.

DODSON ROAD

Dodson Road is one of the special goals of "west of the mountain" birders. Along this 23-mile road through flat, dry habitat lives a wonderland of avian species. Numerous access roads to boat launch areas are fairly well-marked; all have interesting birds. These areas are unique as they are part of the Columbia Basin's major desert riparian habitat. Jackrabbit, coyote, beaver, muskrat, mink, and a few mule deer are some of the mammals found here.

Starting in Ephrata, the first 13 miles of Dodson Road are less interesting, but still productive. Common Ravens nest on the high utility towers, and songbirds can be found in gullies and around tree clumps. At 11.5 miles from Ephrata, turning west for 3.5 miles on "3 NW" brings you to the Winchester Wasteway Area. Several species of waterfowl nest here, including Great Basin Canada Goose; Gadwall; Northern Pintail; American Wigeon; Green-winged, Blue-winged, and Cinnamon Teal; Mallard; Northern Shoveler; Canvasback; and others.

After the I-90 intersection, Dodson continues another ten miles through the Desert Habitat Management Area to Frenchman Hills Road. About three miles after I-90, small lakes—potholes—start appearing on both sides of the road. These ponds can be filled with all kinds of waterfowl; American Avocets; Black-necked Stilts; shorebirds; herons; egrets; Caspian, Forster's, and Black Terns; and California and Ring-billed Gulls—a magnificent plethora of water birds.

Nearby in scrubby trees, Swainson's Hawks nest, and their thin cry can be heard as they circle overhead. The sage areas are generally reliable for Sage Thrasher, Lark Sparrow, and Loggerhead Shrike. Further on, poplars and Russian olive trees appear on the west side. Long-eared Owls have nested here off and on for years. Soon, Russian olives appear on the east side, and at times the owls are seen here. Just before the eastern line of trees is a Burrowing Owl nesting site in the sagebrush on the other side of a fence. The male is often on a fence post in early spring. Back in the sage areas along the road watch for possible Grasshopper, Lark, Sage, and Savannah Sparrows.

At the intersection of Dodson and Frenchman Hills roads, turn west. Frenchman Hills Lake, Sand Lake, and a string of wetlands form the Frenchman Hills Wasteway. Waterfowl, including grebes, are abundant here late in the summer. In recent years, American White Pelicans have been seen; cormorants and loons are found in lesser numbers. American Avocets, Black-necked Stilts, Greater Yellowlegs, and Spotted Sandpiper are found in the wet meadows. The Russian olives support many species including Northern Oriole, Black-billed Magpie, Yellow and Wilson's Warblers, Yellow-breasted Chat, American Goldfinch, and many others. Past the wet area and in the sage-sand dune habitat are several Burrowing Owl nest sites.

Throughout the length of Dodson Road, watch for a variety of raptors. Both Bald and Golden Eagles can be seen, along with Red-tailed and Rough-legged Hawks, occasional Ferruginous Hawk, American Kestrel, Northern Harrier, and, to a far lesser degree, accipiters, Osprey, and Turkey Vulture. Dodson Road also can be accessed from the south through the Lower Crab Creek area. Dodson meets SH 26 about three miles east of Royal City.

QUINCY HABITAT MANAGEMENT AREA

Frenchman Coulee is another favorite of local birders; it is in the southern unit of the Quincy HMA. The road going down the coulee is a section of US 10, the Old Vantage Highway, that winds down to the now-sunken Old Vantage Bridge. At the top, the huge cattail marsh is alive with Yellow-headed and Red-winged Blackbirds, Marsh Wrens, Pied-billed Grebes, and American Coot. The ditches by the side of the road sometimes host Cinnamon Teal and Common

Snipe. A little further, Violet-green Swallows and White-throated Swifts soar and "chitter" along the cliff sides. A bit further, a wonderful half-circle of basalt pillars emerges, one of the most photographed rock formations in Washington.

Frenchman Coulee is reached via I-90 east of the Vantage Bridge. About six miles after the bridge, turn off the freeway, immediately go left under the freeway, then straight as the road goes through the huge cattail marsh. Turn left at the abandoned farm with large trees (check these trees for interesting songbirds); this is the road to the coulee. The rest of Quincy HMA can be reached by taking I-90 to George, turning north on SH 281, and then taking CR 3 or CR 5 northwest.

MOSES COULEE

Chief Moses and his followers farmed this massive coulee bottom, planting pumpkins, corn, and potatoes, but it wasn't long before others came to pasture horses and to take a "shortcut" through the coulee. After the wagon road, the Great Northern Railroad built a branch line from the Columbia River through the coulee to Mansfield. Palisades was once a thriving town when the railroad was built. It is now a quiet patch of green hosting the local school below the fortress-like basaltic pillars after which it was named. The western end of the coulee is well-farmed now, but a few miles past Palisades, the giant Billingsley Ranch takes over most of the coulee.

Moses Coulee is home to nesting Golden Eagles. One cliff area we have monitored for years has six nests. Other cliffs have eagles that have used the same aerie for years. Rock Dove, American Kestrel, Prairie Falcon, Red-tailed Hawk, and Great Horned and Common Barn-Owls also make good use of these 800-foot-high ramparts. White-throated Swifts and Cliff Swallows are quite common on the cliffs, and Bank, Northern Rough-winged, Tree, and Violet-green Swallows also can be found in the valley.

When coming into the coulee from the Columbia River end, scan the fields, utility posts and wires, and scree slopes for a wonderful array of species. Great Blue Heron; Common Nighthawk; Belted Kingfisher; Killdeer; Ring-billed and California Gulls; Mourning Dove; California Quail; Common Raven; Western Meadowlark;

Mountain Bluebird; Eastern and Western Kingbirds; Black-billed Magpie; Northern Oriole; Loggerhead Shrike; Lazuli Bunting; Yellow-headed, Brewer's, and Red-winged Blackbirds; and American Goldfinch are just a few of the species to be found.

In winter, Northern Pintail, Mallard, and American Wigeon can be found in half-frozen puddles in the fields; and Northern Harrier, Rough-legged and Red-tailed Hawks, Golden Eagle, American Kestrel, Common Raven, Ring-necked Pheasant, California Quail, Western Meadowlark, Northern Shrike, Horned Lark, White-crowned Sparrow, and many others can be found. Golden Eagles often are involved in courtship displays in February. Canada Geese and Sandhill Cranes migrate over the Coulee by the hundreds in spring and fall and sometimes settle to rest in the fields toward the northern end of the coulee (nearer US 2).

Continuing through the coulee, the road turns to gravel, small farms thin out, and the beginnings of the vast Billingsley Ranch are encountered. The county road goes through the ranch—drive very slowly—then climbs up through rocky outcroppings to another level of the coulee. Canyon Wrens sing here; Chukars, quail, and pheasants roam the sage and rabbitbrush; and Chipping Sparrows and Say's Phoebe can be found. More Golden Eagles and other raptors nest on these cliffs.

Spring and early summer are most lively in Moses Coulee, but any time of year is productive for birds of interest. Moses Coulee can be accessed from the north, west, or south. From US 2 in the north, turn south near Milepost 172 and west of the Jameson Lake Road (you are in Moses Coulee at this point). Continue through the coulee several miles. At "24 NW" turn west and follow this road down into the canyon and through Palisades. From the west, take SH 28 south out of Wenatchee. Continue four miles past Rock Island Dam, then turn east at the sign to Palisades. The southern route would be to head northwest out of Ephrata on Sagebrush Flat Road. After about nine miles, turn west on "24 NW," which leads into the western arm of the coulee.

Chapter 10
Blue Mountains

The Blue Mountains are situated in the far southeastern corner of Washington. They are a northward projection of Oregon's Blue Mountains, which, in turn, are an extension of the Rocky Mountains. For millions of years, the Blues formed the western continental headlands into the Pacific Ocean. Through various periods of volcanic and ice age activity, the land lifted, then drew back under the sea. Eventually, the Cascade Mountains to the west rose up and shut out the sea from what is now the inland area. The upheaval of basalt that is the Blue Mountains has been deeply eroded by streams and rivers and gives a rugged profile of peaks and passes. Although not superbly high—only a few peaks are over 6,000 feet—the mountains are beautiful and isolated.

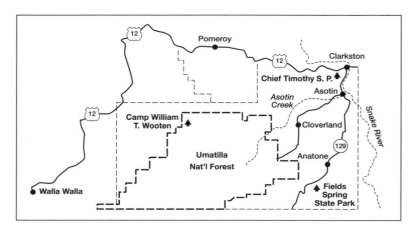

Blue Mountains

The Blue Mountains are mostly in the Umatilla National Forest, and much of the land is part of the Wenaha-Tucannon Wilderness Area. More than 150 miles of trails through forests of ponderosa pine, larch, and Douglas-fir make backpacking popular. Dolly Varden and rainbow trout lure fishermen to this diverse spot, and the canyons of the Snake and Grande Ronde rivers, with their high, wheat-covered plateaus alive with raptors in the winter and songbirds in summer, lure birders. Indian petroglyphs are found along the canyon walls.

Wildlife such as mule deer, white-tailed deer, Rocky Mountain elk, and bighorn sheep can be seen in the region. Wild Turkeys and Chukars have been introduced, and Mountain Quail can be seen regularly. It is the only region in the state where you can see Green-tailed Towhees.

There are intermittent access roads, most of them gravel, leading into the Blue Mountains from Pomeroy, Dayton, and Clarkston on US 12, and from Asotin and Fields Spring State Park on SH 129. Ranger stations at Walla Walla and Pomeroy are good sources of information about roads and facilities.

BLUE MOUNTAIN HABITAT MANAGEMENT AREAS

Asotin Creek Habitat Management Area

The Asotin Creek HMA includes outstanding Chukar habitat and important winter range for elk. Asotin (AH-sow-tin) got its name from the Nez Perce name "Hashotin," meaning "Eel Creek" due to the many eels once found here. This 9,296-acre wildlife area has three main roads: Lick Fork, North Fork, and South Fork. There is no access during the elk calving season. The South Fork Road connects to the Wenatchee Guard Station and makes a great birding loop trip when the snow is gone. Mountain Quail sometimes are seen in this area.

Lick Fork Road. This is the most reliable site in the county for Lewis' Woodpecker. There are about five miles of riparian habitat, some open fields that attract many raptors, and forest where the road ends at the county line. Lick Fork Road continues on and connects to

US 12 at Pomeroy. In the open areas watch for American Kestrel, Red-tailed Hawk, Northern Harrier, and, in winter, Rough-legged Hawk. Chukar; Mourning Dove; Great Horned Owl; Vaux's Swift; Downy and Hairy Woodpeckers; possibly Red-naped Sapsucker; Western Wood-Pewee; Dusky Flycatcher; Black-billed Magpie; House and Canyon Wrens; American Robin; Warbling Vireo; Lazuli Bunting; Chipping, Brewer's, Vesper, White-crowned, and Lark Sparrows; and Northern Oriole also can be found along Lick Fork Road.

North Fork Road. North Fork follows Asotin Creek for about four miles. The first mile has several marshy areas where Sora are common. Yellow-breasted Chat and American Pipit can be heard singing in May and early June. This area is excellent for warblers such as Orange-crowned, Nashville, Yellow, Yellow-rumped, MacGillivray's, and Wilson's. Both kinglets are here, along with Cedar Waxwing, Ruffed Grouse, Northern Pygmy-Owl, Calliope Hummingbird, Belted Kingfisher, Willow and Hammond's Flycatchers, and Violet-green Swallow.

South Fork Road. The South Fork Road has excellent riparian habitat and is abundant in warblers, vireos, wrens, and Black-headed Grosbeak. For years, an American Pipit has nested under the bridge at the fork. As the road begins to climb, Orange-crowned Warblers become abundant. Western and Mountain Bluebirds and Vesper, Brewer's, and Lark Sparrows are found near the ranch at the top. Where timber surrounds open fields past the ranch, Northern Goshawk, Cooper's Hawk, White-headed Woodpecker, and Brewer's Sparrow have been seen. Continuing on several miles to Wickiup Springs, there are possibilities of Merlin; Wild Turkey; Blue Grouse; Hammond's, Dusky, and Cordilleran Flycatchers; and Townsend's Warbler.

Chief Joseph Habitat Management Area

This is dry, open country located along the Snake River south of Asotin. More than 90 species of non-game birds are found in this 9,176-acre area. The Chief Joseph area reaches from the mouth of Joseph Creek to the Oregon state line. Birding is excellent along the Snake and Grande Ronde rivers with Golden Eagle and Prairie Falcon, several species of waterfowl, plus songbirds in the riparian habi-

Rufous Hummingbird

tats. Three young Peregrine Falcons were hacked from the mouth of the Grande Ronde (where it meets the Snake River) in 1990, with one still seen two years later. Wild Turkeys are reliable along Joseph Creek. To reach the Chief Joseph HMA, go south from Asotin along the Snake River canyon, and cross the Grande Ronde—another beautiful canyon. The Chief Joseph area is on either side of the road from there on. The headquarters is on a signed dirt road going east.

Couse Creek. On the way to Chief Joseph HMA, approximately ten miles from Asotin on the Snake River Road, is Couse Creek. This area is excellent for flycatchers, vireos, and other riparian species.

CLOVERLAND GRADE

Cloverland Road is reached by following Asotin Creek out of the town of Asotin for about 2.5 miles, then heading southwest at the fork. The road eventually heads up, and at the top of the grade are three short, metal grain bins. In the fall, Grasshopper and Savannah Sparrows are common. Great Gray Owls have been seen along this road in the past. The area becomes quite forested near the guard station.

Wenatchee Guard Station

This is one of the few sites in Washington state to have Green-tailed Towhees, but they have been increasingly difficult to find. If not found here, try a small patch of mountain mahogany about two miles back from the guard station on Cloverland Road.

CHIEF TIMOTHY STATE PARK

Chief Timothy State Park is located on a bridged island in the Snake River. It is excellent for grebes and various waterfowl, in season. Special birds of interest seen here have been Great Egret, Black-crowned Night-Heron, American Bittern, Snow and Ross' Geese, and a single sighting of a Barnacle Goose. The park has a nice beach area and boat docks, and launching facilities are close by. There are 66 campsites—33 have hookups, and some facilities are wheelchair-accessible. Chief Timothy State Park is eight miles south of Clarkston on US 12. Information: Chief Timothy SP, Highway 12, Clarkston, WA 99403; (509) 758-9580.

Alpowai Interpretive Center. The interpretive center, part of the state park, depicts the geologic and human history of this location. The Nez Perce Indians, whose ancestors had inhabited the area for 10,000 years or more, and the Lewis and Clark Expedition are both interpreted through displays and audio-visual programs. The mouth of Alpowa Creek, near where the center is located, is a good spot for waterfowl and shorebirds such as Canada Goose, Mallard, Northern Pintail, Blue-winged and Cinnamon Teal, Greater Yellowlegs, Spotted Sandpiper, and others.

© LIBBY MILLS 1975

Gray Jay

ASOTIN

Asotin lies six miles south of Clarkston on US 12 at the mouth of Asotin Creek. It was colonized in 1878, after the Nez Perce Indian War. The town is located in Washington's smallest and most south-easterly county of the same name.

Asotin Graveyard

Asotin Graveyard lies just south of town on SH 129. After leaving town, the highway climbs rapidly. The graveyard is located about halfway up the hill and is the only road that goes off to the east. This is the most reliable place for Grasshopper Sparrows in the county. They are easiest to find in spring when the males are singing or in the fall when the young are about.

Asotin Slough

This Nature Conservancy Reserve is open-country habitat located on the Snake River. The list of birds is impressive: 116 species including rarities such as Black-and-White Warbler, White-winged Crossbill, Harris' Sparrow, and Barred Owl. The reserve is good for owls; Great Horned, Common Barn-Owl, and Northern Pygmy-Owl have been seen. Scan the low basalt cliff areas for Chukar, Canyon Wren, and Rock Dove. The open fields have American Kestrel, Ring-necked Pheasant, California Quail, Mourning Dove, Red-winged and Brewer's Blackbirds, and Chipping Sparrows.

The riparian and brushy habitats have a variety of songbirds and other interesting species. Waterfowl sightings on the river are especially good in winter. Look for Canada Goose, Green-winged Teal, Gadwall, Redhead, Common and Barrow's Goldeneyes, Bufflehead, Hooded and Common Mergansers. The shoreline often has Great Blue Heron, Belted Kingfisher, American Coot, and Ring-billed and other gulls.

To reach Asotin Slough, go about two miles south of Asotin on Snake River Road to just past the ballpark. The slough's parking lot is down a well-marked dirt road to the east; there are Nature Conservancy signs along the way.

SAVAGE ROAD PONDS

The ponds on either side of Savage Road are the only good shore-bird spot in Asotin County. The ponds lie just west of SH 129 about 11 miles south of Asotin. Greater and Lesser Yellowlegs, Spotted Sandpiper, Long-billed Curlew, Western Sandpiper, Short- and Long-billed Dowitchers, Common Snipe, Wilson's Phalarope, and Killdeer all have been recorded. Waterfowl, Great Blue Heron, Sora, Bonaparte's and Ring-billed Gulls, Black Tern, Yellow-headed and Red-winged Blackbird, and American Pipit also have been seen.

ANATONE FLATS

The flat fields and areas around the town of Anatone are worth exploring. Open-country birds such as Bald Eagle, Northern Harrier, and Prairie Falcon have been seen. Gray Partridge, Chukar, Ring-necked Pheasant, California Quail, Rock Dove, Common Nighthawk, Horned Lark, Northern Rough-winged and Cliff Swallows, Vesper and Lark Sparrows, Western Meadowlark, and Brewer's Blackbird are all good possibilities. Anatone is about three miles south of the Savage Road Ponds on SH 129.

FIELDS SPRING STATE PARK

Fields Spring State Park is the woodpecker capital of Washington. Every woodpecker in the state has been recorded here at one time or another. Regulars include Red-naped, Red-breasted, and Williamson's Sapsuckers; Pileated, Downy, Hairy, Three-toed, and White-headed Woodpeckers; and Northern Flicker. Late spring, summer, and early fall are the best seasons, and the areas in front of the Wo He Lo Lodge and along the Puffer Butte Trail are two good spots for seeing them.

It is also a good site for Blue Grouse; Olive-sided, Hammond's, Willow, and Dusky Flycatchers; all three nuthatches; Steller's and Gray Jays; Clark's Nutcracker; Black-billed Magpie; all three chickadees; Townsend's Solitaire; Solitary and Warbling Vireos; an assortment of warblers; Western Tanager; Evening Grosbeak; Cassin's Finch; and Red Crossbill. On the ridge south of the park overlooking

Downy Woodpecker

the Grande Ronde River, Golden Eagle; Red-tailed, Swainson's, Ferruginous, and Rough-legged Hawks; falcons; and Northern Harrier can be seen riding the updrafts, especially in the fall.

The park is located on the north side of Puffer Butte within a Canadian Zone habitat that is consistent with southeastern Washington. A one-mile hiking trail goes to the summit of the 4,500-foot butte where there are spectacular views of the Snake River Canyon, the Wallowa Mountains, and Idaho, Oregon, and Washington. Dense stands of ponderosa pine, Douglas-fir, grand fir, and western larch are predominant, and more than 150 varieties of wildflowers have been listed here. The park borders on what once was an arid transition grassland before farming arrived. Fields Spring State Park is 4.5 miles south of Anatone on SH 129. Information: Fields Spring State Park, Box 86, Anatone, WA 99401; (509) 256-3332.

DEPARTMENT OF FISH AND WILDLIFE ACCESS AREAS

There are two Department of Fish and Wildlife Access Areas in this southeastern corner of the state: the Grande Ronde River Access, which is 24 miles south of Asotin on Snake River Road, and the Snake River Access, which is 22.5 miles south of Asotin, also on Snake River Road. Both have boat launches and are good for waterfowl, raptors, and a variety of landbirds.

W.T. WOOTEN HABITAT MANAGEMENT AREA

The W.T. Wooten HMA lies in the rugged Tucannon Valley of the western Blue Mountains. Sharp, steep ridges, scree slopes, and mesas, which are timbered but with open southern slopes covered by range grasses, make up this 11,185-acre area. This transition zone between dry bunchgrass country and the mountain conifer forests has more than a hint of Rocky Mountain species. Wild Turkey, Blue and Ruffed Grouse, California and Mountain Quail, Chukar, Gray Partridge, Ring-necked Pheasant, and Mourning Dove can be seen here. Eight lakes and the Tucannon River provide habitat for waterfowl and wetland species. Riparian habitats abound with songbirds, and wildflowers are magnificent. Rocky Mountain elk, white-tailed and mule deer, black bear, bighorn sheep, cougar, bobcat, cottontail rabbit, and snowshoe hare also live here. Trout and salmon are found in the streams.

To reach the W.T. Wooten area, take SH 12 about three miles west of Pomeroy to SH 126. Head south on SH 126 to Marengo, then follow signs up the Tucannon River to the W.T. Wooten. The wildlife area is about 15 miles away, and there are many forest roads to explore. Look for a small herd of bighorn sheep on Cummings Ridge, which is about a mile up the valley from the headquarters and east of the road. There are various camping areas along the Tucannon. If you are hiking, as in most of eastern Washington, watch for rattlesnakes.

Appendix 1
A Checklist of Washington Birds

 The Field Card of Washington Birds, as compiled by the Washington Bird Records Committee of the Washington Ornithological Society, stands at 430 species as of March 1993—this includes the accepted sight records listed below. The English and scientific names and taxonomic arrangement follow the *Checklist of North American Birds, Sixth Edition*, 1983, American Ornithologists' Union, as amended through the Thirty-sixth Supplement, 1987.

The following birds are listed on the field card as "sight record only": Wilson's Storm-Petrel, Common Black-headed Gull, Gray-cheeked Thrush, Red-throated Pipit, Blue-winged Warbler, Tennessee Warbler, Northern Parula, Cape May Warbler, Blackburnian Warbler, and Sharp-tailed Sparrow.

These additional species are represented in Washington by single-person sight records which the Washington Bird Records Committee believes are valid: Bristle-thighed Curlew, Great Knot, Ivory Gull, Black-backed Wagtail, White-eyed Vireo, Philadelphia Vireo, Black-throated Blue Warbler, Black-throated Green Warbler, Prairie Warbler, and Kentucky Warbler. Listings such as these are constantly changing as new species are sighted and recorded.

Note: The Washington Birds Records Committee questions the validity of the Northwestern Crow as a species.

Species listed with a • have been recorded on fewer than 15 occasions.

AVES: Birds
GAVIIFORMES: Loons
GAVIIDAE: Loons
    Red-throated Loon
       Gavia stellata

Pacific Loon
G. pacifica
Common Loon
G. immer
Yellow-billed Loon
G. adamsii

PODICIPEDIFORMES:
Grebes
PODICIPEDIDAE: Grebes
Pied-billed Grebe
Podilymbus podiceps
Horned Grebe
Podiceps auritus
Red-necked Grebe
P. grisegena
Eared Grebe
P. nigricollis
Western Grebe
Aechmorphorus accidentalis
Clark's Grebe
A. clarkii

PROCELLARIIFORMES:
Tube-nosed Swimmers
DIOMEDEIDAE: Albatrosses
Short-tailed Albatross•
Diomedea albatrus
Black-footed Albatross
D. nigripes
Laysan Albatross
D. immutabilis
Shy Albatross•
D. cauta
PROCELLARIDAE:
Shearwaters, Petrels
Northern Fulmar
Fulmarus glacialis

Mottled Petrel•
Pterodroma inexpectata
Murphy's Petrel•
P. ultima
Pink-footed Shearwater
Puffinus creatopus
Flesh-footed Shearwater
P. carneipes
Buller's Shearwater
P. bulleri
Sooty Shearwater
P. griseus
Short-tailed Shearwater
P. tenuirostris
Manx Shearwater
P. p. puffinus
HYDROBATIDAE:
Storm-Petrels
Fork-tailed Storm-Petrel
Oceanodroma furcata
Leach's Storm-Petrel
O. leucorhoa

PELECANIFORMES:
Totipalmate Swimmers
PHAETHONTIDAE:
Tropicbirds
Red-billed Tropicbird•
Phaethon rubricauda
SULIDAE: Boobies and Gannets
Blue-footed Booby•
Sula nebouxii
PELECANIDAE: Pelicans
American White Pelican
Pelecanus erythrorhynchos
Brown Pelican
P. occidentalis

PHALACROCORACIDAE:
  Cormorants
  Double-crested cormorant
    Phalacrocorax auritus
  Brandt's Cormorant
    P. penicillatus
  Pelagic Cormorant
    P. pelagicus
FREGATIDAE: Frigatebirds
  Magnificent Frigatebird•
    Fregata magnificens

CICONIIFORMES:
  Herons, Ibises, and Storks
ARDEIDAE: Bitterns and
  Herons
  American Bittern
    Botaurus lentiginosus
  Great Blue Heron
    Ardea herodius
  Great Egret
    Casmerodius albus
  Snowy Egret•
    Egretta thula
  Little Blue Heron•
    E. caerulea
  Cattle Egret
    Bubulcus ibis
  Green Heron
    Butorides virescens
  Black-crowned Night-Heron
    Nycticorax nycticorax
THRESKIORNITHIDAE:
  Ibises and Spoonbills
  White-faced Ibis
    Plegadis chihi

ANSERIFORMES:
  Swans, Geese, and Ducks
ANATIDAE: Swans, Geese, and
  Ducks
  Fulvous Whistling-Duck•
    Dendrocygna bicolor
  Tundra Swan
    Cygnus columbianus
  Trumpeter Swan
    C. buccinator
  Mute Swan•
    C. olor
  Greater White-fronted Goose
    Anser albifrons
  Snow Goose
    Chen caerulescens
  Ross' Goose•
    C. rossii
  Emperor Goose
    C. canagica
  Brant
    Branta bernicla
  Canada Goose
    B. canadensis
  Wood Duck
    Aix sponsa
  Green-winged Teal
    Anas crecca
  Falcated Teal•
    A. falcata
  American Black Duck
    A. rubripes
  Mallard
    A. platyrhynchos
  Northern Pintail
    A. acuta
  Garganey•
    A. querquedula

Blue-winged Teal
  A. discors
Cinnamon Teal
  A. cyanoptera
Northern Shoveler
  A. clypeata
Gadwall
  A. strepera
Eurasian Wigeon
  A. penelope
American Wigeon
  A. americana
Canvasback
  Aythya valisineria
Redhead
  A. americana
Ring-necked Duck
  A. collaris
Tufted Duck
  A. fuligula
Greater Scaup
  A. marila
Lesser Scaup
  A. affinis
King Eider•
  Somateria spectabilis
Steller's Eider•
  Polysticta stelleri
Harlequin Duck
  Histrionicus histrionicus
Oldsquaw
  Clangula hyemalis
Black Scoter
  Melanitta nigra
Surf Scoter
  M. perspicillata
White-winged Scoter
  M. fusca

Common Goldeneye
  Bucephala clangula
Barrow's Goldeneye
  B. islandica
Bufflehead
  B. albeola
Smew•
  Mergellus albellus
Hooded Merganser
  Lophodytes cucullatus
Common Merganser
  Mergus merganser
Red-breasted Merganser
  M. serrator
Ruddy Duck
  Oxyura jamaicensis

**FALCONIFORMES:
Diurnal Birds of Prey**
CATHARTIDAE: American
  Vultures
  Turkey Vulture
    Cathartes aura
ACCIPITRIDAE:
Kites, Hawks, and Eagles
  Osprey
    Pandion haliaetus
  White-tailed Kite
    Elanus leucurus
  Bald Eagle
    Haliaeetus leucocephalus
  Northern Harrier
    Circus cyaneus
  Sharp-shinned Hawk
    Accipiter striatus
  Cooper's Hawk
    A. cooperii

Northern Goshawk
  A. gentilis
Red-shouldered Hawk•
  Buteo lineatus
Broad-winged Hawk•
  B. platypterus
Swainson's Hawk
  B. swainsoni
Red-tailed Hawk
  B. jamaicensus
Ferruginous Hawk
  B. regalis
Rough-legged Hawk
  B. lagopus
Golden Eagle
  Aquila chrysaetos
FALCONIDAE:
Caracaras and Falcons
  American Kestrel
    Falco sparverius
  Merlin
    F. columbarius
  Peregrine Falcon
    F. peregrinus
  Gyrfalcon
    F. rusticolus
  Prairie Falcon
    F. mexicanus

GALLIFORMES:
  Gallinaceous Birds
PHASIANIDAE:
Grouse, Turkeys, and Quail
  Gray Partridge
    Perdix perdix
  Chukar
    Alectoris chukar

Ring-necked Pheasant
  Phasianus colchicus
Spruce Grouse
  Dendragapusj canadensis
Blue Grouse
  D. obscurus
White-tailed Ptarmigan
  Lagopus leucurus
Ruffed Grouse
  Bonasa umbellus
Sage Grouse
  Centrocercus urophasianus
Sharp-tailed Grouse
  Tympanuchus phasianellus
Wild Turkey
  Meleagris gallopavo
Northern Bobwhite
  Colinus virginianus
Scaled Quail
  Callipepla squamata
California Quail
  C. californica
Mountain Quail
  Oreortyx pictus

GRUIFORMES: Cranes and
  Rails
RALLIDAE:
Rails, Gallinules, and Coots
  Yellow Rail•
    Coturnicops noveboracensis
  Virginia Rail
    Rallus limicola
  Sora
    Porzana carolina
  American Coot
    Fulica americana

GRUIDAE: Cranes
  Sandhill Crane
    Grus canadensis
CHARADRIIFORMES:
Shorebirds, Gulls, and Alcids
CHARADRIIDAE: Plovers
  Black-bellied Plover
    Pluvialis squatarola
  American Golden-Plover
    P. dominica
  Pacific Golden-Plover
    P. fulva
  Snowy Plover
    Charadrius alexandrinus
  Semipalmated Plover
    C. semipalmatus
  Piping Plover•
    C. melodus
  Killdeer
    C. vociferus
  Mountain Plover•
    C. montanus
  Eurasian Dotterel•
    C. morinellus
HAEMATOPODIDAE:
  Oystercatchers
  Black Oystercatcher
    Haematopus bachmani
RECURVIROSTRIDAE:
Stilts and Avocets
  Black-necked Stilt
    Himantopus mexicanus
  American Avocet
    Recurvirostra americana
SCOLOPACIDAE:
Sandpipers and Phalaropes
  Greater Yellowlegs
    Tringa melanoleuca

Lesser Yellowlegs
  T. flavipes
Solitary Sandpiper
  T. solitaria
Willet
  Catoptrophorus
    semipalmatus
Wandering Tattler
  Heteroscelus incanus
Gray-tailed Tattler•
  H. brevipes
Spotted Sandpiper
  Actitis macularia
Upland Sandpiper
  Bartramia longicauda
Whimbrel
  Numenius phaeopus
Long-billed Curlew
  N. americanus
Hudsonian Godwit•
  Limosa haemastica
Bar-tailed Godwit
  L. lapponica
Marbled Godwit
  L. fedoa
Ruddy Turnstone
  Arenaria interpres
Black Turnstone
  A. melanocephala
Surfbird
  Aphriza virgata
Red Knot
  Calidris canutus
Sanderling
  C. alba
Semipalmated Sandpiper
  C. pusilla

Western Sandpiper
C. mauri
Least Sandpiper
C. minutilla
White-rumped Sandpiper•
C. fuscicollis
Baird's Sandpiper
C. bairdii
Pectoral Sandpiper
C. melanotus
Sharp-tailed Sandpiper
C. acuminata
Rock Sandpiper
C. ptilocnemis
Dunlin
C. alpina
Curlew Sandpiper•
C. ferruginea
Stilt Sandpiper
C. himantopus
Buff-breasted Sandpiper
Tryngites subruficollis
Ruff
Philomachus pugnax
Short-billed Dowitcher
Limnodromus griseus
Long-billed Dowitcher
L. scolopaceus
Common Snipe
Gallinago gallinago
Wilson's Phalarope
Phalaropus tricolor
Red-necked Phalarope
P. lobatus
Red Phalarope
P. fulicaria

LARIDAE: Skuas, Jaegers,
Gulls, Terns, and Skimmers
Pomarine Jaeger
Stercorarius pomarinus
Parasitic Jaeger
S. parasiticus
Long-tailed Jaeger
S. longicaudus
South Polar Skua
Catharacta maccormicki
Laughing Gull•
Larus atricilla
Franklin's Gull
L. pipixcan
Little Gull
L. minutus
Bonaparte's Gull
L. philadelphia
Heermann's Gull
L. heermanni
Mew Gull
L. canus
Ring-billed Gull
L. delawarensis
California Gull
L. californicus
Herring Gull
L. argentatus
Thayer's Gull
L. thayeri
Slaty-backed Gull•
L. schistisagus
Western Gull
L. occidentalis
Glaucous-winged Gull
L. glaucescens

Glaucous Gull
  L. hyperboreus
Black-legged Kittiwake
  Rissa tridactyla
Red-legged Kittiwake•
  R. brevirostris
Sabine's Gull
  Xema sabini
Caspian Tern
  Sterna caspia
Elegant Tern
  S. elegans
Common Tern
  S. hirundo
Arctic Tern
  S. paradisaea
Forster's Tern
  S. forsteri
Least Tern•
  S. antillarum
Black Tern
  Chlidonias niger
ALCIDAE: Auks and Relatives
  Common Murre
    Uria aalge
  Thick-billed Murre•
    U. lomvia
  Pigeon Guillemot
    Cepphus columba
  Marbled Murrelet
    Brachyramphus marmoratus
  Kittlitz's Murrelet•
    B. brevirostris
  Xantus' Murrelet
    *Synthliboramphus
      hypoleucus*
  Ancient Murrelet
    S. antiquus

Cassin's Auklet
  Ptychoramphus aleuticus
Parakeet Auklet•
  Cyclorrhynchus psittacula
Rhinocerous Auklet
  Cerorhinca monocerata
Tufted Puffin
  Fratercula cirrhata
Horned Puffin•
  F. corniculata

COLUMBIFORMES:
Pigeons and Doves
Columbidae: Pigeons and Doves
  Rock Dove
    Columba livia
  Band-tailed Pigeon
    C. fasciata
  White-winged Dove•
    Zenaida asiatica
  Mourning Dove
    Z. macroura

CUCULIFORMES:
Cuckoos and Anis
CUCULIDAE: Cuckoos and Anis
  Black-billed Cuckoo•
    Coccyzus erythropthalmus
  Yellow-billed Cuckoo•
    C. americanus

STRIGIFORMES: Owls
TYTONIDAE: Barn-Owls
  Common Barn-Owl
    Tyto alba
STRIGIDAE: Typical Owls
  Flammulated Owl
    Otus flammeolus

Western Screech-Owl
  O. kennicottii
Great Horned Owl
  Bubo virginianus
Snowy Owl
  Nyctea scandiaca
Northern Hawk-Owl•
  Surnia ulula
Northern Pygmy-Owl
  Glaucidium gnoma
Burrowing Owl
  Athene cunicularia
Spotted Owl
  Strix occidentalis
Barred Owl
  S. varia
Great Gray Owl•
  S. nebulosa
Long-eared Owl
  Asio otus
Short-eared Owl
  A. flammeus
Boreal Owl
  Aegolius funereus
Northern Saw-whet Owl
  A. acadicus

**CAPRIMULGIFORMES:
  Goatsuckers**
CAPRIMULGIDAE: Goatsuckers
  Common Nighthawk
    Chordeiles acutipennis
  Common Poorwill
    Phalaenoptilus nuttallii

**APODIFORMES: Swifts and
  Hummingbirds**
APODIDAE: Swifts

Black Swift
  Cypseloides niger
Vaux's Swift
  C. vauxi
White-throated Swift
  Aeronautes saxatalis
TROCHILIDAE: Hummingbirds
  Black-chinned Hummingbird
    Archilochis alexandri
  Anna's Hummingbird
    Calypte anna
  Calliope Hummingbird
    Stellula calliope
  Rufous Hummingbird
    Selasphorus platycercus
  Allen's Hummingbird•
    S. sasin

**CORACIIFORMES:
  Kingfishers**
ALCEDINIDAE: Kingfishers
  Belted Kingfisher
    Ceryle alcyon

PICIFORMES: Woodpeckers
PICIDAE: Woodpeckers
  Lewis' Woodpecker
    Melanerpes lewis
  Acorn Woodpecker
    M. formicivorus
  Yellow-bellied Sapsucker•
    Sphyrapicus varius
  Red-naped Sapsucker
    Sphyrapicus nuchalis
  Red-breasted Sapsucker
    S. ruber
  Williamson's Sapsucker
    S. thyroideus

Downy Woodpecker
Picoides pubescens
Hairy Woodpecker
P. villosus
White-headed Woodpecker
P. albolarvatus
Three-toed Woodpecker
P. tridctylus
Black-backed Woodpecker
P. arcticus
Northern Flicker
Colaptes auratus
Pileated Woodpecker
Dryocopus pileatus

PASSERIFORMES: Passerine Birds
TYRANNIDAE: Tyrant Flycatchers
Olive-sided Flycatcher
Contopus borealis
Western Wood-Pewee
C. sordidulus
Willow Flycatcher
Empidonax traillii
Least Flycatcher
E. minimus
Hammond's Flycatcher
E. hammondii
Dusky Flycatcher
E. oberholseri
Gray Flycatcher
E. wrightii
Pacific-slope Flycatcher
E. difficilis
Black Phoebe•
Sayornis nigricans

Eastern Phoebe•
S. phoebe
Say's Phoebe
S. saya
Vermillion Flycatcher•
Pyrocephalus rubinus
Ash-throated Flycatcher
Myiarchus tyrannulus
Tropical Kingbird•
Tyrannus melancholicus
Western Kingbird
T. verticalis
Eastern Kingbird
T. tyrannus
Scissor-tailed Flycatcher•
T. forficatus
ALAUDIDAE: Larks
Eurasian Skylark
Alauda arvensis
Horned Lark
Eremophila alpestris
HIRUNDINIDAE: Swallows
Purple Martin
Progne subis
Tree Swallow
Tachycineta bicolor
Violet-green Swallow
T. thalassina
Northern Rough-winged Swallow
Stelgidopteryx serripennis
Bank Swallow
Riparia riparia
Cliff Swallow
Hirundo pyrrhonota
Barn Swallow
H. rustica

CORVIDAE: Jays, Crows, and
Magpies
Gray Jay
Perisoreus canadensis
Steller's Jay
Cyanocitta stelleri
Blue Jay
C. cristata
Scrub Jay
Aphelocoma coerulescens
Pinyon Jay•
Gymnorhinus cyanocephalus
Clark's Nutcracker
Nucifraga columbiana
Black-billed Magpie
Pica pica
American Crow
Corvus brachyrhynchos
Northwestern Crow
C. caurinus
Common Raven
C. corax
PARIDAE: Titmice and
Chickadees
Black-capped Chickadee
Parus atricapillus
Mountain Chickadee
P. gambeli
Boreal Chickadee
P. hudsonicus
Chestnut-backed Chickadee
P. rufescens
AEGITHALIDAE: Bushtits
Bushtit
Psaltriparus minimus
SITTIDAE: Nuthatches
Red-breasted Nuthatch
Sitta canadensis

White-breasted Nuthatch
S. carolinensis
Pygmy Nuthatch
S. Pygmaea
CERTHIIDAE: Creepers
Brown Creeper
Certhia americana
TROGLODYTIDAE: Wrens
Rock Wren
Salpinctes obsoletus
Canyon Wren
Catherpes mexicanus
Bewick's Wren
Thryomanes bewickii
House Wren
Troglodytes aedon
Winter Wren
T. troglodytes
Marsh Wren
Cistothorus palustris
CINCLIDAE: Dippers
American Dipper
Cinclus mexicanus
MUSCICAPIDAE: Muscicapids
Golden-crowned Kinglet
Regulus satrapa
Ruby-crowned Kinglet
R. calendula
Blue-gray Gnatcatcher•
Polioptila caerulea
Western Bluebird
Sialia mexicana
Mountain Bluebird
S. currucoides
Townsend's Solitaire
Myadestes townsendi
Veery
Catharus fuscescens

Swainson's Thrush
  C. ustulatus
Hermit Thrush
  C. guttatus
American Robin
  Turdus migratorius
Varied Thrush
  Ixoreus naevius
MIMIDAE: Mockingbirds and
  Thrashers
Gray Catbird
  Dumetella carolinensis
Northern Mockingbird
  Mimus polyglottos
Sage Thrasher
  Oreoscoptes montanus
PRUNELLIDAE: Accentors
Siberian Accentor•
  Prunella montanella
MOTACILLIDAE: Pipits and
  Wagtails
Yellow Wagtail•
  Motacilla flava
White Wagtail•
  Motacilla alba
American Pipit
  A. rubescens
BOMBYCILLIDAE: Waxwings
Bohemian Waxwing
  Bombycilla garrulus
Cedar Waxwing
  B. cedrorum
LANIIDAE: Shrikes
Northern Shrike
  Lanius excubitor
Loggerhead Shrike
  L. ludovicianus

STURNIDAE: Starlings
European Starling
  Sturnus vulgaris
VIREONIDAE: Vireos
Solitary Vireo
  Vireo solitarius
Hutton's Vireo
  V. huttoni
Warbling Vireo
  V. gilvus
Red-eyed Vireo
  V. olivaceus
EMBERIZIDAE: Emberizids
Orange-crowned Warbler
  V. celata
Nashville Warbler
  V. ruficappila
Yellow Warbler
  Dendroica petechia
Chestnut-sided Warbler•
  D. pensylvanica
Magnolia Warbler•
  D. magnolia
Yellow-rumped Warbler
  D. coronata
Black-throated Gray Warbler
  D. nigrescens
Townsend's Warbler
  D. townsendi
Hermit Warbler
  D. occidentalis
Palm Warbler
  D. palmarum
Blackpoll Warbler•
  D. striata
Black-and-White Warbler•
  Mniotilta varia

American Redstart
Setophaga ruticilla
Prothonotary Warbler•
Protonotaria citrea
Ovenbird•
Seiurus aurocapillus
Northern Waterthrush
S. noveboracensis
MacGillivray's Warbler
Oporornis tolmiei
Common Yellowthroat
Geothlypis trichas
Hooded Warbler•
Wilsonia citrina
Wilson's Warbler
W. pusilla
Yellow-breasted Chat
Icteria virens
Western Tanager
Piranga ludoviciana
Rose-breasted Grosbeak•
Pheucticus ludovicianus
Black-headed Grosbeak
P. melanocephalus
Lazuli Bunting
Passerina amoena
Indigo Bunting•
P. cyanea
Dickcissel•
Spiza americana
Green-tailed Towhee
Piplo chlorurus
Rufous-sided Towhee
P. erythrophthalmus
American Tree Sparrow
Spizella arborea
Chipping Sparrow
S. passerina

Clay-colored Sparrow•
S. pallida
Brewer's Sparrow
S. breweri
Vesper Sparrow
Pooecetes gramineus
Lark Sparrow
Chondestes grammacus
Black-throated Sparrow
Amphispiza bilineata
Sage Sparrow
A. belli
Lark Bunting•
Calamospiza melanocorys
Savannah Sparrow
Passerculus sandwichensis
Grasshopper Sparrow
Ammodramus savannarum
Le Conte's Sparrow•
A. leconteii
Fox Sparrow
Passerella iliaca
Song Sparrow
Melospiza melodia
Lincoln's Sparrow
M. lincolnii
Swamp Sparrow
M. georgiana
White-throated Sparrow
Zonotrichia albicollis
Golden-crowned Sparrow
Z. atricapilla
White-crowned Sparrow
Z. leucophrys
Harris' Sparrow
Z. querula
Dark-eyed Junco
Junco hyemalis

Lapland Longspur
Calcarius lapponicus
Chestnut-collared Longspur•
C. ornatus
Rustic Bunting•
Emberiza rustica
Snow Bunting
Plectrophenax nivalis
McKay's Bunting•
P. hyperboreus
Bobolink
Dolichonyx oryzivorus
Red-winged Blackbird
Agelaius phoeniceus
Western Meadowlark
Sturnella neglecta
Yellow-headed Blackbird
Xanthocephalus
xanthocephalus
Rusty Blackbird•
Euphagus carolinus
Brewer's Blackbird
E. cyanocephalus
Great-tailed Grackle•
Quiscalus mexicanus
Common Grackle•
Q. quiscula
Brown-headed Cowbird
Molothrus ater
Orchard Oriole•
Icterus spurius
Hooded Oriole•
I. cucullatus
Northern Oriole
Icterus spurius

Scott's Oriole•
I. parisorum

FRINGILLIDAE: Finches
Brambling•
Fringilla montifringilla
Gray-crowned Rosy Finch
Leucosticte tephrocotis
Pine Grosbeak
Pinicola enucleator
Purple Finch
Carpodacus purpureus
Cassin's Finch
C. cassinii
House Finch
C. mexicanus
Red Crossbill
Loxia curvirostra
White-winged Crossbill
L. leucoptera
Common Redpoll
Carduelis flammea
Pine Siskin
C. pinus
Lesser Goldfinch
C. psaltria
American Goldfinch
C. tristis
Evening Grosbeak
Coccothraustes vespertinus

PASSERIDAE: Weavers
House Sparrow
Passer domesticus

Appendix 2
Contacts for Birders

 RARE BIRD ALERT NUMBERS
Seattle-Statewide: (206) 526-8266
Southeast Washington-Idaho: (208) 882-6195
Oregon: (503) 292-0661
Vancouver, British Columbia: (604) 737-9910

WASHINGTON ORNITHOLOGICAL SOCIETY

WOS was founded in 1988 to increase knowledge about the birds of Washington and to enhance communication among all persons interested in those birds. Further information and checklists (25¢) are available from:

Washington Ornithological Society
P.O. Box 85786
Seattle, Washington 98145

WASHINGTON CHAPTERS OF THE NATIONAL AUDUBON SOCIETY

There are 24 chapters of the National Audubon Society in Washington. All have regular field trips and interesting meetings.

Admiralty Audubon Society
P.O. Box 666
Port Townsend, WA 98368

Black Hills Audubon Society
P.O. Box 2524
Olympia, WA 98507

Blue Mountain Audubon Society
P.O. Box 1106
Walla Walla, WA 99362

Central Basin-Moses Lake A.S.
P.O. Box 86
Moses Lake, WA 98837

Columbia Gorge Audubon Society
P.O. Box 512
Hood River, OR 97031

East Lake Washington A.S.
P.O. Box 3632
Bellevue, WA 98009

Kitsap Audubon Society
P.O. Box 961
Poulsbo, WA 98370

Kittitas Audubon Society
P.O. Box 1443
Ellensburg, WA 98926

Lower Columbia Basin A.S.
P.O. Box 1900
Richland, WA 99352

North Cascades A.S.
P.O. Box 5805
Bellingham, WA 98227

North Central Washington A.S.
P.O. Box 2934 P
Wenatchee, WA 98807

Palouse Audubon Society
P.O. Box 3606, University Station
Moscow, ID 83843-0156

Pilchuck Audubon Society
P.O. Box 11
Everett, WA 98206

Rainier Audubon Society
P.O. Box 778
Auburn, WA 98071

San Juan Islands Audubon
P.O. Box 224
Orcas, WA 98280

Seattle Audubon Society
8028 35th Avenue NE
Seattle, WA 98115

Skagit Audubon Society
2849 Francis Road
Mt. Vernon, WA 98273

Spokane Audubon Society
P.O. Box 9818
Spokane, WA 99209

Tahoma Audubon Society
2601 70th Ave. W., Suite E
Tacoma, WA 98466-5430

Vancouver Audubon Society
Box 1966
Vancouver, WA 98668

Vashon-Maury Island Audubon
P.O. Box 876
Vashon Island, WA 98070

Whidbey Audubon Society
P.O. Box 1012
Oak Harbor, WA 98277

Willapa Hills Audubon
P.O. Box 93
Longview, WA 98632

Yakima Valley Audubon
P.O. Box 2823
Yakima, WA 98907

Other important National Audubon Society addresses that may be of help:

Washington State Office, N.A.S.   Western Regional Office, N.A.S.
P.O. Box 462   555 Audubon Place
Olympia, WA 98507   Sacramento, CA 95825

The Hawk Migration Association of North America has been collecting raptor migration data on the North American continent since the early 1970s. Its growing database provides invaluable research opportunities for understanding migration behavior and monitoring raptor populations.

> Hawk Migration Association of North America
> P.O. Box 3482
> Lynchburg, VA 24503
>
> HMANA Pacific Northwest Region
> 6135 NE 193rd Place
> Seattle, WA 98155

The Trumpeter Swan Society, a North American society, plus its Washington State Swan Working Group, were organized to help biologists monitor the recovery of the Trumpeter Swan. The Washington group can be contacted at:

> The Trumpeter Swan Society
> 14112 First Avenue West
> Everett, WA 98208
> (206) 787-0258

The Olympic Vulture Study is an independent research project in cooperation with volunteers in British Columbia to study the migration of Turkey Vultures from Canada.

> Olympic Vulture Study
> 22622 53 Avenue SE
> Bothell, WA 98021

Falcon Research Group: A non-profit group doing falcon research in the Pacific Northwest and involved with the reintroduction of nesting Peregrine Falcons to Seattle.

> Falcon Research Group
> P.O. Box 248
> Bow, WA 98232

Washington Birder: An independent quarterly newsletter about birding activities in Washington state; includes a site or species guide in each issue. It is published as an additional source of information for birders interested in adding to their state and county lists while contributing to our knowledge of Washington's bird distribution.

> Washington Birder
> P.O. Box 486
> Wauna, WA 98395

Founded in 1951, **The Nature Conservancy** focuses on the scientific identification and protection of biodiversity. It strives to buy ecologically important lands from willing sellers. At present, the Conservancy owns and manages more than 1,200 U.S. nature preserves, the largest private system of nature sanctuaries in the world.

> The Nature Conservancy
> Seattle Office
> 207 Pine Street, Suite 1100
> Seattle, WA 98101
> (206) 343-4344

Washington State Department of Fish and Wildlife: More than 850,000 acres of land for wildlife habitat and wildlife-related recreation is managed, owned, or leased by this department. It provides information on wildlife viewing opportunities, and hunting and freshwater fishing information and regulations.

> Washington State Department of Fish and Wildlife
> 600 Capitol Way, GJ-11

Olympia, Washington 98504
(360) 902-2200

Washington State Parks and Recreation Commission: Free
brochures on all of Washington's 110 state parks are available from
this office; many areas have bird check lists for the asking. This
department also has a directory of various local park districts found
throughout the state.

Washington State Parks and Recreation Commission
Public Affairs Office
7150 Cleanwater Lane, KY-11
Olympia, Washington 98504-5711
(360) 753-2027

The Washington State Department of Natural Resources has a
variety of maps and brochures on the lands that it administers including a guide to DNR campgrounds.

Washington State Department of Natural Resources
Division of Recreation
120 E. Union, Room 109, EK-12
Olympia, Washington 98504
(360) 753-2400

The state department of economic development publishes a cal-
endar of monthly events in Washington and also has a variety of publications on travel and tourism.

Washington Dept. of Commerce and Economic Development
Tourism Development Division
101 General Administration Building, AX-13
Olympia, Washington 98504
(360) 586-2088 or (360) 586-2102

Washington has a wealth of nationally administered natural areas to
visit: three national parks including Mount Rainier NP, North Cascades NP, and Olympic NP, six national forests that encompass 30
wilderness areas, one national volcanic monument at Mount St.

Helens, six national historic park/trail/sites, and three national recreation areas. All offer good birding and some excellent brochures. For further information write or call:

> U. S. Forest Service/National Park Service
> Outdoor Recreation Information Center
> 915 Second Avenue, Suite 442
> Seattle, Washington 98174
> (206) 220-7450

You may also contact the individual national parks or forests directly:

> Mount Rainier National Park: (360) 569-2211
> Olympic National Park: (360) 452-0330
> North Cascades National Park: (360) 856-5700
> Mt. Baker-Snoqualmie National Forest: (206) 775-9702
> Wenatchee National Forest: (509) 662-4335
> Okanogan National Forest: (509) 826-3275
> Gifford Pinchot National Forest: (360) 750-5000
> Olympic National Forest: (360) 956-2400
> Mt. St. Helens National Volcanic Monument: (360) 274-2100

There are 21 national wildlife refuges in Washington. For more information about the National Wildlife Refuge System, individual refuges, or to volunteer your services to refuges, write the U.S. Fish and Wildlife Service at the following address.

> U.S. Fish and Wildlife Service
> Eastside Federal Complex
> 911 NE 11th Avenue
> Portland, OR 97232-4181
> (503) 231-6121

To receive an excellent brochure on the National Wildlife Refuges of Puget Sound and Coastal Washington, write:

> U.S. Dept. of the Interior/Fish & Wildlife Service
> Nisqually National Wildlife Refuge

100 Brown Farm Road
Olympia, WA 98506

Nearly 340,000 acres of the state's land is administered by the U.S. Bureau of Land Management. The BLM is reponsible for managing public lands and their resources under a multiple-use policy. The Watchable Wildlife program is administered by the BLM. For information on their various projects:

U.S. Bureau of Land Management
East 4217 Main
Spokane, WA 99202
(509) 353-2570

To obtain an official highway map of Washington, write to:

Department of Transportation
Public Affairs Office
Transportation Building, KF-01
Olympia, WA 98504
(360) 753-2150

Washington has top zoological exhibits, some featuring animals in their northwest environment.

Woodland Park Zoo
5500 Phinney Avenue North
Seattle, WA 98103
(206) 684-4800

Northwest Trek Wildlife Park
11610 Trek Drive East
Eatonville, WA 98328
(360) 847-1901

Pt. Defiance Zoo and Aquarium
5400 North Pearl
Tacoma, WA 98407
(206) 591-5335

If your interest is in exploring and learning more about the Pacific Northwest, there are many organizations that provide programs and field seminars.

Olympic Park Institute
HC 62 Box 9T
Port Angeles, WA 98362
(360) 928-3720

Island Institute
4004 58th Place SW
Seattle, WA 98116
(206) 463-6722

North Cascades Institute
2105 Highway 20
Sedro Woolley, WA 98284
(360) 856-5700 (ext. 209)

The Mountaineers is an outdoor club that supports protection of the Northwest environment. It has an excellent stock of guidebooks and information about hiking, camping, and wildlife. For a free catalogue:

The Mountaineers
300 Third Avenue West
Seattle, WA 98119
(206) 284-6310

Other groups that may have helpful information are:

Washington State Outfitters and Guides Association
c/o High Country Outfitters
23836 SE 24th
Issaquah, WA 98027
(206) 392-6107

Trade Association of Sea Kayaking (TASK)
P.O. 84114
Seattle, WA 98124
(206) 621-1018

Sierra Club
Cascade Chapter
1516 Melrose Avenue
Seattle, WA 98122
(206) 625-0632

Appendix 3
Selected References

 **BIRD DISTRIBUTION IN
WASHINGTON STATE**

Alcorn, *Northwest Birds—Distribution and Eggs.* Tacoma: Western Media Printing and Publications, 1978.

Angell, T. and Balcomb, K.C. III. *Marine Birds and Mammals of Puget Sound.* Seattle: University of Washington Press, 1982.

Butler and Marsh, *Birding in Southcentral Washington.* Yakima: Yakima Valley Audubon Society, 1983.

Ennor, H.R. *Birds of the Tri-Cities and Vicinity.* Richland: Lower Columbia Basin Audubon Society, 1991.

Gordon, D.G. *The Audubon Society Field Guide to the Bald Eagle.* Seattle: Sasquatch Books, 1991.

Hunn, E.S. *Birding in Seattle and King County (Trailside Series).* Seattle: Seattle Audubon Society, 1982.

Jewett, S.G. et al. *Birds of Washington.* Seattle: University of Washington Press, 1953.

Larrison, E.J. *Birds of the Pacific Northwest.* Moscow: University Press of Idaho, 1981.

Lewis, M.G. and Sharpe, F.A. *Birding in the San Juan Islands.* Seattle: The Mountaineers, 1987.

Morse, B. *A Birder's Guide to Ocean Shores, Washington.* Seattle: R.W. Morse Company, 1993.

Nehls, H.B. *Familiar Birds of the Northwest.* Portland: Portland Audubon Society, 1981.

Paulson, D. *Shorebirds of the Pacific Northwest.* Seattle: University of Washington, 1993.

Portman, S. *Birds of Sun Mountain and the Methow Valley.* Sally Portman, 1988.

Wahl, T.R. and Paulson, D.R. *A Guide to Bird-Finding in Washington,* Revised edition. Bellingham: T.R. Wahl, 1991.

Walton, R.K. and Lawson, R.W. *Birding by Ear: Western Guide to Bird Song Identification* (Peterson Field Guide Series). Boston: Houghton Mifflin Co., 1990.

Zimmer K.J. *The Western Bird Watcher.* Englewood Cliffs: Prentice-Hall, 1985.

GENERAL BIRD IDENTIFICATION

Clark, W.S. *A Field Guide to Hawks of North America* (Peterson Field Guide Series). Boston: Houghton Mifflin Co., 1987.

Ehrlich, P.R. et al. *The Birder's Handbook.* New York: Simon & Schuster, Inc., 1988.

Farrand, J. Jr., Ed. *The Audubon Society Master Guide to Birding,* Volumes 1, 2, 3. New York: Alfred A. Knopf, Inc., 1983.

Harrison, H.H. *A Field Guide to Birds' Nests Found West of the Mississippi River* (Peterson Field Guide Series). Boston: Houghton Mifflin Co., 1979.

Kaufman, K. *Advanced Birding* (Peterson Field Guide Series). Boston: Houghton Mifflin Co., 1990.

National Geographic Society. *Field Guide to the Birds of North America,* 2nd ed. Washington: National Geographic Society, 1987.

Peterson, R.T. *A Field Guide to Western Birds* (Peterson Field Guide Series), 3rd ed. Boston: Houghton Mifflin Co., 1990.

Robbins, Chandler S. et al. *Birds of North America* (Golden Field Guide Series), Revised expanded ed. New York: Golden Press, 1983.

MISCELLANEOUS REFERENCES

Alt, D.D. and Hyndman, D.W. *Roadside Geology of Washington* (Roadside Geology Series). Missoula: Mountain Press, 1984.

DeLorme Mapping Company. *Washington Atlas & Gazetteer.* 2nd ed. Freeport: DeLorme Mapping Company, 1992.

Dittmar Family. *Visitors' Guide to Ancient Forests of Western Washington.* Washington, D.C.: The Wilderness Society, 1990.

Hooper, David. *Exploring Washington's Wild Olympic Coast.* Seattle: The Mountaineers, 1993.

Kirk, R. and Alexander, C. *Exploring Washington's Past, A Road Guide to History.* Seattle: University of Washington Press, 1990.

Kritzman, E.B. *Little Mammals of the Pacific Northwest.* Seattle: Pacific Search Press, 1977.

Kruckeberg, A.R. *The Natural History of Puget Sound Country.* Seattle: University of Washington Press, 1991.

La Tourrette, J. *Washington Wildlife Viewing Guide.* Helena: Falcon Press & Defenders of Wildlife, Washington, D.C., 1992.

Niehaus, T.F. *A Field Guide to Pacific States Wildflowers* (Peterson Field Guide Series). Boston: Houghton Mifflin Co., 1976.

Saling, A. *The Great Northwest Nature Factbook.* Bothell: Alaska Northwest Books, 1991.

Shea, P., Antczak, E., and Feaster, L. *Access America: An Atlas of the National Parks for Visitors with Disabilities.* Northern Cartographic, Inc., 1988.

Stienstra, T. *Pacific Northwest Camping.* 2nd ed. San Francisco: Foghorn Press, 1990.

Thollander, E. *Back Roads of Washington,* Updated edition. Seattle: Sasquatch Books, 1992.

Underhill, J.E. (Ted). *Roadside Wildflowers of the Northwest.* Vancouver: Hancock House Publishers Ltd., 1981.

Whitney, S.R. *A Field Guide to the Cascades & Olympics.* Seattle: The Mountaineers, 1983.

Index of Birds

This index is of English names only. The last page for each species refers to the page in Appendix 1, *A Checklist of Washington Birds*, where scientific order, family, genus, and species names are listed. Illustrations are listed in bold.

Index of Birds **315**

Index of Locations

Maps are listed in bold.